Trust in the Lord with all your heart,
and do not rely on your own understanding;
think about Him in all your ways,
and He will guide you on the right paths.

—

PROVERBS 3:5-6 HOLMAN CSB

The Holy Bible, King James Version

The Holy Bible, New King James Version (NKJV) Copyright © 1982 by Thomas Nelson, Inc. Used by permission.

New century Version®. (NCV) Copyright   © 1987, 1988, 1991 by Word Publishing, a division of Thomas Nelson, Inc. All rights reserved. Used by permission.

The Holman Christian Standard Bible™ (Holman CSB) Copyright © 1999, 2000, 2001 by Holman Bible Publishers. Used by permission.

The Holy Bible, New International Version®. (NIV) Copyright © 1973, 1978, 1984 International Bible Society. Used by permission of Zondervan. All rights reserved.

The Holy Bible. New Living Translation (NLT) copyright © 1996 Tyndale Charitable Trust. Used by permission of Tyndale House Publishers.

The New American Standard Bible®, (NASB) Copyright © 1960, 1962, 1963, 1968, 1971, 1972, 1973, 1975, 1977, 1995 by The Lockman Foundation. Used by permission.

Scripture taken from The Message. (MSG) Copyright © 1993, 1994, 1995, 1996, 2000, 2001, 2002. Used by permission of NavPress Publishing Group.

Cover Design by Kim Russell / Wahoo Designs
Page Layout by Bart Dawson

ISBN 978-1-60587-122-6

INTRODUCTION

Whether you realize it or not, your life is a journey. When you make that journey with God, you win massive rewards here on earth and (more importantly) in heaven. So if you're smart, you'll make a habit of spending time once a day every day with your Creator. When you do, you'll soon discover that God will help you make better decisions, decisions that will improve of your own life and the lives of your friends and family.

This book contains 365 chapters, one for each day of the year. During the next 12 months, try this experiment: Read a chapter each day—and while you're at it, put at least one good idea into your head and your heart, at least one nugget of inspiration for the upcoming day. By giving God a few minutes each morning, you can change the direction of your thoughts and the quality of your choices.

Your daily devotional time can be habit-forming, and should be. The first few minutes of each day are invaluable—if you treat them that way and offer them to God, you'll never regret it.

READ THE BIBLE IN A YEAR

Reading the Bible from cover to cover in 365 days is a worthy goal for every Christian, including you. If you complete the suggested Bible readings found on each page of this book, you will, in 365 days, finish both the Old and New Testaments.

Each day provides yet another opportunity to study God's Word, to follow His path, and reacquaint yourself with His promises. When you do these things, you will be richly blessed. So take the time to read His Word once a day, every day. No exceptions.

AT LEAST ONCE A DAY, EVERY DAY, WITH GOD

Therefore, get your minds ready for action, being self-disciplined, and set your hope completely on the grace to be brought to you at the revelation of Jesus Christ.

1 Peter 1:13 Holman CSB

Are you willing to spend a few minutes every day with God? Are you willing to spend a few quiet moments each morning studying God's Word, or are you too busy for that? The answer, of course, is that you can find time for God . . . and you should.

Scottish-born evangelist Henry Drummond correctly observed, "Ten minutes spent in Christ's company every day—even two minutes—will make the whole day different." How true. If you dedicate even a few minutes each morning to a time of devotional reading and prayer, you will change the tone and direction of your day.

Are you seeking to change some aspect of your life? Do you seek to improve the condition of your spiritual, physical, or emotional health? Do you desire the peace that can be yours through Christ? If so, ask for God's help and ask for it many times each day . . . starting with a steady diet of God's wisdom, God's truth, and God's love.

If I should neglect prayer but a single day, I should lose a great deal of the fire of faith.

Martin Luther

A TIMELY TIP

God is available to you every morning . . . and you should make yourself available to Him.

YOUR JOURNEY WITH GOD

There is no wisdom, understanding, or advice that can succeed against the Lord.

Proverbs 21:30 NCV

Does God have a plan for your life? Of course He does! Every day of your life is a journey with Him, and He's trying to lead you along a path of His choosing . . . but He won't force you to follow. God has given you free will, the opportunity to make decisions for yourself. The choices are yours: either you will choose to obey His Word and seek His will, or you will choose to follow a different path.

This morning, as you spend a few quiet moments with your Heavenly Father, ask Him to guide you on today's journey. God's plans for you may be far bigger than you imagine, but He may be waiting for you to make the next move—so today, make that move prayerfully, faithfully, and carefully. And after you've made your move, trust God to make His.

The one supreme business of life is to find God's plan for your life and live it.

E. Stanley Jones

The only way you can experience abundant life is to surrender your plans to Him.

Charles Stanley

A TIMELY TIP

If you're graduating into a new phase of life, be sure to make God your partner. If you do, He'll guide your steps, He'll help carry your burdens, and He'll help you focus on the things that really matter.

TRUSTING THE FUTURE TO GOD

"I say this because I know what I am planning for you," says the Lord. "I have good plans for you, not plans to hurt you. I will give you hope and a good future."

Jeremiah 29:11 NCV

How bright is your future? Well, if you're a faithful believer, God's plans for you are so bright that you'd better wear shades. But here's an important question: How bright do you believe your future to be? Are you expecting a terrific tomorrow, or are you dreading a terrible one? The answer you give will have a powerful impact on the way tomorrow turns out.

Do you trust in the ultimate goodness of God's plan for your life? Will you face tomorrow's challenges with optimism and hope? You should. After all, God created you for a very important reason: His reason. And you still have important work to do: His work.

Today, as you live in the present and look to the future, remember that God has an amazing plan for you. Act—and believe—accordingly.

Never be afraid to trust an unknown future to a known God.

Corrie ten Boom

Our future may look fearfully intimidating, yet we can look up to the Engineer of the Universe, confident that nothing escapes His attention or slips out of the control of those strong hands.

Elisabeth Elliot

A TIMELY TIP

If you follow in Christ's footsteps, your future is amazingly bright. So don't delay—follow Jesus today!

STEWARDSHIP OF GOD'S GIFTS

God has given gifts to each of you from his great variety of spiritual gifts. Manage them well so that God's generosity can flow through you.

1 Peter 4:10 NLT

The gifts that you possess are gifts from the Giver of all things good. Do you have a spiritual gift? Share it. Do you have a testimony about the things that Christ has done for you? Don't leave your story untold. Do you possess financial resources? Share them. Do you have particular talents? Hone your skills and use them for God's glory.

When you hoard the treasures that God has given you, you live in rebellion against His commandments. But, when you obey God by sharing His gifts freely and without fanfare, you invite Him to bless you more and more. Today, be a faithful steward of your talents and treasures. And then prepare yourself for even greater blessings that are sure to come.

You are the only person on earth who can use your ability.

Zig Ziglar

Great relief and satisfaction can come from seeking God's priorities for us in each season, discerning what is "best" in the midst of many noble opportunities, and pouring our most excellent energies into those things.

Beth Moore

A TIMELY TIP

God has given you a unique array of talents and opportunities. If you use your gifts wisely, they're multiplied. If you misuse your gifts—or ignore them altogether—they are lost. God is anxious for you to use your gifts . . . are you?

DABBLERS BEWARE

I do not consider myself yet to have taken hold of it. But one thing I do: Forgetting what is behind and straining toward what is ahead, I press on toward the goal to win the prize for which God has called me heavenward in Christ Jesus.

Philippians 3:13-14 NIV

Is Christ the focus of your life? Are you fired with enthusiasm for Him? Are you an energized Christian who allows God's Son to reign over every aspect of your day? Make no mistake: that's exactly what God intends for you to do.

God has given you the gift of eternal life through His Son. In response to God's priceless gift, you are instructed to focus your thoughts, your prayers, and your energies upon God and His only begotten Son. To do so, you must resist the subtle yet powerful temptation to become a "spiritual dabbler."

A person who dabbles in the Christian faith is unwilling to place God in His rightful place: above all other things. Resist that temptation; make God the cornerstone and the touchstone of your life. When you do, He will give you all the strength and wisdom you need to live victoriously for Him.

Give me the person who says, "This one thing I do, and not these fifty things I dabble in."

D. L. Moody

Jesus challenges you and me to keep our focus daily on the cross of His will if we want to be His disciples.

Anne Graham Lotz

A TIMELY TIP

First focus on God . . . and then everything else will come into focus.

HOW OFTEN DO YOU ASK?

Ask and it will be given to you; seek and you will find; knock and the door will be opened to you. For everyone who asks receives; he who seeks finds; and to him who knocks, the door will be opened.

Matthew 7:7-8 NIV

How often do you ask for God's help? Occasionally? Intermittently? Whenever you experience a crisis? Hopefully not. Hopefully, you have developed the habit of asking for God's assistance early and often. And hopefully, you have learned to seek His guidance in every aspect of your life.

God has promised that when you ask for His help, He will not withhold it. So ask. Ask Him to meet the needs of your day. Ask Him for wisdom. Ask Him to lead you, to protect you, and to correct you. And trust the answers He gives.

God stands at the door and waits. When you knock on His door, He answers. Your task, of course, is to seek His guidance prayerfully, confidently, and often.

If you want more from life, ask more from God.

Marie T. Freeman

When trials come your way—as inevitably they will—do not run away. Run to your God and Father.

Kay Arthur

A TIMELY TIP

If you want more from life, ask more from God. If you're seeking a worthy goal, ask for God's help—and keep asking—until He answers your prayers.

FOR GOD SO LOVED THE WORLD

This is how much God loved the world: He gave his Son, his one and only Son. And this is why: so that no one need be destroyed; by believing in him anyone can have a whole and lasting life.

John 3:16 MSG

For believers, death is not an ending; it is a beginning; for believers, the grave is not a final resting-place, it is a place of transition. For believers, death is not a dark journey into nothingness; it is a homecoming. God sent His Son as a sacrifice for our sins. Through Jesus, we are redeemed. By welcoming Christ into our hearts, we have received the precious, unfathomable gift of eternal life. Let us praise God for His Son. The One from Galilee has saved us from our sins so that we might live courageously, die triumphantly, and live again—eternally.

Considering how I prepare for my children when I know they are coming home, I love to think of the preparations God is making for my homecoming one day. He knows the colors I love, the scenery I enjoy, the things that make me happy, all the personal details.

Anne Graham Lotz

Eventually, many of us will meet for the first time, and in Christ we are always sure that Christians never meet for the last time!

Vance Havner

A TIMELY TIP

God offers you a priceless gift: the gift of eternal life. If you have not already done so, accept God's gift today—tomorrow may be too late.

WHO SHOULD YOU PLEASE?

A tranquil heart is life to the body, but jealousy is rottenness to the bones.

Proverbs 14:30 Holman CSB

Sometimes, it's very tempting to be a people-pleaser. But usually, it's the wrong thing to do.

When you worry too much about pleasing dates or friends, you may not worry enough about pleasing God—and when you fail to please God, you inevitably pay a very high price for our mistaken priorities.

Whom will you try to please today: God or your friends? Your obligation is most certainly not to your peers or to your date. Your obligation is to an all-knowing and perfect God. Trust Him always. Love Him always. Praise Him always. And seek to please Him and only Him. Always.

It is comfortable to know that we are responsible to God and not to man. It is a small matter to be judged of man's judgement.

Lottie Moon

Ambition! We must be careful what we mean by it. If it means the desire to get ahead of other people—which is what I think it does mean—then it is bad. If it simply means wanting to do a thing well, then it is good. It isn't wrong for an actor to want to act his part as well as it can possibly be acted, but the wish to have his name in bigger type than the other actors is a bad one.

C. S. Lewis

A TIMELY TIP

When it comes to doing the right thing, you must never be afraid to stand up and be counted.

DO THE RIGHT THING

You can't pick and choose in these things, specializing in keeping one or two things in God's law and ignoring others.

James 2:10 MSG

I f you continue to date somebody who behaves foolishly or impulsive-ly, then sooner or later, you'll probably find yourself doing impulsive things, too. And that's bad . . . very bad. So here's an ironclad rule for maintaining your self-respect and your sanity: If you find yourself out on a date with an impulsive person who's pressuring you to betray your values, go home and go home fast. Otherwise, before you know it, you'll be in more trouble than you can imagine.

When you feel pressured to do things—or to compromise yourself—in ways that lead you away from God, you're heading straight for major-league problems. The best time to decide how you'll behave yourself is before you go out on a date (not during a date!). So don't do the "easy" thing and don't do the impulsive thing. Do the right thing, and do it every time.

When your good behavior speaks for itself . . . don't interrupt.

Anonymous

Study the Bible and observe how the persons behaved and how God dealt with them. There is explicit teaching on every condition of life.

Corrie ten Boom

A TIMELY TIP

If you're dating someone who doesn't consider your feelings, you're dating the wrong person.

TODAY'S BIBLE READING
Old Testament: Genesis 26-27
New Testament: Matthew 8:1-20

GOD'S WISDOM:
AN ENDLESS FOUNTAIN

Understanding is like a fountain which gives life to those who use it.

Proverbs 16:22 NCV

Wisdom is like a savings account: If you add to it consistently, then eventually you will have accumulated a great sum. The secret to success is consistency.

Do you seek wisdom for yourself and for your family? Then you must keep learning, and you must keep motivating them to do likewise. The ultimate source of wisdom, of course, is the Word of God. When you study God's Word and live according to His commandments, you will accumulate wisdom day by day. And finally, with God's help, you'll have enough wisdom to keep and enough left over to share.

Most of us go through life praying a little, planning a little, jockeying for position, hoping but never being quite certain of anything, and always secretly afraid that we will miss the way. This is a tragic waste of truth and never gives rest to the heart. There is a better way. It is to repudiate our own wisdom and take instead the infinite wisdom of God.

A. W. Tozer

Wisdom is the God-given ability to see life with rare objectivity and to handle life with rare stability.

Charles Swindoll

A TIMELY TIP

Learning about God's truth is "head knowledge" and it is incomplete. Learning and living in accordance with God's truth is "head-and-heart knowledge" . . . and it is complete.

LIVING WITH THE UNEXPECTED

Do not boast about tomorrow, for you do not know what a day may bring forth.
Proverbs 27:1 NKJV

The old saying is both familiar and true: "Man proposes and God disposes." Proverbs 27:1 remind us that our world unfolds according to God's plans, not our wishes. Thus, boasting about future events is to be avoided by those who acknowledge God's sovereignty over all things.

Are you planning for a better tomorrow for yourself and your family? If so, you are to be congratulated: God rewards forethought in the same way that He often punishes impulsiveness. But as you make your plans, do so with humility, with gratitude, and with trust in your Heavenly Father. His hand directs the future; to think otherwise is both arrogant and naïve.

Like little children on Christmas Eve, we know that lovely surprises are in the making. We can't see them. We have simply been told, and we believe. Tomorrow we shall see.

Elisabeth Elliot

You have a glorious future in Christ! Live every moment in His power and love

Vonette Bright

A TIMELY TIP

The future isn't some pie-in-the-sky dream. Hope for the future is simply one aspect of trusting God.

THE PROBLEM OF SIN

Stay awake and pray, so that you won't enter into temptation. The spirit is willing, but the flesh is weak.

Matthew 26:41 Holman CSB

How hard is it to bump into temptation in this crazy world? Not very hard. The devil, it seems, is out on the street, working 24/7, causing pain and heartache in more ways than ever before. We, as Christians, must remain vigilant. Not only must we resist Satan when he confronts us, but we must also avoid those places where Satan can most easily tempt us. And, if we are to avoid the unending temptations of this world, we must arm ourselves with the Word of God.

In a letter to believers, Peter offers a stern warning: "Your adversary, the devil, prowls around like a roaring lion, seeking someone to devour" (1 Peter 5:8 NASB). What was true in New Testament times is equally true in our own. Satan tempts his prey and then devours them (and it's up to you—and only you—to make sure that you're not one of the ones being devoured!).

As believing Christians, we must beware because temptations are everywhere. Satan is determined to win; we must be equally determined that he does not.

It is not the Word hidden in the head that keeps us from sin. It is the Word hidden in the heart.

Vance Havner

A TIMELY TIP

Because you live in a temptation-filled world, you must guard your eyes, your thoughts, and your heart—all day, every day.

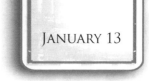

YOUR TO-DO LIST . . . AND GOD'S

Come near to God, and God will come near to you. You sinners, clean sin out of your lives. You who are trying to follow God and the world at the same time, make your thinking pure.

James 4:8 NCV

Have you fervently asked God to help prioritize your life? Have you asked Him for guidance and for the courage to do the things that you know need to be done? If so, then you're continually inviting your Creator to reveal Himself in a variety of ways. As a follower of Christ, you must do no less.

When you make God's priorities your priorities, you will receive God's abundance and His peace. When you make God a full partner in every aspect of your life, He will lead you along the proper path: His path. When you allow God to reign over your heart, He will honor you with spiritual blessings that are simply too numerous to count. So, as you plan for the day ahead, make God's will your ultimate priority. When you do, every other priority will have a tendency to fall neatly into place.

Our Lord is searching for people who will make a difference. Christians dare not dissolve into the background or blend into the neutral scenery of the world.

Charles Swindoll

A TIMELY TIP

Make time for God. Even if your day is filled to the brim with obligations and priorities, no priority is greater than our obligation to our Creator. Make sure to give Him the time He deserves, not only on Sundays, but also on every other day of the week.

FINDING COMFORT

I was very worried, but you comforted me . . . .

Psalm 94:19 NCV

If you are a person with lots of obligations and plenty of responsibilities, it is simply a fact of life: You worry. From time to time, you worry about health, about money, about safety, about family, and about countless other concerns, some great and some small.

Where is the best place to take your worries? Take them to God. Take your troubles to Him; take your fears to Him; take your doubts to Him; take your weaknesses to Him; take your sorrows to Him . . . and leave them all there. Seek protection from the One who offers you eternal salvation; build your spiritual house upon the Rock that cannot be moved.

Give your cares to Him who cares for the flowers of the field. Rest assured He will also care for you.

C. H. Spurgeon

The more you give your mental burdens to the Lord, the more exciting it becomes to see how God will handle things that are impossible for you to do anything about.

Charles Swindoll

A TIMELY TIP

Work hard, pray harder, and if you have any worries, take them to God—and leave them there.

GOD CARES

For the Lord your God is the God of gods and Lord of lords, the great, mighty, and awesome God.

Deuteronomy 10:17 Holman CSB

I t's a promise that is made over and over again in the Bible: Whatever "it" is, God can handle it.

Life isn't always easy. Far from it! Sometimes, life can be very, very tough. But even then, even during our darkest moments, we're protected by a loving Heavenly Father. When we're worried, God can reassure us; when we're sad, God can comfort us. When our hearts are broken, God is not just near; He is here. So we must lift our thoughts and prayers to Him. When we do, He will answer our prayers. Why? Because He is our shepherd, and He has promised to protect us now and forever.

The next time you're disappointed, don't panic. Don't give up. Just be patient and let God remind you he's still in control.

Max Lucado

The great love of God is an ocean without a bottom or a shore.

C. H. Spurgeon

A TIMELY TIP

God deserves first place in your life . . . and you deserve the experience of putting Him there.

FINDING FULFILLMENT IN ALL THE RIGHT PLACES

I am the Gate. Anyone who goes through me will be cared for—will freely go in and out, and find pasture. A thief is only there to steal and kill and destroy. I came so they can have real and eternal life, more and better life than they ever dreamed of. I am the Good Shepherd. The Good Shepherd puts the sheep before himself, sacrifices himself if necessary.

John 10:9-11 MSG

Where can we find contentment? Is it a result of wealth, or power, or beauty, or fame? Hardly. Genuine contentment is a gift from God to those who trust Him and follow His commandments.

Our modern world seems preoccupied with the search for happiness. We are bombarded with messages telling us that happiness depends upon the acquisition of material possessions. These messages are false. Enduring peace is not the result of our acquisitions; it is a spiritual gift from God to those who obey Him and accept His will.

If we don't find contentment in God, we will never find it anywhere else. But, if we seek Him and obey Him, we will be blessed with an inner peace that is beyond human understanding. When God dwells at the center of our lives, peace and contentment will belong to us just as surely as we belong to God.

We will never be happy until we make God the source of our fulfillment and the answer to our longings.

Stormie Omartian

A TIMELY TIP

Be contented where you are, even if it's not exactly where you want to end up. God has something wonderful in store for you—and remember that God's timing is perfect—so be patient, trust God, do your best, and expect the best.

SELF-ESTEEM 101

That is why we can say with confidence, "The Lord is my helper, so I will not be afraid. What can mere mortals do to me?"

Hebrews 13:6 NLT

Sometimes, it's hard to feel good about yourself, especially since you live in a society that keeps sending out the message that you've got to be perfect.

Are you your own worst critic? And in response to that criticism, are you constantly trying to transform yourself into a person who meets society's expectations, but not God's expectations? If so, it's time to become a little more understanding of the person in the mirror.

Millions of words have been written about various ways to improve self-esteem. Yet, maintaining a healthy self-image is, to a surprising extent, a matter of doing a few simple things: 1. Obeying God 2. Thinking healthy thoughts 3. Finding things to do that please your Creator and yourself. 4. Finding encouraging friends who reinforce your sense of self-worth, friends who urge you to behave yourself and believe in yourself. When you do these four things, your self-image will tend to take care of itself.

Being loved by Him whose opinion matters most gives us the security to risk loving, too—even loving ourselves.

Gloria Gaither

A TIMELY TIP

Until you learn when, where, and how to say "No," you'll make yourself miserable. So, the best time to learn how to say no to the things you don't need is now.

YOUR PARTNERSHIP WITH GOD

God is working in you to help you want to do and be able to do what pleases him.

Philippians 2:13 NCV

D o you want the best that life has to offer? If so, then you must form a partnership with God.

You are God's work-in-progress. God wants to mold your heart and guide your path, but because He created you as a creature of free will, He will not force you to become His. That choice is yours alone, and it is a choice that should be reflected in every decision you make and every step you take.

Today, as you encounter the challenges of everyday life, strengthen your partnership with God through prayer, through obedience, through praise, through thanksgiving, and through service. God is the ultimate partner, and He wants to be your partner in every aspect of your life. Please don't turn Him down.

No matter what we are going through, no matter how long the waiting for answers, of one thing we may be sure. God is faithful. He keeps His promises. What He starts, He finishes . . . including His perfect work in us.

Gloria Gaither

Our Lord never drew power from Himself, He drew it always from His Father.

Oswald Chambers

A TIMELY TIP

Perhaps you have become wrapped up in the world's problems or your own problems. If so, it's time to focus more on your spiritual blessings as you open yourself up to God. When you do, God will bless you and comfort you.

GUARD YOUR THOUGHTS

Those who are pure in their thinking are happy, because they will be with God.

Matthew 5:8 NCV

Paul Valéry observed, "We hope vaguely but dread precisely." How true. All too often, we allow the worries of everyday life to overwhelm our thoughts and cloud our vision. What's needed is clearer perspective, renewed faith, and a different focus.

When we focus on the frustrations of today or the uncertainties of tomorrow, we rob ourselves of peace in the present moment. But, when we focus on God's grace, and when we trust in the ultimate wisdom of God's plan for our lives, our worries no longer tyrannize us.

Today, remember that God is infinitely greater than the challenges that you face. Remember also that your thoughts are profoundly powerful, so guard them accordingly.

Attitude is the mind's paintbrush; it can color any situation.

Barbara Johnson

People who do not develop and practice good thinking often find themselves at the mercy of their circumstances.

John Maxwell

A TIMELY TIP

Your thoughts have the power to lift you up or bring you down, so you should guard your thoughts very carefully.

FINISHING THE WORK

It is better to finish something than to start it. It is better to be patient than to be proud.

Ecclesiastes 7:8 NCV

As you continue to seek God's purpose for your life, you will undoubtedly experience your fair share of disappointments, detours, false starts, and failures. When you do, don't become discouraged: God's not finished with you yet.

The old saying is as true today as it was when it was first spoken: "Life is a marathon, not a sprint." That's why wise travelers select a traveling companion who never tires and never falters. That partner, of course, is your Heavenly Father.

Are you tired? Ask God for strength. Are you discouraged? Believe in His promises. Are you defeated? Pray as if everything depended upon God, and work as if everything depended upon you. And finally, have faith that you play an important role in God's great plan for mankind—because you do.

Perseverance is more than endurance. It is endurance combined with absolute assurance and certainty that what we are looking for is going to happen.

Oswald Chambers

By perseverance the snail reached the ark.

C. H. Spurgeon

A TIMELY TIP

Life is difficult and success requires effort—so perseverance pays big dividends.

WHEN THE BOSS ISN'T WATCHING

Go to the ant, O sluggard. Observe her ways and be wise: which, having no chief, officer or ruler, prepares her food in the summer and gathers her provision in the harvest. How long will you lie down, O sluggard? When will you arise from your sleep?

Proverbs 6:6-9 NASB

The Bible instructs us that we can learn an important lesson of a surprising source: ants. Ants are among nature's most industrious creatures. They do their work without supervision and without hesitation. We should do likewise.

God's Word is clear: We are instructed to work diligently and faithfully. We are told that the fields are ripe for the harvest, that the workers are few, and that the importance of our work is profound. Let us labor, then, for our Master without hesitation and without complaint. Nighttime is coming. Until it does, let us honor our Heavenly Father with grateful hearts and willing hands.

If you want to reach your potential, you need to add a strong work ethic to your talent.

John Maxwell

Ordinary work, which is what most of us do most of the time, is ordained by God every bit as much as is the extraordinary.

Elisabeth Elliot

A TIMELY TIP

Today, take a hard look at your work habits. Is your work pleasing to God, and are you making the most of the skills and opportunities that He has given you? If so, congratulations on your hard work. If not, today is a great day to start working harder, or smarter, or both.

DEPENDING UPON GOD

Depend on the Lord and his strength; always go to him for help. Remember the miracles he has done; remember his wonders and his decisions.

Psalm 105:4-5 NCV

God is a never-ending source of strength and courage if we call upon Him. When we are weary, He gives us strength. When we see no hope, God reminds us of His promises. When we grieve, God wipes away our tears.

Do you feel overwhelmed by today's responsibilities? Do you feel pressured by the ever-increasing demands of 21st-century life? Then turn your concerns and your prayers over to God. He knows your needs, and He has promised to meet those needs. Whatever your circumstances, God will protect you and care for you . . . if you let Him. Invite Him into your heart and allow Him to renew your spirits. When you trust Him and Him alone, He will never fail you.

The strength that we claim from God's Word does not depend on circumstances. Circumstances will be difficult, but our strength will be sufficient.

Corrie ten Boom

You needn't worry about not feeling brave. Our Lord didn't—see the scene in Gethsemane. How thankful I am that when God became man He did not choose to become a man of iron nerves; that would not have helped weaklings like you and me nearly so much.

C. S. Lewis

A TIMELY TIP

When you are tired, fearful, or discouraged, God can restore your strength.

SPIRITUAL WEALTH

Trust in your money and down you go! But the godly flourish like leaves in spring.

Proverbs 11:28 NLT

Sometimes it's hard being a Christian, especially when the world keeps pumping out messages that are contrary to your faith.

The media is working around the clock in an attempt to rearrange your priorities. The media says that your appearance is all-important, that your clothes are all-important, that your relationships with the opposite sex are all-important, and that partying is all-important. But guess what? Those messages are lies. The "all-important" things in your life have little to do with parties and appearances. The all-important things in life have to do with your faith, your family, and your future. Period.

Are you willing to stand up for your faith? Are you willing to stand up and be counted, not just in church, where it's relatively easy to be a Christian, but also out there in the "real" world, where it's hard? Hopefully so, because you owe it to God and you owe it to yourself.

All those who look to draw their satisfaction from the wells of the world will soon be thirsty again!

Anne Graham Lotz

A fish would never be happy living on land, because it was made for water. An eagle could never feel satisfied if it wasn't allowed to fly. You will never feel completely satisfied on earth, because you were made for more.

Rick Warren

A TIMELY TIP

The media is pumping out messages that are contrary to your best interests, messages that are often totally untrue. So if you're smart, you'll develop a "media-filter" that separates truth from fiction.

LAUGHING WITH LIFE

A joyful heart makes a face cheerful.

Proverbs 15:13 Holman CSB

Laughter is medicine for the soul, but sometimes, amid the stresses of the day, we forget to take our medicine. Instead of viewing our world with a mixture of optimism and humor, we allow worries and distractions to rob us of the joy that God intends for our lives.

So the next time you find yourself dwelling upon the negatives of life, refocus your attention to things positive. The next time you find yourself falling prey to the blight of pessimism, stop yourself and turn your thoughts around. And, if you see your glass as "half-empty," rest assured that your spiritual vision is impaired. With God, your glass is never half empty. With God as your protector and Christ as your Savior, your glass is filled to the brim and overflowing . . . forever.

Today, as you go about your daily activities, approach life with a smile on your lips and hope in your heart. And laugh every chance you get. After all, God created laughter for a reason . . . and Father indeed knows best. So laugh!

I think everybody ought to be a laughing Christian. I'm convinced that there's just one place where there's not any laughter, and that's hell.

Jerry Clower

A TIMELY TIP

If you can't see the joy and humor in everyday life . . . you're not paying attention to the right things. Remember the donut-maker's creed: "As you travel through life brother, whatever be your goal, keep your eye upon the donut, and not upon the hole."

WHEN WE DON'T UNDERSTAND

Now we see a dim reflection, as if we were looking into a mirror, but then we shall see clearly. Now I know only a part, but then I will know fully, as God has known me.

1 Corinthians 13:12 NCV

As humans with limited understanding, we can never fully comprehend the hand of God. But as believers in a benevolent God, we must always trust the heart of our Heavenly Father.

Before His crucifixion, Jesus went to the Mount of Olives and poured out His heart to God (Luke 22). Jesus knew of the agony that He was destined to endure, but He also knew that God's will must be done. We, like our Savior, face trials that bring fear and trembling to the very depths of our souls, but like Christ, we, too, must ultimately seek God's will, not our own.

As this day unfolds, seek God's will for your own life and obey His Word. When you entrust your life to Him completely and without reservation, He will give you the strength to meet any challenge, the courage to face any trial, and the wisdom to live in His righteousness and in His peace.

A religion that is small enough for our understanding would not be big enough for our needs.

Corrie ten Boom

There are a lot of things in life that are difficult to understand. Faith allows the soul to go beyond what the eyes can see.

John Maxwell

A TIMELY TIP

Today, challenge your faith by promising yourself and your Creator that you will worship Him seven days a week, not just on Sunday.

TODAY'S BIBLE READING
Old Testament: Exodus 13-14
New Testament: Matthew 18:1-20

FAITH-FILLED CHRISTIAN

Cast your burden on the Lord, and He will support you; He will never allow the righteous to be shaken.

Psalm 55:22 Holman CSB

Pessimism and Christianity don't mix. Why? Because Christians have every reason to be optimistic about life here on earth and life eternal. As C. H. Spurgeon observed, "Our hope in Christ for the future is the mainstream of our joy." But sometimes, we fall prey to worry, frustration, anxiety, or sheer exhaustion, and our hearts become heavy. What's needed is plenty of rest, a large dose of perspective, and God's healing touch, but not necessarily in that order.

Today, make this promise to yourself and keep it: vow to be a hope-filled Christian. Think optimistically about your life, your profession, your future, and your students. Trust your hopes, not your fears. Take time to celebrate God's glorious creation. And then, when you've filled your heart with hope and gladness, share your optimism with others. They'll be better for it, and so will you. But not necessarily in that order.

Christ can put a spring in your step and a thrill in your heart. Optimism and cheerfulness are products of knowing Christ.

Billy Graham

A TIMELY TIP

Be a realistic optimist. Your attitude toward the future will help create your future. So think realistically about yourself and your situation while making a conscious effort to focus on hopes, not fears. When you do, you'll put the self-fulfilling prophecy to work for you.

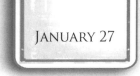
WHATEVER IT IS, GOD IS BIGGER

Jesus turned around and said to her, "Daughter, be encouraged! Your faith has made you well." And the woman was healed at that moment.

Matthew 9:22 NLT

Genuine faith is never meant to be locked up in the heart of a believer; to the contrary, it is meant to be shared with the world. But, if you sincerely seek to share your faith, you must first find it.

When a suffering woman sought healing by merely touching the hem of His cloak, Jesus replied, "Daughter, be of good comfort; thy faith hath made thee whole" (Matthew 9:22 KJV). The message to believers of every generation is clear: live by faith today and every day.

How can you strengthen your faith? Through praise, through worship, through Bible study, and through prayer. And, as your faith becomes stronger, you will find ways to share it with your friends, your family, and with the world. When you place your faith, your trust, indeed your life in the hands of Christ Jesus, you'll be amazed at the marvelous things He can do with you and through you; so trust God's plans. With Him, all things are possible, and whatever "it" is, God is bigger.

The Christian life is one of faith, where we find ourselves routinely overdriving our headlights but knowing it's okay because God is in control and has a purpose behind it.

Bill Hybels

A TIMELY TIP

If you don't have faith, you'll never move mountains. But if you do have faith, there's no limit to the things that you and God, working together, can accomplish.

TODAY IS YOUR CLASSROOM

If you teach the wise, they will get knowledge.

Proverbs 21:11 NCV

Today is your classroom: what will you learn? Will you use today's experiences as tools for personal growth, or will you ignore the lessons that life and God are trying to teach you? Will you carefully study God's Word, and will you apply His teachings to the experiences of everyday life? The events of today have much to teach. You have much to learn. May you live—and learn—accordingly.

God's plan for our guidance is for us to grow gradually in wisdom before we get to the crossroads.

Bill Hybels

The more wisdom enters our hearts, the more we will be able to trust our hearts in difficult situations.

John Eldredge

A TIMELY TIP

Your future depends, to a very great extent, upon you. So keep learning and keep growing personally, intellectually, emotionally, and spiritually.

MID-COURSE CORRECTIONS

The wise see danger ahead and avoid it, but fools keep going and get into trouble.

Proverbs 22:3 NCV

In our fast-paced world, everyday life has become an exercise in managing change. Our circumstances change; our relationships change; our bodies change. We grow older every day, as does our world. Thankfully, God does not change. He is eternal, as are the truths that are found in His Holy Word.

Are you facing one of life's inevitable "mid-course corrections"? If so, you must place your faith, your trust, and your life in the hands of the One who does not change: your Heavenly Father. He is the unmoving rock upon which you must construct this day and every day. When you do, you are secure.

The God who orchestrates the universe has a good many things to consider that have not occurred to me, and it is well that I leave them to Him.

Elisabeth Elliot

Having a doctrine pass before the mind is not what the Bible means by knowing the truth. It's only when it reaches down deep into the heart that the truth begins to set us free, just as a key must penetrate a lock to turn it, or as rainfall must saturate the earth down to the roots in order for your garden to grow.

John Eldredge

A TIMELY TIP

Don't be satisfied with the acquisition of knowledge . . . strive to acquire wisdom. As Beth Moore correctly observed, "A big difference exists between a head full of knowledge and the words of God literally abiding in us."

GOD'S SURPRISING PLANS

But as it is written: What no eye has seen and no ear has heard, and what has never come into a man's heart, is what God has prepared for those who love Him.

1 Corinthians 2:9 Holman CSB

God has plans for your life, wonderful, surprising plans . . . but He won't force those plans upon you. To the contrary, He has given you free will, the ability to make decisions on your own. With that freedom to choose comes the responsibility of living with the consequences of the choices you make.

If you seek to live in accordance with God's will for your life—and you should—then you will live in accordance with His commandments. You will study God's Word, and you will be watchful for His signs. You will associate with fellow Christians who will encourage your spiritual growth, and you will listen to that inner voice that speaks to you in the quiet moments of your daily devotionals.

God intends to use you in wonderful, unexpected ways if you let Him. The decision to seek God's plan and to follow it is yours and yours alone. The consequences of that decision have implications that are both profound and eternal, so choose carefully.

Even when we cannot see the why and wherefore of God's dealings, we know that there is love in and behind them, so we can rejoice always.

J. I. Packer

A TIMELY TIP

Carve out time to thank God for His blessings. Take time out of every day (not just on Sundays) to praise God and thank Him for His gifts.

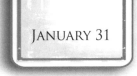

TODAY: A DAY OF CELEBRATION

Always be full of joy in the Lord. I say it again—rejoice!

Philippians 4:4 NLT

What is the best day to celebrate life? This one! Today and every day should be a time for celebration as we consider the Good News of God's gift: salvation through Jesus Christ.

What do you expect from the day ahead? Are you expecting God to do wonderful things, or are you living beneath a cloud of worry and doubt?

The familiar words of Psalm 118:24 remind us of a profound yet simple truth: "This is the day which the LORD has made." Our duty, as believers, is to rejoice in God's marvelous creation. For Christians, every day begins and ends with God and His Son. Christ came to this earth to give us abundant life and eternal salvation. We give thanks to our Maker when we treasure each day. So with no further ado, let the celebration begin!

Joy comes not from what we have but from what we are.

C. H. Spurgeon

A smile is the light in the window of your face that tells people your at home.

Barbara Johnson

A TIMELY TIP

If you don't feel like celebrating, start counting your blessings. Before long, you'll realize that you have plenty of reasons to celebrate.

THE MIGHTY WORKS OF THOSE WHO BELIEVE

I assure you: The one who believes in Me will also do the works that I do. And he will do even greater works than these, because I am going to the Father.

John 14:12 Holman CSB

When you invite Christ to rule over your heart, you avail yourself of His power. And make no mistake about it: You and Christ, working together, can do miraculous things. In fact, miraculous things are exactly what Christ intends for you to do, but He won't force you to do great things on His behalf. The decision to become a full-fledged participant in His power is a decision that you must make for yourself.

The words of John 14:12 make this promise: when you put absolute faith in Christ, you can share in His power. Today, trust the Savior's promise and expect a miracle in His name.

We must understand that the first and chief thing—for everyone who would do the work of Jesus—is to believe, and in doing so, to become linked to Him, the Almighty One . . . and then, to pray the prayer of faith in His Name.

Andrew Murray

We are saved by faith alone, but faith is never alone.

John Calvin

A TIMELY TIP

Wherever you happen to be, give your best effort. Giving your best is habit-forming, and it's a habit you need to acquire.

WHY AM I HERE?

May He grant you according to your heart's desire, and fulfill all your purpose.

Psalm 20:4 NKJV

"**W**hy did God put me here?" It's an easy question to ask and, at times, a very difficult question to answer. As you seek to answer that question, God's purposes will not always be clear to you. Sometimes you may wander aimlessly in a wilderness of your own making. And sometimes, you may struggle mightily against God in a vain effort to find success and happiness through your own means, not His.

Are you earnestly seeking to discern God's purpose for your life? If so, these pages are intended as a reminder of several important facts: 1. God has a plan for your life; 2. If you seek that plan sincerely and prayerfully, you will find it; 3. When you discover God's purpose for your life, you will experience abundance, peace, joy, and power—God's power. And that's the only kind of power that really matters.

God custom-designed you with your unique combination of personality, temperament, talents, and background, and He wants to harness and use these in His mission to reach this messed-up world.

Bill Hybels

Their distress is due entirely to their deliberate determination to use themselves for a purpose other than God's.

Oswald Chambers

A TIMELY TIP

God has a plan for your life, a definite purpose that you can fulfill . . . or not. Your challenge is to pray for God's guidance and to follow wherever He leads.

TODAY'S BIBLE READING
Old Testament: Exodus 31-33
New Testament: Matthew 22:23-46

TRUST HIM

Trust the Lord with all your heart, and don't depend on your own understanding. Remember the Lord in all you do, and he will give you success.

Proverbs 3:5-6 NCV

As the journey through this life unfolds day by day, we are confronted with situations that we simply don't understand. But God does. And He has a reason for everything that He does. Furthermore, God doesn't explain Himself in ways that we, as mortals with limited insight and clouded vision, can comprehend. So, instead of understanding every aspect of God's unfolding plan for our lives and our universe, we must be satisfied to trust Him completely. We cannot know God's motivations, nor can we understand His actions. We can, however, trust Him, and we must.

God is God. He knows what he is doing. When you can't trace his hand, trust his heart.

Max Lucado

Trusting God completely means having faith that he knows what is best for your life. You expect him to keep his promises, help you with problems, and do the impossible when necessary.

Rick Warren

A TIMELY TIP

It's simple: depend upon God. Remember the words of Vance Havner: "We must live in all kinds of days, both high days and low days, in simple dependence upon Christ as the branch on the vine. This is the supreme experience."

FAITH ABOVE FEELINGS

Now the just shall live by faith.

Hebrews 10:38 NKJV

Hebrews 10:38 teaches that we should live by faith. Yet sometimes, despite our best intentions, negative feelings can rob us of the peace and abundance that would otherwise be ours through Christ. When anger or anxiety separates us from the spiritual blessings that God has in store, we must rethink our priorities and renew our faith. And we must place faith above feelings. Human emotions are highly variable, decidedly unpredictable, and often unreliable. Our emotions are like the weather, only far more fickle. So we must learn to live by faith, not by the ups and downs of our own emotional roller coasters.

Sometime during this day, you will probably be gripped by a strong negative emotion. Distrust it. Reign it in. Test it. And turn it over to God. Your emotions will inevitably change; God will not. So trust Him completely as you watch your feelings slowly evaporate into thin air—which, of course, they will.

We are to live by faith, not feelings.

Kay Arthur

Only God can move mountains, but faith and prayer can move God.

E. M. Bounds

A TIMELY TIP

Feelings come and feelings go, but God never changes. So when you have a choice between trusting your feelings or trusting God, trust God.

BEYOND ENVY

We can't afford to waste a minute, must not squander these precious daylight hours in frivolity and indulgence, in sleeping around and dissipation, in bickering and grabbing everything in sight. Get out of bed and get dressed! Don't loiter and linger, waiting until the very last minute. Dress yourselves in Christ, and be up and about!

Romans 13:13-14 MSG

B ecause we are frail, imperfect human beings, we are sometimes envious of others. But God's Word warns us that envy is sin. Thus, we must guard ourselves against the natural tendency to feel resentment and jealousy when other people experience good fortune.

As believers, we have absolutely no reason to be envious of any people on earth. After all, as Christians we are already recipients of the greatest gift in all creation: God's grace. We have been promised the gift of eternal life through God's only begotten Son, and we must count that gift as our most precious possession.

Rather than succumbing to the sin of envy, we should focus on the marvelous things that God has done for us—starting with Christ's sacrifice. And we must refrain from preoccupying ourselves with the blessings that God has chosen to give others.

So here's a surefire formula for a happier, healthier life: Count your own blessings and let your neighbors count theirs. It's the godly way to live.

Discontent dries up the soul.

Elisabeth Elliot

A TIMELY TIP

You can be envious, or you can be happy, but you can't be both. Envy and happiness can't live at the same time in the same brain.

PREPARING FOR LIFE . . . AND DEATH

Alive, I'm Christ's messenger; dead, I'm his bounty. Life versus even more life! I can't lose.

Philippians 1:21 MSG

God has given you the gift of life. How will you use that gift? Will you allow God's Son to reign over your heart? And will you treat each day as a precious treasure from your Heavenly Father? You should, and, hopefully, you will.

Every day that we live, we should be preparing to die. If we seek to live purposeful, productive lives, we will be ever mindful that our time here on earth is limited, and we will conduct ourselves accordingly.

Life is a glorious opportunity, but it is also shockingly brief. We must serve God each day as if it were our last day. When we do, we prepare ourselves for the inevitable end of life on here earth, and or the victory that is certain to follow.

Death marks the beginning, not the end. It is our journey to God.

Billy Graham

I haven't lost my wife Sara because I know where she is. You haven't lost anything if you know where it is. Death can hide but not divide.

Vance Havner

A TIMELY TIP

People love talking about religion, and everybody has their own opinions, but ultimately only one opinion counts . . . God's. Think about God's promise of eternal life—and what that promise means to you.

ENTHUSIASM FOR YOUR JOURNEY

Do your work with enthusiasm. Work as if you were serving the Lord, not as if you were serving only men and women.

Ephesians 6:7 NCV

Do you see each day as a glorious opportunity to serve God and to do His will? Are you enthused about life, or do you struggle through each day giving scarcely a thought to God's blessings? Are you constantly praising God for His gifts, and are you sharing His Good News with the world? And are you excited about the possibilities for service that God has placed before you, whether at home, at work, at church, or at school? You should be.

You are the recipient of Christ's sacrificial love. Accept it enthusiastically and share it fervently. Jesus deserves your enthusiasm; the world deserves it; and you deserve the experience of sharing it.

Enthusiasm, like the flu, is contagious—we get it from one another.

Barbara Johnson

The proper perspective creates within us a spirit of reaching outside of ourselves with joy and enthusiasm.

Luci Swindoll

A TIMELY TIP

When you become genuinely enthused about your life and your faith, you'll guard your heart and improve your life.

BODY CARE

Don't you know that you are God's temple and that God's Spirit lives in you?

1 Corinthians 3:16 NCV

How do you treat your body? Do you treat it with the reverence and respect it deserves, or do you take it more or less for granted? Well, the Bible has clear instructions about the way you should take care of the miraculous body that God has given you.

God's Word teaches us that our bodies are "temples" that belong to God (1 Corinthians 6:19-20). We are commanded (not encouraged, not advised—we are commanded!) to treat our bodies with respect and honor. We do so by making wise choices and by making those choices consistently over an extended period of time.

Do you sincerely seek to improve the overall quality of your life and your health? Then promise yourself—and God—that you will begin making the kind of wise choices that will lead to a longer, healthier, happier life. The responsibility for those choices is yours. And so are the rewards.

God wants you to give Him your body. Some people do foolish things with their bodies. God wants your body as a holy sacrifice.

Warren Wiersbe

If you desire to improve your physical well-being and your emotional outlook, increasing your faith can help you.

John Maxwell

A TIMELY TIP

God needs you, and He's given you a marvelous gift: your body. Taking care of that body is your responsibility. Don't shirk that responsibility!

ENTRUSTING OUR HOPES TO GOD

You, Lord, give true peace to those who depend on you, because they trust you.

Isaiah 26:3 NCV

Have you ever felt hope for the future slipping away? If so, you have temporarily lost sight of the hope that we, as believers, must place in the promises of our Heavenly Father. If you are feeling discouraged, worried, or worse, remember the words of Psalm 31:24: "Be of good courage, and He shall strengthen your heart, all you who hope in the Lord" (NKJV).

Of course, we will face disappointments and failures, but these are only temporary defeats. Of course, this world can be a place of trials and tribulations, but we are secure. God has promised us peace, joy, and eternal life. And God keeps His promises today, tomorrow, and forever.

Everything that is done in the world is done by hope.

Martin Luther

God's Word never said we were not to grieve our losses. It says we are not to grieve as those who have no hope (1 Thessalonians 4:13). Big Difference.

Beth Moore

A TIMELY TIP

Since God has promised to guide and protect you—now and forever—you should never lose hope.

A POWER BEYOND UNDERSTANDING

I pray also that you will have greater understanding in your heart so you will know the hope to which he has called us and that you will know how rich and glorious are the blessings God has promised his holy people. And you will know that God's power is very great for us who believe.

Ephesians 1:18-19 NCV

Ours is a God of infinite possibilities. But sometimes, because of limited faith and limited understanding, we wrongly assume that God cannot or will not intervene in the affairs of mankind. Such assumptions are simply wrong.

Are you afraid to ask God to do big things in your life? Is your faith threadbare and worn? If so, it's time to abandon your doubts and reclaim your faith in God's promises.

God's Holy Word makes it clear: absolutely nothing is impossible for the Lord. And since the Bible means what it says, you can be comforted in the knowledge that the Creator of the universe can do miraculous things in your own life and in the lives of your loved ones. Your challenge, as a believer, is to take God at His word, and to expect the miraculous.

He upholds the whole creation, founded the earth, and still sustains it by the word of his power. What cannot he do in the affairs of families and kingdoms, far beyond our conception and expectation, who hangs the earth upon nothing?

Matthew Henry

A TIMELY TIP

God wants to bless you abundantly and eternally. When you trust God completely and obey Him faithfully, you will be blessed.

YOUR PLANS, GOD'S PLANS

You reveal the path of life to me; in Your presence is abundant joy; in Your right hand are eternal pleasures.

Psalm 16:11 Holman CSB

"What on earth does God intend for me to do with my life?" It's an easy question to ask but, for many of us, a difficult question to answer. Why? Because God's purposes aren't always clear to us. Sometimes we wander aimlessly in a wilderness of our own making. And sometimes, we struggle mightily against God in an unsuccessful attempt to find success and happiness through our own means, not His.

Are you genuinely trying to figure out God's purpose for your life? If so, you can be sure that with God's help, you will eventually discover it. So keep praying, and keep watching. And rest assured: God's got big plans for you . . . very big plans.

One of the wonderful things about being a Christian is the knowledge that God has a plan for our lives.

Warren Wiersbe

Jesus was the Savior Who would deliver them not only from the bondage of sin but also from meaningless wandering through life.

Anne Graham Lotz

A TIMELY TIP

Discovering God's purpose for your life requires a willingness to be open. God's plan is unfolding day by day. If you keep your eyes and your heart open, He'll reveal His plans. God has big things in store for you, but He may have quite a few lessons to teach you before you are fully prepared to do His will and fulfill His purposes.

A FAITH BIGGER THAN FEAR

Do not let your hearts be troubled. Trust in God; trust also in me. In my Father's house are many rooms; if it were not so, I would have told you. I am going there to prepare a place for you.

John 14:1-2 NIV

American clergyman Edward Everett Hale observed, "Some people bear three kinds of trouble—the ones they've had, the ones they have, and the ones they expect to have." How true. But a better strategy for you is this: accept the past, live in the present, and place the future in God's capable hands.

As you face the challenges of everyday life, you may be comforted by this fact: Trouble, of every kind, is temporary. Yet God's grace is eternal. And worries, of every kind, are temporary. But God's love is everlasting. The troubles that concern you will pass. God remains. And with these thoughts in mind, it's now time for you to place today's troubles in their proper perspective.

Worry and anxiety are sand in the machinery of life; faith is the oil.

E. Stanley Jones

Worry makes you forget who's in charge.

Max Lucado

A TIMELY TIP

An important part of becoming a more mature Christian is learning to worry less and to trust God more.

FEBRUARY 13

TODAY'S BIBLE READING
Old Testament: Leviticus 11-12
New Testament: Matthew 27:54-66

GOOD TREASURE FROM A GOOD HEART

A good person produces good deeds and words season after season.

Matthew 12:35 MSG

How can we demonstrate our love for God? By accepting His Son as our personal Savior and by placing Christ squarely at the center of our lives and our hearts. Jesus said that if we are to love Him, we must obey His commandments (John 14:15). Thus, our obedience to the Master is an expression of our love for Him.

In Ephesians 2:10 we read, "For we are His workmanship, created in Christ Jesus for good works" (NKJV). These words instructive: We are not saved by good works, but for good works. Good works are not the root, but rather the fruit of our salvation.

Today, let the fruits of your stewardship be a clear demonstration of your love for Christ. When you do, your good heart will bring forth many good things for yourself and for God. Christ has given you spiritual abundance and eternal life. You, in turn, owe Him good treasure from a single obedient heart . . . yours.

There is but one good; that is God. Everything else is good when it looks to Him and bad when it turns from Him.

C. S. Lewis

A TIMELY TIP

When you're trying to decide how to treat another person, ask yourself this question: "How would I feel if somebody treated me that way?" Then, treat the other person the way that you would want to be treated.

JESUS IS FIRST

First pay attention to me, and then relax. Now you can take it easy—you're in good hands.

Proverbs 1:33 MSG

Here's one last tip for your dating life: behave yourself like a Christian every day of the week, not just on Sundays. In other words, make Jesus a priority in every aspect of your life, including your dating life.

Jesus made an extreme sacrifice for you. Are you willing to make changes in your life for Him? Can you honestly say that you're passionate about your faith and that you're really following Jesus? Hopefully so. But if you're preoccupied with other things—or if you're strictly a one-day-a-week Christian—then you're in need of a big time spiritual makeover.

Jesus doesn't want you to be a run-of-the-mill, follow-the-crowd kind of believer. Jesus wants you to be a "new creation" through Him. And that's exactly what you should want for yourself, too.

So remember this: you're the recipient of Christ's love. Accept it enthusiastically and demonstrate your love with words and actions. Jesus deserves your heart—give it to Him today, tomorrow, and forever, Amen.

A disciple is a follower of Christ. That means you take on His priorities as your own. His agenda becomes your agenda. His mission becomes your mission.

Charles Stanley

A TIMELY TIP

Place God first in every aspect of your life, including your dating life: He deserves first place, and any relationship that doesn't put Him there is the wrong relationship for you. (Exodus 20:3)

TODAY'S BIBLE READING
Old Testament: Leviticus 15-16
New Testament: Mark 1:1-28

FINDING (AND TRUSTING) MENTORS

A wise man will listen and increase his learning, and a discerning man will obtain guidance.

Proverbs 1:5 Holman CSB

D
o you seek to become wise? Then you must acknowledge that you are not wise enough on your own. When you face an important decision, you must first study God's Word, and you should also seek the counsel of trusted friends and mentors.

When we arrive at the inevitable crossroads of life, God inevitably sends righteous men and women to guide us if we let them. If we are willing to listen and to learn, then we, too, will become wise. And God will bless our endeavors.

The fruit of wisdom is Christlikeness, peace, humility, and love. And, the root of it is faith in Christ as the manifested wisdom of God.

J. I. Packer

The process of living seems to consist in coming to realize truths so ancient and simple that, if stated, they sound like barren platitudes. They cannot sound otherwise to those who have not had the relevant experience: that is why there is no real teaching of such truths possible and every generation starts from scratch.

C. S. Lewis

A TIMELY TIP

Wisdom 101: If you're looking for wisdom (financial or otherwise), the Book of Proverbs is a wonderful place to start. It has 31 chapters, one for each day of the month. If you read Proverbs regularly, and if you take its teachings to heart, you'll gain timeless wisdom from God's unchanging Word.

DEMONSTRATING YOUR FAITH

So brothers and sisters, be careful that none of you has an evil, unbelieving heart that will turn you away from the living God. But encourage each other every day while it is "today." Help each other so none of you will become hardened because sin has tricked you.

Hebrews 3:13 NCV

Let's face facts: those of us who are Christians should be willing to talk about the things that Christ has done for us. Our personal testimonies are vitally important, but sometimes, because of shyness or insecurities, we're afraid to share our experiences. And that's unfortunate.

In his second letter to Timothy, Paul shares a message to believers of every generation when he writes, "God has not given us a spirit of timidity" (1:7). Paul's meaning is crystal clear: When sharing our testimonies, we must be courageous and unashamed.

We live in a world that desperately needs the healing message of Christ Jesus. Every believer, each in his or her own way, bears responsibility for sharing the Good News of our Savior. And it is important to remember that we bear testimony through both words and actions.

If you seek to be a radical follower of Christ, then it's time for you to share your testimony with others. So today, preach the Gospel through your words and your deeds . . . but not necessarily in that order.

How many people have you made homesick for God?

Oswald Chambers

A TIMELY TIP

Have you made the decision to allow Christ to reign over your heart? If so, you have an important story to tell: yours.

THE DAILY PATH

Then He said to them all, "If anyone wants to come with Me, he must deny himself, take up his cross daily, and follow Me."

Luke 9:23 Holman CSB

There's an old saying—trite but true—"Today is the first day of the rest of your life." As you get closer to graduation, you will be beginning a new life. Perhaps it will be time to move on to the halls of higher learning, or perhaps you'll be venturing into the workplace. Whatever your situation will be, remember that this day, like every day, holds boundless possibilities if you are wise enough and observant enough to claim them.

For Christian believers, every day begins and ends with God and His Son. Christ came to this earth to give us abundant life and eternal salvation. Our task is to accept Christ's grace with joy in our hearts and praise on our lips. Believers who fashion their days around Jesus are transformed: They see the world differently, they act differently, and they feel differently about themselves and their neighbors.

Christians face the inevitable challenges and disappointments of each day armed with the joy of Christ and the promise of salvation. So whatever this day holds for you, begin it and end it with God as your partner and Christ as your Savior. And throughout the day, give thanks to the One who created you and saved you. God's love for you is infinite. Accept it joyously and be thankful.

With each new dawn, life delivers a package to your front door, rings your doorbell, and runs.

Charles Swindoll

A TIMELY TIP

Remember that today is a wonderful, one-of-a-kind gift from God. Challenge yourself to treat it that way.

EXPECTING THE IMPOSSIBLE

Is anything impossible for the Lord?

Genesis 18:14 Holman CSB

D o you believe that God is at work in the world? And do you also believe that nothing is impossible for Him? If so, then you also believe that God is perfectly capable of doing things that you, as a mere human being with limited vision and limited understanding, would deem to be utterly impossible. And that's precisely what God does.

Since He created our universe out of nothingness, God has made a habit of doing miraculous things. And He still works miracles today. Expect Him to work miracles in your own life, and then be watchful. With God, absolutely nothing is impossible, including an amazing assortment of miracles that He stands ready, willing, and able to perform for you and yours.

If all things are possible with God, then all things are possible to him who believes in him.

Corrie ten Boom

When you believe that nothing significant can happen through you, you have said more about your belief in God than you have said about yourself.

Henry Blackaby

A TIMELY TIP

Focus on possibilities, not roadblocks. The road of life contains a number of potholes and stumbling blocks. Of course you will encounter them from time to time. But, don't invest large quantities of your life focusing on past misfortunes. On the road of life, regret is a dead end.

THE JOYS OF A CLEAR CONSCIENCE

Let us come near to God with a sincere heart and a sure faith, because we have been made free from a guilty conscience, and our bodies have been washed with pure water.

Hebrews 10:22 NCV

Few things in life torment us more than a guilty conscience. And, few things in life provide more contentment than the knowledge that we are obeying God's commandments. A clear conscience is one of the rewards we earn when we obey God's Word and follow His will. When we follow God's will and accept His gift of salvation, our earthly rewards are never-ceasing, and our heavenly rewards are everlasting.

A good conscience is a continual feast.

Francis Bacon

Your conscience is your alarm system. It's your protection.

Charles Stanley

A TIMELY TIP

If you're not sure what to do . . . slow down and listen to your conscience. That little voice inside your head is remarkably dependable, but you can't depend upon it if you never listen to it. So stop, listen, and learn—your conscience is almost always right!

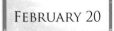

ARE YOU DATING? BE PICKY!

Do not be mismatched with unbelievers. For what partnership is there between righteousness and lawlessness? Or what fellowship does light have with darkness?

2 Corinthians 6:14 Holman CSB

I f you're still searching for that special someone, be patient, be prudent, and be picky. Look for someone whose values you respect, whose behavior you approve of, and whose faith you admire. Remember that appearances can be deceiving and tempting, so watch your step. And when it comes to the important task of building a lifetime relationship, pray about it!

If you happen to be one of those very lucky persons who has already fallen madly in love, say a great big thanks to the Matchmaker in heaven. But if you haven't yet found your love, don't fret. Just keep trusting God, and keep yourself open to the direction in which He is leading you. And remember: When it comes to selecting someone, God wants to give His approval—or not—but He won't give it until He's asked. So ask, listen, and decide accordingly.

When feeling becomes the dominant force in a relationship, the relationship is bound for trouble because feelings change.

Ed Young

Either God's Word keeps you from sin, or sin keeps you from God's Word.

Corrie ten Boom

A TIMELY TIP

Look beyond appearances. Judging other people solely by appearances is tempting, but it's foolish, shortsighted, immature, and ultimately destructive. So don't do it.

WHEN WE ARE BLESSED, WE ARE TESTED

Blessed in the man who does not walk in the counsel of the wicked or stand in the way of sinners or sit in the seat of mockers. But his delight is in the law of the LORD, and on his law he meditates day and night. He is like a tree planted by streams of water, which yields its fruit in season and whose leaf does not wither. Whatever he does prospers.

Psalm 1:1-3 NIV

Sometimes, we are tested more in times of plenty than we are in times of privation. When we experience life's difficult days, we may be more likely to turn our thoughts and hearts to God. But in times of plenty, when the sun is shining and our minds are at ease, we may be tempted to believe that our good fortune is entirely of our own making. Nothing could be further from the truth. God plays a hand in every aspect of everyday life, and for the blessings that we receive, we must offer thanks and praise to Him, not to ourselves.

Have you been blessed by God? Are you enjoying the abundance He has promised? If so, praise Him for His gifts. Praise Him faithfully and humbly. And don't, for a single moment, allow a prideful heart to separate you from blessings of your loving Father.

Blessings can either humble us and draw us closer to God or allow us to become full of pride and self-sufficiency.

Jim Cymbala

A TIMELY TIP

Carve out time to thank God for His blessings. Take time out of every day (not just on Sundays) to praise God and thank Him for His gifts.

THE COURAGE TO FOLLOW GOD

Be strong and courageous, and do the work. Don't be afraid or discouraged, for
the Lord God, my God, is with you. He won't leave you or forsake you.

1 Chronicles 28:20 Holman CSB

Because we are saved by a risen Christ, we can have hope for the future, no matter how desperate our circumstances may seem. After all, God has promised that we are His throughout eternity. And, He has told us that we must place our hopes in Him.

Today, summon the courage to follow God. Even if the path seems difficult, even if your heart is fearful, trust your Heavenly Father and follow Him. Trust Him with your day and your life. Do His work, care for His children, and share His Good News. Let Him guide your steps. He will not lead you astray.

Down through the centuries, in times of trouble and trial, God has brought courage to the hearts of those who love Him. The Bible is filled with assurances of God's help and comfort in every kind of trouble which might cause fears to arise in the human heart. You can look ahead with promise, hope, and joy.

Billy Graham

The amazing thing about Jesus is that He doesn't just patch up our lives, He gives us a brand new sheet, a clean slate to start over, all new.

Gloria Gaither

A TIMELY TIP

Is your courage being tested? Cling tightly to God's promises, and pray. God can give you the strength to meet any challenge, and that's exactly what you should ask Him to do.

WELCOMING THE NEW YOU

You were taught to leave your old self—to stop living the evil way you lived before. That old self becomes worse, because people are fooled by the evil things they want to do. But you were taught to be made new in your hearts, to become a new person. That new person is made to be like God—made to be truly good and holy.

Ephesians 4:22–24 NCV

Think, for a moment, about the "old" you, the person you were before you invited Christ to reign over your heart. Now, think about the "new" you, the person you have become since then. Is there a difference between the "old" you and the "new and improved" version? There should be! And that difference should be noticeable not only to you but also to others.

The Bible clearly teaches that when we welcome Christ into our hearts, we become new creations through Him. Our challenge, of course, is to behave ourselves like new creations. When we do, God fills our hearts, He blesses our endeavors, and transforms our lives . . . forever.

No man is ever the same after God has laid His hand upon him.

A. W. Tozer

The amazing thing about Jesus is that He doesn't just patch up our lives, He gives us a brand new sheet, a clean slate to start over, all new.

Gloria Gaither

A TIMELY TIP

Unless you're a radically different person because of your relationship with Jesus, your faith isn't what it could be . . . or should be.

A HEALTHY FEAR

Reverence for the Lord is the foundation of true wisdom. The rewards of wisdom come to all who obey him.

Psalm 111:10 NLT

The Bible instructs us that a healthy fear of the Lord is the foundation of wisdom. Yet sometimes, in our shortsightedness, we fail to show respect for our Creator because we fail to obey Him. When we do, our disobedience always has consequences, and sometimes those consequences are severe.

When we honor the Father by obeying His commandments, we receive His love and His grace. Today, let us demonstrate our respect for God by developing a healthy fear of disobeying Him.

A healthy fear of God will do much to deter us from sin.

Charles Swindoll

When true believers are awed by the greatness of God and by the privilege of becoming His children, then they become sincerely motivated, effective evangelists.

Bill Hybels

A TIMELY TIP

When you possess a healthy fear of God, He will guide your steps and guard your heart.

THE ULTIMATE ARMOR

Finally, be strong in the Lord and in his mighty power. Put on the full armor of God so that you can take your stand against the devil's schemes.

Ephesians 6:10-11 NIV

In a world filled with dangers and temptations, God is the ultimate armor. In a world filled with misleading messages, God's Word is the ultimate truth. In a world filled with more frustrations than we can count, God's Son offers the ultimate peace. Will you accept God's peace and wear God's armor against the dangers of our world?

Sometimes, in the crush of everyday life, God may seem far away, but He is not. God is everywhere you have ever been and everywhere you will ever go. He is with you night and day; He knows your thoughts and your prayers. His is your ultimate Protector. And, when you earnestly seek His protection, you will find it because He is here—always—waiting patiently for you to reach out to Him.

God walks with us. He scoops us up in His arms or simply sits with us in silent strength until we cannot avoid the awesome recognition that yes, even now, He is here.

Gloria Gaither

As we join together in prayer, we draw on God's enabling might in a way that multiplies our own efforts many times over.

Shirley Dobson

A TIMELY TIP

Of this you can be sure: God's faithfulness is steadfast, unwavering, and eternal.

USING OUR GIFTS

I remind you to keep using the gift God gave you . . . . Now let it grow, as a small flame grows into a fire.

2 Timothy 1:6 NCV

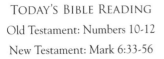

Face it: you've got an array of talents that need to be refined. All people possess special gifts—bestowed from the Father above—and you are no exception. But, your particular gift is no guarantee of success; it must be cultivated—by you—or it will go unused . . . and God's gift to you will be squandered.

Are you willing to do the hard work that's required to discover your talents and to develop them? If you are wise, you'll answer "yes." After all, if you don't make the most of your talents, who has the most to lose? You do!

So make a promise to yourself that you will earnestly seek to discover the talents that God has given you. Then, nourish those talents and make them grow. Finally, vow to share your gifts with the world for as long as God gives you the power to do so. After all, the best way to say "Thank You" for God's gifts is to use them.

The Lord has abundantly blessed me all of my life. I'm not trying to pay Him back for all of His wonderful gifts; I just realize that He gave them to me to give away.

Lisa Whelchel

A TIMELY TIP

You are the sole owner of your own set of talents and opportunities. God has given you your own particular gifts—the rest is up to you.

OUR PURPOSES, GOD'S PURPOSES

For we are His making, created in Christ Jesus for good works, which God prepared ahead of time so that we should walk in them.

Ephesians 2:10 Holman CSB

Whenever we struggle against God's plans, we suffer. When we resist God's calling, our efforts bear little fruit. Our best strategy, therefore, is to seek God's wisdom and to follow Him wherever He chooses to lead. When we do so, we are blessed.

When we align ourselves with God's purposes, we avail ourselves of His power and His peace. But how can we know precisely what God's intentions are? The answer, of course, is that even the most well-intentioned believers face periods of uncertainty and doubt about the direction of their lives. So, too, will you.

When you arrive at one of life's inevitable crossroads, that is precisely the moment when you should turn your thoughts and prayers toward God. When you do, He will make Himself known to you in a time and manner of His choosing.

God will help us become the people we are meant to be, if only we will ask Him.

Hannah Whitall Smith

You cannot be the person God meant you to be, and you cannot live the life he meant you to live, unless you live from the heart.

John Eldredge

A TIMELY TIP

God has a wonderful plan for your life. And the time to start looking for that plan—and living it—is now.

THOUGHTFUL WORDS

The wise don't tell everything they know, but the foolish talk too much and are ruined.

Proverbs 10:14 NCV

Think . . . pause . . . then speak: How wise is the person who can communicate in this way. But all too often, in the rush to have ourselves heard, we speak first and think next . . . with unfortunate results.

God's Word reminds us that, "Reckless words pierce like a sword, but the tongue of the wise brings healing" (Proverbs 12:18 NIV). If we seek to be a source of encouragement to friends and family, then we must measure our words carefully. Words are important: they can hurt or heal. Words can uplift us or discourage us, and reckless words, spoken in haste, cannot be erased.

Today, seek to encourage all who cross your path. Measure your words carefully. Speak wisely, not impulsively. Use words of kindness and praise, not words of anger or derision. Remember that you have the power to heal others or to injure them, to lift others up or to hold them back. When you lift them up, your wisdom will bring healing and comfort to a world that needs both.

Like dynamite, God's power is only latent power until it is released. You can release God's dynamite power into people's lives and the world through faith, your words, and prayer.

Bill Bright

A TIMELY TIP

God understands the importance of the words you speak . . . and so must you.

POPULARITY CONTESTS

Do you think I am trying to make people accept me? No, God is the One I am trying to please. Am I trying to please people? If I still wanted to please people, I would not be a servant of Christ.

Galatians 1:10 NCV

A re you a people-pleaser or a God-pleaser? Hopefully, you're far more concerned with pleasing God than you are with pleasing your friends. But face facts: even if you're a devoted Christian, you're still going to feel the urge to impress your friends and acquaintances—and sometimes that urge will be strong.

Peer pressure can be good or bad, depending upon who your peers are and how they behave. If your friends encourage you to follow God's will and to obey His commandments, then you'll experience positive peer pressure, and that's a good thing. But, if your friends encourage you to do foolish things, then you're facing a different kind of peer pressure . . . and you'd better beware.

To sum it up, here's your choice: you can choose to please God first, or you can fall victim to peer pressure. The choice is yours—and so are the consequences.

Long ago I ceased to count heads. Truth is often in the minority in this evil world.

C. H. Spurgeon

Comparison is the root of all feelings of inferiority.

James Dobson

A TIMELY TIP

Your world is loaded up with pressures, some good and some bad. Your big challenge is to know the difference and act accordingly.

SELF-DEFEATING ANGER

When you are angry, do not sin, and be sure to stop being angry before the end of the day. Do not give the devil a way to defeat you.

Ephesians 4:26–27 NCV

When you allow yourself to become angry, you are certain to defeat at least one person: yourself. When you allow the minor frustrations of everyday life to hijack your emotions, you do harm to yourself and to your loved ones. So today and every day, guard yourself against the kind of angry thinking that inevitably takes a toll on your emotions and your relationships.

When you strike out in anger, you may miss the other person, but you will always hit yourself.

Jim Gallery

Anger breeds remorse in the heart, discord in the home, bitterness in the community, and confusion in the state.

Billy Graham

A Timely Tip

When you lose your temper . . . you lose.

SLOW DOWN

Careful planning puts you ahead in the long run; hurry and scurry puts you further behind.

Proverbs 21:5 MSG

Everybody knows you're a very busy person. But here's a question: are you able to squeeze time into your hectic schedule for God? Hopefully so! But if you're one of those who rush through the day with scarcely a single moment to talk with your Creator, it's time to reshuffle your priorities.

You live in a noisy world, a world filled with distractions, frustrations, temptations, and complications. But if you allow the distractions of everyday life to distract you from God's peace, you're doing yourself a big disservice. So here's some good advice: instead of rushing nonstop through the day, slow yourself down long enough to have a few quiet minutes with God.

Nothing is more important than the time you spend with your Heavenly Father. Absolutely nothing. So be still and claim the inner peace that is your spiritual birthright: the peace of Jesus Christ. It is offered freely; it has been paid for in full; it is yours for the asking. So ask. And then share.

The foe of opportunity is preoccupation. Just when God sends along a chance to turn a great victory for mankind, some of us are too busy puttering around to notice it.

A. W. Tozer

A TIMELY TIP

Do first things first, and keep your focus on high-priority tasks. And remember this: your highest priority should be your relationship with God and His Son.

THE DANGERS OF PRIDE

Pride leads only to shame; it is wise to be humble.

Proverbs 11:2 NCV

The words from Proverbs 11 remind us that pride and destruction are traveling partners. But as imperfect human beings, we are tempted to puff out our chests and crow about our own accomplishments. When we do so, we delude ourselves.

As Christians, we have a profound reason to be humble: We have been refashioned and saved by Jesus Christ, and that salvation came not because of our own good works but because of God's grace. Thus, we are not "self-made"; we are "God-made" and "Christ-saved." How, then, can we be boastful? The answer, of course, is simple: if we are honest with ourselves and with our God, we cannot be boastful. In the quiet moments, when we search the depths of our own hearts, we know that whatever "it" is, God did that. And He deserves the credit.

The Lord sends no one away empty except those who are full of themselves.

D. L. Moody

The Bible never says that God resists a drunkard, a thief, or even a murderer, but he does resist the proud. Every kind of sin can be cleansed and forgiven if we humble ourselves and confess it to the Lord.

Jim Cymbala

A TIMELY TIP

All of your talents and abilities come from God. Give Him thanks, and give Him the glory.

FORGIVENESS AND SPIRITUAL GROWTH

Be gentle with one another, sensitive. Forgive one another as quickly and thoroughly as God in Christ forgave you.

Ephesians 4:32 MSG

Are you the kind of person who has a tough time forgiving and forgetting? If so, welcome to the club. Most of us find it difficult to forgive the people who have hurt us. And that's too bad because life would be much simpler if we could forgive people "once and for all" and be done with it. Yet forgiveness is seldom that easy. Usually, the decision to forgive is straightforward, but the process of forgiving is more difficult. Forgiveness is a journey that requires effort, time, perseverance, and prayer.

If there exists even one person whom you have not forgiven (and that includes yourself), obey God's commandment: forgive that person today. And remember that bitterness, anger, and regret are not part of God's plan for your life. Forgiveness is.

If you sincerely wish to forgive someone, pray for that person. And then pray for yourself by asking God to heal your heart. Don't expect forgiveness to be easy or quick, but rest assured: with God as your partner, you can forgive . . . and you will.

It is better to forgive and forget than to resent and remember.

Barbara Johnson

A TIMELY TIP

Until you learn how to forgive, you're locked inside a prison of your own making.

PERSEVERING FOR GOD

Therefore, my dear brothers, be steadfast, immovable, always abounding in the Lord's work, knowing that your labor in the Lord is not in vain.

1 Corinthians 15:58 Holman CSB

Are you a person who doesn't give up easily, or are you quick to bail out when the going gets tough? If you've developed the unfortunate habit of giving up at the first sign of trouble, it's probably time for you to have a heart-to-heart talk with that person you see every time you look in the mirror.

A well-lived life is like a marathon, not a sprint—it calls for preparation, determination, and lots of perseverance. As an example of perfect perseverance, you need look no further than your Savior, Jesus Christ.

Jesus finished what He began. Despite His suffering and despite the shame of the cross, Jesus was steadfast in His faithfulness to God. You, too, should remain faithful, especially when times are tough.

Are you facing a difficult situation? If so, remember this: whatever your problem, God can handle it. Your job is to keep persevering until He does.

Every achievement worth remembering is stained with the blood of diligence and scarred by the wounds of disappointment.

Charles Swindoll

When God is silent, you have only one reasonable option—trust Him; hang in there; wait on Him. He may be quiet, but He has not quit on you.

Charles Stanley

A TIMELY TIP

Life is an exercise in perseverance. If you persevere, you win.

CHOICES MATTER

But Daniel purposed in his heart that he would not defile himself . . . .

Daniel 1:8 KJV

Your life is a series of choices. From the instant you wake up in the morning until the moment you nod off to sleep at night, you make lots of decisions: decisions about the things you do, decisions about the words you speak, and decisions about the thoughts you choose to think. Simply put, the quality of those decisions determines the quality of your life.

So, if you sincerely want to lead a life that is pleasing to God, you must make choices that are pleasing to Him. And you know what? He deserves no less . . . and neither, for that matter, do you.

There may be no trumpet sound or loud applause when we make a right decision, just a calm sense of resolution and peace.

Gloria Gaither

Life is a series of choices between the bad, the good, and the best. Everything depends on how we choose.

Vance Havner

A TIMELY TIP

If you've got a decision to make, the first thing you should do is slow down and check it out with God.

ENERGY FOR TODAY

Let us lay aside every weight and the sin that so easily ensnares us, and run with endurance the race that lies before us, keeping our eyes on Jesus, the source and perfecter of our faith.

Hebrews 12:1-2 Holman CSB

All of us have moments when we feel drained. All of us suffer through difficult days, trying times, and perplexing periods of our lives. Thankfully, God stands ready and willing to give us comfort and strength if we turn to Him.

Burning the candle at both ends is tempting but potentially destructive. Instead, we should place first things first by saying no to the things that we simply don't have the time or the energy to do. As we establish our priorities, we should turn to God and to His Holy Word for guidance.

If you're a person with too many demands and too few hours in which to meet them, don't fret. Instead, focus upon God and upon His love for you. Then, ask Him for the wisdom to prioritize your life and the strength to fulfill your responsibilities. God will give you the energy to do the most important things on today's to-do list . . . if you ask Him. So ask Him.

Where there is much prayer, there will be much of the Spirit; where there is much of the Spirit, there will be ever-increasing power.

Andrew Murray

A TIMELY TIP

Feeling exhausted? Try this: Start getting more sleep each night; begin a program of regular, sensible exercise; avoid harmful food and drink; and turn your problems over to God . . . and the greatest of these is "turn your problems over to God."

CHOOSING WISELY

The thing you should want most is God's kingdom and doing what God wants. Then all these other things you need will be given to you.

Matthew 6:33 NCV

The choices you make will determine the quality and direction of your life. And that includes all the choices you make about your dating life. As an informed citizen of the 21st century, you have every reason to make wise choices. But sometimes, when the pressures of the dating world threaten to grind you up and spit you out, you may feel tempted to make decisions that are displeasing to God. When you do, you'll suffer in more ways than you can imagine.

So, as you pause to consider the kind of Christian you are—and the kind of Christian you want to become—ask yourself whether you're sitting on the fence or standing in the light. And then, if you sincerely want to follow in the footsteps of the One from Galilee, make choices that are pleasing to Him. He deserves no less . . . and neither, for that matter, do you.

Life is pretty much like a cafeteria line—it offers us many choices, both good and bad. The Christian must have a spiritual radar that detects the difference not only between bad and good but also among good, better, and best.

Dennis Swanberg

A TIMELY TIP

Little decisions, when taken together over a long period of time, can have big consequences. So remember that when it comes to matters of health, school, dating, or spirituality, there are no small decisions.

WHEN YOU ARE HURT

We take the good days from God—why not also the bad days?

Job 2:10 MSG

Face it: sometimes people can be very cruel. And when people are unkind to you or to your friends, you may be tempted to strike back in anger. Don't do it! Instead, remember that God corrects other people's behaviors in His own way, and He doesn't need your help. And remember that God has commanded you to forgive others, just as you, too, must sometimes seek forgiveness from them.

So, when other people are cruel, as they most certainly will be from time to time, what should you do? 1. Politely speak up for yourself (and for people who can't speak up for themselves); 2. Forgive everybody as quickly as you can; 3. Leave the rest up to God, and 4. Get on with your life.

Some folks cause happiness wherever they go, others whenever they go.

Barbara Johnson

The scrutiny we give other people should be for ourselves.

Oswald Chambers

A TIMELY TIP

Plenty of young people (and plenty of adults, too) can be plenty cruel, but you should never be.

RECEIVING GOD IN THE PRESENT TENSE

Love the Lord your God with all your heart, with all your soul, and with all your strength.

Deuteronomy 6:5 Holman CSB

God's love for you is deeper and more profound than you can imagine. God's love for you is so great that He sent His only Son to this earth to die for your sins and to offer you the priceless gift of eternal life. Now, you must decide whether or not to accept God's gift. Will you ignore it or embrace it? Will you return it or neglect it? Will you accept Christ's love and build a lifelong relationship with Him, or will you turn away from Him and take a different path?

Your decision to allow Christ to reign over your heart is the pivotal decision of your life. It is a decision that you cannot ignore. It is a decision that is yours and yours alone. Accept God's gift now: allow His Son to preside over your heart, your thoughts, and your life, starting this very instant.

Jesus is the personal approach from the unseen God coming so near that he becomes inescapable. You don't have to find him—you just have to consent to be found.

E. Stanley Jones

It's your heart that Jesus longs for: your will to be made His own with self on the cross forever, and Jesus alone on the throne.

Ruth Bell Graham

A TIMELY TIP

The ultimate choice for you is the choice to invite God's Son into your heart. Choose wisely . . . and immediately.

WISDOM IS AS WISDOM DOES

A foolish person enjoys doing wrong, but a person with understanding enjoys doing what is wise.

Proverbs 10:23 NCV

D o you seek to become wise? If so, you must behave wisely. Wisdom is as wisdom does.

High-sounding platitudes are as common as table salt. Aphorisms are everywhere. Parables proliferate. No matter. Wisdom is denominated not by words, but by deeds.

Do you wish to walk among the wise? If so, you must walk wisely. There is simply no other way.

The best evidence of our having the truth is our walking in the truth.

Matthew Henry

There are some things that can be learned by the head, but Christ crucified can only be learned by the heart.

C. H. Spurgeon

A TIMELY TIP

If you want to be really smart, you've got to behave wisely . . . It's as simple as that.

A SOCIETY BRIMMING WITH TEMPTATIONS

But remember that the temptations that come into your life are no different from what others experience. And God is faithful. He will keep the temptation from becoming so strong that you can't stand up against it. When you are tempted, he will show you a way out so that you will not give in to it.

1 Corinthians 10:13 NLT

Face facts: you live in a temptation-filled world. The devil is hard at work in your neighborhood, and so are his helpers. Here in the 21st Century, the bad guys are working around the clock to lead you astray. That's why you must remain vigilant.

In a letter to believers, Peter offers a stern warning: "Your adversary, the devil, prowls around like a roaring lion, seeking someone to devour" (I Peter 5:8 NASB). What was true in New Testament times is equally true in our own. Satan tempts his prey and then devours them (and it's up to you—and only you—to make sure that you're not one of the ones being devoured!).

As a believer who seeks a radical relationship with Jesus, you must beware because temptations are everywhere. Satan is determined to win; you must be equally determined that he does not.

Temptation always carries with it some bait that appeals to our natural desires. The bait not only attracts us, but it also hides the fact that yielding to the desire will eventually bring sorrow and punishment.

Warren Wiersbe

A TIMELY TIP

Here in the 21st century, the road to ruin is big, fast, wide, and crowded. Steer clear.

A NEW LIFE

You have been born again, and this new life did not come from something that dies, but from something that cannot die. You were born again through God's living message that continues forever.

2 Peter 1:23 NCV

God's Word is clear: When we genuinely invite Him to reign over our hearts, and when we accept His transforming love, we are forever changed. When we welcome Christ into our hearts, an old life ends and a new way of living—along with a completely new way of viewing the world—begins.

Each morning offers a fresh opportunity to invite Christ, yet once again, to rule over our hearts and our days. Each morning presents yet another opportunity to take up His cross and follow in His footsteps. Today, let us rejoice in the new life that is ours through Christ, and let us follow Him, step by step, on the path that He first walked.

You were born with tremendous potential. When you were born again through faith in Jesus Christ, God added spiritual gifts to your natural talents.

Warren Wiersbe

When I met Christ, I felt that I had swallowed sunshine.

E. Stanley Jones

A TIMELY TIP

When you allow Christ to rule your heart, you take a risk (by giving up many things that the world values) in order to earn a priceless reward (by earning peace here on earth and eternal life in heaven).

DREAMS NOT WORTH CHASING

Those who work their land will have plenty of food, but the ones who chase empty dreams instead will end up poor.

Proverbs 28:19 NCV

Some of our most important dreams are the ones we abandon. Some of our most important goals are the ones we don't attain. Sometimes, our most important journeys are the ones that we take to the winding conclusion of what seem to be dead-end streets. Thankfully, with God there are no dead ends; there are only opportunities to learn, to yield, to trust, to serve, and to grow.

The next time you experience one of life's inevitable disappointments, don't despair and don't be afraid to try "Plan B." Consider every setback an opportunity to choose a different, more appropriate path. Have faith that God may indeed be leading you in an entirely different direction, a direction of His choosing. And as you take your next step, remember that what looks like a dead end to you may, in fact, be the fast lane according to God.

Set goals so big that unless God helps you, you will be a miserable failure.

Bill Bright

Resisting His will for your life will cause you to doubt.

Anne Graham Lotz

A TIMELY TIP

Making your dreams come true requires work. John Maxwell writes, "The gap between your vision and your present reality can only be filled through a commitment to maximize your potential." Enough said.

A LIFETIME OF SPIRITUAL GROWTH

You are God's children whom he loves, so try to be like him. Live a life of love just as Christ loved us and gave himself for us as a sweet-smelling offering and sacrifice to God.

Ephesians 5:1 NCV

The journey toward spiritual maturity lasts a lifetime: As Christians, we can and should continue to grow in the love and the knowledge of our Savior as long as we live. Norman Vincent Peale had simple advice for believers of all ages: "Ask the God who made you to keep remaking you." That advice, of course, is perfectly sound, but too often ignored.

When we cease to grow, either emotionally or spiritually, we do ourselves and our families a profound disservice. But, if we study God's Word, if we obey His commandments, and if we live in the center of His will, we will not be "stagnant" believers; we will, instead, be growing Christians . . . and that's exactly what God wants for our lives.

In those quiet moments when we open our hearts to God, the Creator who made us keeps remaking us. He gives us direction, perspective, wisdom, and courage. And, the appropriate moment to accept His spiritual gifts is always this one.

God wants to revolutionize our lives—by showing us how knowing Him can be the most powerful force to help us become all we want to be.

Bill Hybels

A TIMELY TIP

Wherever you are in your spiritual journey, it's always the right time to take another step toward God.

BEYOND ANXIETY

Anxiety in a man's heart weighs it down, but a good word cheers it up.

Proverbs 12:25 Holman CSB

God calls us to live above and beyond anxiety. God calls us to live by faith, not by fear. He instructs us to trust Him completely, this day and forever. But sometimes, trusting God is difficult, especially when we become caught up in the incessant demands of an anxious world.

When you feel anxious—and you will—return your thoughts to God's love. Then, take your concerns to Him in prayer, and to the best of your ability, leave them there. Whatever "it" is, God is big enough to handle it. Let Him. Now.

The thing that preserves a man from panic is his relationship to God.

Oswald Chambers

One of the main missions of God is to free us from the debilitating bonds of fear and anxiety. God's heart is broken when He sees us so demoralized and weighed down by fear.

Bill Hybels

A TIMELY TIP

You have worries, but God has solutions. Your challenge is to trust Him to solve the problems that you can't.

NEVER GIVE UP

Even though good people may be bothered by trouble seven times, they are never defeated.

Proverbs 24:16 NCV

D

o you sincerely want to live a life that is pleasing to God? If so, you must remember that life is not a sprint, it's a marathon that calls for preparation, determination, and lots of perseverance.

Are you one of those people who doesn't give up easily, or are you quick to bail out when the going gets tough? If you've developed the unfortunate habit of giving up at the first sign of trouble, it's probably time for you to have a heart-to-heart talk with the person you see every time you look in the mirror.

Jesus finished what He began, and so should you. Despite His suffering and despite the shame of the cross, Jesus was steadfast in His faithfulness to God. You, too, must remain faithful, especially when times are tough.

Do you want to build a closer relationship with God? Then don't give up. And if you're facing a difficult situation, remember this: whatever your problem, God can handle it. Your job is to keep persevering until He does.

That is the source of Jeremiah's living persistence, his creative constancy. He was up before the sun, listening to God's word. Rising early, he was quiet and attentive before his Lord. Long before the yelling started, the mocking, the complaining, there was this centering, discovering, exploring time with God.

Eugene Peterson

A TIMELY TIP

If things don't work out at first, don't quit. If you never try, you'll never know how good you can be.

THE IMPORTANCE OF WORDS

So then, rid yourselves of all evil, all lying, hypocrisy, jealousy, and evil speech. As newborn babies want milk, you should want the pure and simple teaching. By it you can grow up and be saved.

1 Peter 2:1–2 NCV

How important are the words we speak? More important than we realize. Our words have echoes that extend beyond place or time. If our words are encouraging, we can lift others up; if our words are hurtful, we can hold others back.

Do you seek to be a source of encouragement to others? And, do you seek to be a worthy ambassador for Christ? If so, you must speak words that are worthy of your Savior. So avoid angry outbursts. Refrain from impulsive outpourings. Terminate tantrums. Instead, speak words of encouragement and hope to your family and friends, who, by the way, most certainly need all the hope and encouragement they can find.

Words. Do you fully understand their power? Can any of us really grasp the mighty force behind the things we say? Do we stop and think before we speak, considering the potency of the words we utter?

Joni Eareckson Tada

The things that we feel most deeply we ought to learn to be silent about, at least until we have talked them over thoroughly with God.

Elisabeth Elliot

A TIMELY TIP

You can guard your heart by paying careful attention to the words you speak. So measure your words carefully and prayerfully.

MAKING THE MOST OF WHATEVER COMES

A man's heart plans his way, but the Lord determines his steps.

Proverbs 16:9 Holman CSB

God's hand shapes the world, and it shapes your life. So wherever you find yourself—whether on the mountaintop or in the darkest valley—remember that God is there, too. And He's ready to help.

Are you willing to accept God's help by prayerfully opening your heart to Him? And are you willing to conform your will to His? If so, then you can be certain that you and God, working together, will make the most of whatever comes your way.

Great opportunities often disguise themselves in small tasks.

Rick Warren

Worry is the senseless process of cluttering up tomorrow's opportunities with leftover problems from today.

Barbara Johnson

A TIMELY TIP

God gives us opportunities for a reason . . . to use them. And, God wants you to make the most out of all the opportunities He sends your way. Billy Graham observed, "Life is a glorious opportunity." That's sound advice, so keep looking for your opportunities until you find them, and when you find them, take advantage of them sooner rather than later.

OUR ACTIONS REVEAL OUR BELIEFS

Therefore by their fruits you will know them.

Matthew 7:20 NKJV

E nglish clergyman Thomas Fuller observed, "He does not believe who does not live according to his beliefs." These words are most certainly true. We may proclaim our beliefs to our hearts' content, but our proclamations will mean nothing—to others or to ourselves—unless we accompany our words with deeds that match. The sermons that we live are far more compelling than the ones we preach.

Like it or not, your life is an accurate reflection of your creed. If this fact gives you some cause for concern, don't bother talking about the changes that you intend to make—make them. And then, when your good deeds speak for themselves—as they most certainly will—don't interrupt.

What you do reveals what you believe about God, regardless of what you say. When God reveals what He has purposed to do, you face a crisis—a decision time. God and the world can tell from your response what you really believe about God.

Henry Blackaby

Obedience is the natural outcome of belief.

C. H. Spurgeon

A TIMELY TIP

How can you guard your steps? By walking with Jesus every day of your life.

ACCEPTANCE FOR TODAY

To You, O my Strength, I will sing praises; for God is my defense, my God of mercy.

Psalm 59:17 NKJV

Manmade plans are fallible; God's plans are not. Yet whenever life takes an unexpected turn, we are tempted to fall into the spiritual traps of worry, self-pity, or bitterness. God intends that we do otherwise.

The old saying is familiar: "Forgive and forget." But when we have been hurt badly, forgiveness is often difficult and forgetting is downright impossible. Since we can't forget yesterday's troubles, we should learn from them. Yesterday has much to teach us about tomorrow. We may learn from the past, but we should never live in the past. God has given each of us a glorious day: this one. And it's up to each of us to use this day as faithful stewards, not as embittered historians.

So if you're trying to forget the past, don't waste your time. Instead, try a different approach: learn to accept the past and live in the present. Then, you can focus your thoughts and your energies, not on the struggles of yesterday, but instead on the profound opportunities that God has placed before you today.

Acceptance is resting in God's goodness, believing that He has all things under His control.

Charles Swindoll

A TIMELY TIP

You should learn from the past, but you should never allow yourself to become stuck there. Once you have made peace with the past, you are then free to live more fully in the present . . . and that's precisely what you should do.

DOING THE RIGHT THING

Do what is right and good in the Lord's sight, so that you may prosper and so that you may enter and possess the good land the Lord your God swore to [give] your fathers.

Deuteronomy 6:18 Holman CSB

Oswald Chambers, the author of the Christian classic devotional text *My Utmost for His Highest*, advised, "Never support an experience which does not have God as its source, and faith in God as its result." These words serve as a powerful reminder that, as Christians, we are called to walk with God and obey His commandments. But, we live in a world that presents us with countless temptations to stray far from God's path. We Christians, when confronted with sin, have clear instructions: Walk—or better yet run—in the opposite direction.

Today, take every step of your journey with God as your traveling companion. Read His Word and follow His commandments. Support only those activities that further God's kingdom and your spiritual growth. Be an example of righteous living to your friends, to your neighbors, and to your children. Then, reap the blessings that God has promised to all those who live according to His will and His Word.

We must appropriate the tender mercy of God every day after conversion, or problems quickly develop. We need his grace daily in order to live a righteous life.

Jim Cymbala

A TIMELY TIP

Because God is just, He rewards good behavior just as surely as He punishes sin. And there aren't any loopholes.

A HEART PREPARED FOR PRAYER

But when you are praying, first forgive anyone you are holding a grudge against, so that your Father in heaven will forgive your sins, too.

Mark 11:25 NLT

Life is a patchwork of successes and failures, victories and defeats, joys and sorrows. When we experience life's inevitable disappointments, we may become embittered, but God instructs us to do otherwise. God understands the futility of bitterness, and He knows that without forgiveness, we can never enjoy the spiritual abundance that He offers us through the person of His Son Jesus.

Christ's teachings are straightforward: Before we offer our prayers to God, we should cleanse ourselves of bitterness, hatred, jealousy, and regret. When we do so, we can petition God with pure hearts.

Be so preoccupied with good will that you haven't room for ill will.

E. Stanley Jones

Bitterness is a spiritual cancer, a rapidly growing malignancy that can consume your life. Bitterness cannot be ignored but must be healed at the very core, and only Christ can heal bitterness.

Beth Moore

A TIMELY TIP

The Bible warns that bitterness is both dangerous and self-destructive.

THE RICHES OF HIS GRACE

In Him we have redemption through His blood, the forgiveness of our trespasses, according to the riches of His grace that He lavished on us with all wisdom and understanding.

Ephesians 1:7-8 Holman CSB

We are saved not by our own righteousness, but by God's grace. God's priceless gift of eternal life is not a reward for our good deeds; it is a manifestation of God's infinite love for those who worship Him and accept His Son as their Savior.

Are you absolutely certain that you have accepted the gift of salvation? If not, drop to your knees this very instant and accept Christ as your personal Savior. And, if you are already the thankful recipient of eternal life through Christ Jesus, use this day as an opportunity to share your testimony with friends and family members.

Jesus is the sovereign friend and ultimate Savior of mankind. Christ showed enduring love for us by willingly sacrificing His own life so that we might have eternal life. Let us love Him, praise Him, and share His message of salvation with our neighbors and with the world.

The Gospel is not so much a demand as it is an offer, an offer of new life to man by the grace of God.

E. Stanley Jones

In the depths of our sin, Christ died for us. He did not wait for persons to get as close as possible through obedience to the law and righteous living.

Beth Moore

A TIMELY TIP

Remember that His grace is enough . . . God promises that His grace is sufficient for your needs. Believe Him.

MATERIAL AND SPIRITUAL POSSESSIONS

And how do you benefit if you gain the whole world but lose your own soul in the process? Is anything worth more than your soul?

Mark 8:36-37 NLT

Earthly riches are temporary: here today and soon gone forever. Spiritual riches, on the other hand, are permanent: ours today, ours tomorrow, ours throughout eternity. Yet all too often, we focus our thoughts and energies on the accumulation of earthly treasures, leaving precious little time to accumulate the only treasures that really matter: the spiritual kind.

Our material possessions have the potential to do great good or terrible harm, depending upon how we choose to use them. As believers, our instructions are clear: we must use our possessions in accordance with God's commandments, and we must be faithful stewards of the gifts He has seen fit to bestow upon us.

Today, let us honor God by placing no other gods before Him. God comes first; everything else comes next—and "everything else" most certainly includes all of our earthly possessions.

No one is truly happy if he has what he wants, but only if he wants something he should have.

St. Augustine

A TIMELY TIP

Materialism Made Simple: The world wants you to believe that "money and stuff" can buy happiness. Don't believe it! Genuine happiness comes not from money, but from the things that money can't buy—starting, of course, with your relationship to God and His only begotten Son.

WHERE THE SPIRIT LEADS

The true children of God are those who let God's Spirit lead them.

Romans 8:14 NCV

Paul encourages believers to be filled with the Spirit of God: "Do not be drunk with wine, which will ruin you, but be filled with the Spirit" (Ephesians 5:18). When you are filled with the Holy Spirit, your words and deeds will reflect a love and devotion to Christ. When you are filled with the Holy Spirit, the steps of your life's journey are guided by the Lord. When you allow God's Spirit to work in you and through you, you will be energized and transformed.

Today, allow yourself to be filled with the Spirit of God. And then stand back in amazement as God begins to work miracles in your own life and in the lives of those you love.

The power of God through His Spirit will work within us to the degree that we permit it.

Mrs. Charles E. Cowman

The Holy Spirit is like a living and continually flowing fountain in believers. We have the boundless privilege of tapping into that fountain every time we pray.

Shirley Dobson

A TIMELY TIP

The Holy Spirit is God in us, providing us with all we need to be effective Christians.

THE WISDOM OF KINDNESS

Kind people do themselves a favor, but cruel people bring trouble on themselves.
Proverbs 11:17 NCV

I f we believe the words of Proverbs 11:17—and we should—then we understand that kindness is its own reward. And, if we obey the commandments of our Savior—and we should—we must sow seeds of kindness wherever we go.

Kindness, compassion, and forgiveness are hallmarks of our Christian faith. So today, in honor of the One who first showed compassion for us, let's teach our families and friends the art of kindness through our words and through our deeds. Our loved ones are watching . . . and so is God.

When we do little acts of kindness that make life more bearable for someone else, we are walking in love as the Bible commands us.

Barbara Johnson

When you extend hospitality to others, you're not trying to impress people, you're trying to reflect God to them.

Max Lucado

A TIMELY TIP

Kindness is contagious—make sure that your family and friends catch it from you!

OBEDIENCE AND PRAISE

Praise the Lord! Happy are those who respect the Lord, who want what he commands.

Psalm 112:1 NCV

Psalm 112 links two powerful principles: obedience and praise. One of the most important ways that we can praise God is by obeying Him. As believers who have been saved by a risen Christ, we must worship our Creator, not only with our prayers and our words, but also with our actions.

Are you grateful for God's glorious gifts? Are you thankful for the treasure of eternal life that is yours through the sacrifice of God's Son Jesus? Of course you are. And one of the very best ways to express your gratitude to God is through obedience to the unchanging commandments of His Holy Word.

When you suffer and lose, that does not mean you are being disobedient to God. In fact, it might mean you're right in the center of His will. The path of obedience is often marked by times of suffering and loss.

Charles Swindoll

God does not want the forced obedience of slaves. Instead, He covets the voluntary love and obedience of children who love Him for Himself.

Catherine Marshall

A TIMELY TIP

If you're pleasing God, you'll have more blessings than you can count. If you're rebelling against Him, you'll have more troubles than you can imagine.

CLAIMING CONTENTMENT IN A DISCONTENTED WORLD

Serving God does make us very rich, if we are satisfied with what we have.

1 Timothy 6:6 NCV

The world readily offers us many things, but lasting contentment is not one of them. Genuine contentment cannot be found in material possessions, earthly power, human relationships, or transitory fame. Genuine contentment starts with God and His only begotten Son . . . and ends there.

Do you seek the contentment and peace that only God can offer? Then welcome His Son into your heart. Allow Christ to rule over every aspect of your day: talk with Him; walk with Him; be with Him; praise Him. When you do, you will discover the peace and contentment that only God can give.

The key to contentment is to consider. Consider who you are and be satisfied with that. Consider what you have and be satisfied with that. Consider what God's doing and be satisfied with that.

Luci Swindoll

You've heard the saying, "Life is what you make it." That means we have a choice. We can choose to have a life full of frustration and fear, but we can just as easily choose one of joy and contentment.

Dennis Swanberg

A TIMELY TIP

Because you are loved and protected by God, you should be contented, whatever your circumstances.

WHAT CAN I LEARN TODAY?

It takes knowledge to fill a home with rare and beautiful treasures.

Proverbs 24:4 NCV

I f we are to grow as Christians, we need both knowledge and wisdom. Knowledge is found in textbooks. Wisdom, on the other hand, is found in God's Holy Word and in the carefully-chosen words of loving parents, family members, and friends. Knowledge is an important building block in a well-lived life, and it pays rich dividends both personally and professionally. But, wisdom is even more important because it refashions not only the mind, but also the heart.

A big difference exists between a head full of knowledge and the words of God literally abiding in us.

Beth Moore

The doorstep to the temple of wisdom is a knowledge of our own ignorance.

C. H. Spurgeon

A TIMELY TIP

Need knowledge? Study God's Word and spend time with knowledgeable people.

PATIENCE WITH OTHERS AND ONE'S SELF

God has chosen you and made you his holy people. He loves you. So always do these things: Show mercy to others, be kind, humble, gentle, and patient.

Colossians 3:12 NCV

The dictionary defines the word *patience* as "the ability to be calm, tolerant, and understanding." If that describes you, you can skip the rest of this page. But, if you're like most of us, you'd better keep reading.

For most of us, patience is a hard thing to master. Why? Because we have lots of things we want, and we want them NOW (if not sooner). But the Bible tells us that we must learn to wait patiently for the things that God has in store for us.

The next time you find your patience tested to the limit, remember that the world unfolds according to God's timetable, not yours. Sometimes, you must wait patiently, and that's as it should be. After all, think how patient God has been with you!

The times we find ourselves having to wait on others may be the perfect opportunities to train ourselves to wait on the Lord.

Joni Eareckson Tada

You can't step in front of God and not get in trouble. When He says, "Go three steps," don't go four.

Charles Stanley

A TIMELY TIP

Patience pays. Impatience costs. Behave accordingly.

BEYOND OUR FEARS

He replied, "You of little faith, why are you so afraid?" Then he got up and rebuked the winds and the waves, and it was completely calm.

Matthew 8:26 NIV

A frightening storm rose quickly on the Sea of Galilee, and the disciples were afraid. Because of their limited faith, they feared for their lives. When they turned to Jesus, He calmed the waters and He rebuked His disciples for their lack of faith in Him.

On occasion, we, like the disciples, are frightened by the inevitable storms of life. Why are we afraid? Because we, like the disciples, possess imperfect faith.

When we genuinely accept God's promises as absolute truth, when we trust Him with life-here-on-earth and life eternal, we have little to fear. Faith in God is the antidote to worry. Faith in God is the foundation of courage and the source of power. Today, let us trust God more completely and, by doing so, move beyond our fears to a place of abundance, assurance, and peace.

Fear is a self-imposed prison that will keep you from becoming what God intends for you to be.

Rick Warren

Only believe, don't fear. Our Master, Jesus, always watches over us, and no matter what the persecution, Jesus will surely overcome it.

Lottie Moon

A TIMELY TIP

Don't give up on God. And remember: He will never give up on you or your family.

STUDYING GOD'S WORD

As newborn babies want milk, you should want the pure and simple teaching. By it you can grow up and be saved.

1 Peter 2:2 NCV

When it comes to your faith, God doesn't intend for you to stand still. He wants you to keep moving and growing. In fact, God's plan for you includes a lifetime of prayer, praise, and spiritual growth.

As a Christian, you should continue to grow in the love and the knowledge of your Savior as long as you live. How? By studying God's Word every day, by obeying His commandments, and by allowing His Son to reign over your heart, that's how.

Are you continually seeking to become a more mature believer? Hopefully so, because that's exactly what you owe to yourself and to God . . . but not necessarily in that order.

You are free to choose, but the choices you make today will determine what you will have, what you will be, and what you will do in the tomorrow of your life.

Zig Ziglar

A TIMELY TIP

Today, think about the quality of the choices that you've made recently. Are these choices helping you become a more mature Christian? If so, don't change. If not, think about the quality of your decisions, the consequences of those decisions, and the steps that you can take to make better decisions.

TODAY'S BIBLE READING
Old Testament: Judges 20-21
New Testament: Luke 8:41-56

AMAZING GRACE

Saving is all [God's] idea, and all his work. All we do is trust him enough to let him do it. It's God's idea from start to finish! We don't play the major role. If we did, we'd probably go around bragging that we'd done the whole thing! No, we neither make nor save ourselves. God does both the making and the saving.

Ephesians 2:8-9 MSG

Here's the great news: God's grace is not earned . . . and thank goodness it's not! If God's grace were some sort of reward for good behavior, none of us could earn enough brownie points to win the big prize. But it doesn't work that way. Grace is a free offer from God. By accepting that offer, we transform our lives today and forever.

God's grace is not just any old gift; it's the ultimate gift, and we owe Him our eternal gratitude. Our Heavenly Father is waiting patiently for each of us to accept His Son and receive His grace. Let us accept that gift today so that we might enjoy God's presence now and throughout all eternity.

To believe is to take freely what God gives freely.

C. H. Spurgeon

Number one, God brought me here. It is by His will that I am in this place. In that fact I will rest. Number two, He will keep me here in His love and give me grace to behave as His child. Number three, He will make the trial a blessing, teaching me the lessons He intends for me to learn and working in me the grace He means to bestow. Number four, in His good time He can bring me out again. How and when, He knows. So, let me say I am here.

Andrew Murray

A TIMELY TIP

God's grace isn't earned, but freely given—what an amazing, humbling gift.

GOD'S GOLDEN RULE

Here is a simple, rule-of-thumb for behavior: Ask yourself what you want people to do for you, then grab the initiative and do it for them. Add up God's Law and Prophets and this is what you get.

Matthew 7:12 MSG

The words of Matthew 7:12 remind us that, as believers in Christ, we are commanded to treat others as we wish to be treated. This commandment is, indeed, the Golden Rule for Christians of every generation. When we weave the thread of kindness into the very fabric of our lives, we give glory to the One who gave His life for ours.

Because we are imperfect human beings, we are, on occasion, selfish, thoughtless, or cruel. But God commands us to behave otherwise. He teaches us to rise above our own imperfections and to treat others with unselfishness and love. When we observe God's Golden Rule, we help build His kingdom here on earth. And, when we share the love of Christ, we share a priceless gift; may we share it today and every day that we live.

It's not difficult to make an impact on your world. All you really have to do is put the needs of others ahead of your own. You can make a difference with a little time and a big heart.

James Dobson

Reject the road to cynicism.

Catherine Marshall

A TIMELY TIP

When you understand that Christianity is about servanthood, other people become your focus and your ministry.

TRUST IN A LOVING FATHER

If God is for us, who is against us?

Romans 8:31 Holman CSB

What do you expect from the day ahead? Are you expecting God to do wonderful things, or are you living beneath a cloud of apprehension and doubt? The familiar words of Psalm 118:24 remind us of a profound yet simple truth: "This is the day which the LORD hath made; we will rejoice and be glad in it" (KJV).

For Christian believers, every day begins and ends with God's Son and God's promises. When we accept Christ into our hearts, God promises us the opportunity for earthly peace and spiritual abundance. But more importantly, God promises us the priceless gift of eternal life.

As we face the inevitable challenges of life-here-on-earth, we must arm ourselves with the promises of God's Holy Word. When we do, we can expect the best, not only for the day ahead, but also for all eternity.

How changed our lives would be if we could only fly through the days on wings of surrender and trust!

Hannah Whitall Smith

The passwords that open the gates into the refuge of God are the soul-wrenching words that flow out of our hearts when we finally decide to trust God.

Bill Hybels

A TIMELY TIP

One of the most important lessons that you can ever learn is to trust God for everything, and that includes timing . . . In other words, you should trust God to decide the best time for things to happen. Sometimes it's hard to trust God, but it's always the right thing to do.

THE RIGHT KIND OF WISDOM

Only the Lord gives wisdom; he gives knowledge and understanding.

Proverbs 2:6 NCV

Sometimes, amid the concerns of everyday life, we lose perspective. Life seems out of balance as we confront an array of demands that sap our strength and cloud our thoughts. What's needed is a renewed faith, a fresh perspective, and God's wisdom.

Here in the 21st century, commentary is commonplace and information is everywhere. But the ultimate source of wisdom, the kind of timeless wisdom that God willingly shares with His children, is still available from a single unique source: the Holy Bible.

The wisdom of the world changes with the ever-shifting sands of public opinion. God's wisdom does not. His wisdom is eternal. It never changes. And it most certainly is the wisdom that you must use to plan your day, your life, and your eternal destiny.

If you lack knowledge, go to school. If you lack wisdom, get on your knees.

Vance Havner

A TIMELY TIP

If you own a Bible, you have ready access to God's wisdom. Your job is to read, to understand, and to apply His teachings to your life . . . starting now and ending never.

PATIENCE AND TRUST

Trust in him at all times, O people; pour out your hearts to him, for God is our refuge.

Psalm 62:8 NIV

As individuals, as families, and as a nation, we are impatient for the changes that we so earnestly desire. We want solutions to our problems, and we want them right now! But sometimes, life's greatest challenges defy easy solutions, so we must be patient.

Psalm 37:7 commands us to "Rest in the Lord, and wait patiently for Him" (NKJV). But for most of us, waiting quietly for God is difficult. Why? Because we are imperfect beings who seek solutions to our problems today, if not sooner. We seek to manage our lives according to our own timetables, not God's. To do so is a mistake. Instead of impatiently tapping our fingers, we should fold our fingers and pray. When we do, our Heavenly Father will reward us in His own miraculous way and in His own perfect time.

Be patient. God is using today's difficulties to strengthen you for tomorrow. He is equipping you. The God who makes things grow will help you bear fruit.

Max Lucado

It is wise to wait because God gives clear direction only when we are willing to wait.

Charles Stanley

A TIMELY TIP

Since you want other people to be patient with you, you should be patient with them, too.

HIS PROMISES NEVER FAIL

Patient endurance is what you need now, so you will continue to do God's will. Then you will receive all that he has promised.

Hebrews 10:36 NLT

God has made quite a few promises to you, and He intends to keep every single one of them. You will find these promises in a book like no other: the Holy Bible. The Bible is your roadmap for life here on earth and for life eternal—as a believer, you are called upon to trust its promises, to follow its commandments, and to share its Good News.

God has made promises to all of humanity and to you. God's promises never fail and they never grow old. You must trust those promises and share them with your family, with your friends, and with the world . . . starting now . . . and ending never.

There are four words I wish we would never forget, and they are, "God keeps his word."

Charles Swindoll

Shake the dust from your past, and move forward in His promises.

Kay Arthur

A TIMELY TIP

Today, think about the role that God's Word plays in your life, and think about ways that you can worry less and trust God more.

THE JOY OF SERVING GOD

Enjoy serving the Lord, and he will give you what you want.

Psalm 37:4 NCV

Are you excited about serving God? You should be. As a believer living in today's challenging world, you have countless opportunities to honor your Father in heaven by serving Him.

Far too many Christians seem bored with their faith and stressed by their service. Don't allow yourself to become one of them! Serve God with thanksgiving in your heart and praise on your lips. Make your service to Him a time of celebration and thanksgiving. Worship your Creator by working for Him, joyfully, faithfully, and often.

God wants us to serve Him with a willing spirit, one that would choose no other way.

Beth Moore

Have thy tools ready; God will find thee work.

Charles Kingsley

A TIMELY TIP

The direction of your steps and the quality of your life will be determined by the level of your service.

TODAY'S BIBLE READING
Old Testament: 1 Samuel 13-15
New Testament: Luke 11:37-54

APRIL 11

THE POWER OF PATIENCE

Patience is better than strength. Controlling your temper is better than capturing a city.

Proverbs 16:32 NCV

Temper tantrums are usually unproductive, unattractive, unforgettable, and unnecessary. Perhaps that's why Proverbs 16:32 states that, "Controlling your temper is better than capturing a city."

If you've allowed anger to become a regular visitor at your house, today you must pray for wisdom, for patience, and for a heart that is so filled with love and forgiveness that it contains no room for bitterness. God will help you terminate your tantrums if you ask Him to. And God can help you perfect your ability to be patient if you ask Him to. So ask Him, and then wait patiently for the ever-more-patient you to arrive.

When I am dealing with an all-powerful, all-knowing God, I, as a mere mortal, must offer my petitions not only with persistence, but also with patience. Someday I'll know why.

Ruth Bell Graham

Two signposts of faith: "Slow Down" and "Wait Here."

Charles Stanley

A TIMELY TIP

If you think you're about to say or do something you'll regret later, slow down and take a deep breath, or two deep breaths, or ten, or . . . well you get the idea.

UNRELIABLE THINKING

Do not worry about anything, but pray and ask God for everything you need, always giving thanks.

Philippians 4:6 NCV

Charles Swindoll advises, "When you're on the verge of throwing a pity party thanks to your despairing thoughts, go back to the Word of God." How true. Self-pity is not only an unproductive way to think, it is also an affront to your Father in heaven. God's Word promises that His children can receive abundance, peace, love, and eternal life. These gifts are not earned; they are an outpouring from God, a manifestation of His grace. With these rich blessings, how can we, as believers, feel sorry for ourselves? Self-pity and peace cannot coexist in the same mind. Bitterness and joy cannot coexist in the same heart. Thanksgiving and despair are mutually exclusive. So, if your unreliable thoughts are allowing pain and worry to dominate your life, you must train yourself to think less about your troubles and more about God's blessings. When you stop to think about it, hasn't He given you enough blessings to occupy your thoughts all day, every day, from now on? Of course He has! So focus your mind on Him, and let your worries fend for themselves.

Worry is a cycle of inefficient thoughts whirling around a center of fear.

Corrie ten Boom

I've read the last page of the Bible. It's all going to turn out all right.

Billy Graham

A TIMELY TIP

Focus on your work, not your worries. Worry is never a valid substitute for work, so get out there, do your best, and turn your worries over to God.

WORDS SPEAK LOUDER

In every way be an example of doing good deeds. When you teach, do it with honesty and seriousness.

Titus 2:7 NCV

Our words speak, but our actions speak much more loudly. And whether we like it or not, all of us are role models. Our friends and family members observe our actions; as followers of Christ, we are obliged to act accordingly.

Corrie ten Boom advised, "Don't worry about what you do not understand. Worry about what you do understand in the Bible but do not live by." And that's sound advice because our families and friends are always watching . . . and so, for that matter, is God.

Your life is destined to be an example. The only question is "what kind?"

Marie T. Freeman

There is nothing anybody else can do that can stop God from using us. We can turn everything into a testimony.

Corrie ten Boom

A TIMELY TIP

Today, ask yourself this: If every Christian followed your example, what kind of world would we live in? If you like the answer you receive from the person in the mirror, keep doing what you're doing. But if you find room for improvement, start making those improvements today.

LIVING WITH THE LIVING WORD

Those who listen to instruction will prosper; those who trust the LORD will be happy.

Proverbs 16:20 NLT

Are you sincerely seeking to discover God's will and follow it? If so, study His Word and obey His commandments. The words of Matthew 4:4 remind us that, "Man shall not live by bread alone, but by every word that proceeds from the mouth of God" (NKJV). As believers, we must study the Bible and meditate upon its meaning for our lives. Otherwise, we deprive ourselves of a priceless gift from our Creator.

Jonathan Edwards advised, "Be assiduous in reading the Holy Scriptures. This is the fountain whence all knowledge in divinity must be derived. Therefore let not this treasure lie by you neglected." God's Holy Word is, indeed, a priceless, one-of-a-kind treasure, and a passing acquaintance with the Good Book is insufficient for Christians who seek to obey God's Word and to understand His will. After all, man does not live by bread alone . . .

God has given us all sorts of counsel and direction in his written Word; thank God, we have it written down in black and white.

John Eldredge

Weave the unveiling fabric of God's word through your heart and mind. It will hold strong, even if the rest of life unravels.

Gigi Graham Tchividjian

A TIMELY TIP

Trust God's Word: Charles Swindoll writes, "There are four words I wish we would never forget, and they are, 'God keeps his word.'" And remember: When it comes to studying God's Word, school is always in session.

FINDING THE NEW AND BETTER WAY

When we were baptized, we were buried with Christ and shared his death. So, just as Christ was raised from the dead by the wonderful power of the Father, we also can live a new life.

Romans 6:4 NCV

For faithful Christians, every day begins and ends with God and with His only begotten Son. Christ came to this earth to give us abundant life and eternal salvation. Our task is to accept Christ's grace with joy in our hearts as we receive the "new life" that can be ours through Him.

Believers who fashion their days around Jesus are transformed: They see the world differently; they act differently, and they feel differently about themselves and their neighbors.

Thoughtful believers face the inevitable challenges and disappointments of each day armed with the joy of Christ and the promise of salvation. So whatever this day holds for you, begin it and end it with God as your partner and Christ as your Savior. And throughout the day, give thanks to the One who created you and saved you. God's love for you is infinite. Accept it joyously and be thankful.

We can be victorious, but only if we walk with God.

Beth Moore

I have been all over the world, and I have never met anyone who regretted giving his or her life to Christ.

Billy Graham

A TIMELY TIP

Your life is a priceless opportunity, a gift of incalculable worth. You should thank God for the gift of life . . . and you should use that gift wisely.

THE POWER OF HOPE

I wait quietly before God, for my hope is in him.

Psalm 62:5 NLT

The self-fulfilling prophecy is alive, well, and living at your house. If you trust God and have faith for the future, your optimistic beliefs will give you direction and motivation. That's one reason that you should never lose hope, but certainly not the only reason. The primary reason that you, as a believer, should never lose hope, is because of God's unfailing promises.

Make no mistake about it: thoughts are powerful things. Your thoughts have the power to lift you up or to hold you down. When you acquire the habit of hopeful thinking, you will have acquired a powerful tool for improving your life. So if you find yourself falling into the spiritual traps of worry and discouragement, seek the healing touch of Jesus and the encouraging words of fellow Christians. And if you fall into the terrible habit of negative thinking, think again. After all, God's Word teaches us that Christ can overcome every difficulty (John 16:33). And when God makes a promise, He keeps it.

Hope is nothing more than the expectation of those things which faith has believed to be truly promised by God.

John Calvin

The most profane word we use is "hopeless." When you say a situation or person is hopeless, you are slamming the door in the face of God.

Kathy Troccoli

A TIMELY TIP

Never be afraid to hope—or to ask—for a miracle.

LEARNING HOW TO FORGIVE

Above all, love each other deeply, because love covers over a multitude of sins.

1 Peter 4:8 NIV

Genuine love is an exercise in forgiveness. If we wish to build lasting relationships, we must learn how to forgive. Why? Because our loved ones are imperfect (as are we). How often must we forgive our family and friends? More times than we can count. Why? Because that's what God wants us to do.

Perhaps granting forgiveness is hard for you. If so, you are not alone. Genuine, lasting forgiveness is often difficult to achieve—difficult but not impossible. Thankfully, with God's help, all things are possible, and that includes forgiveness. But, even though God is willing to help, He expects you to do some of the work. And make no mistake: forgiveness is work, which is okay with God. He knows that the payoffs are worth the effort.

Love is not soft as water is; it is solid as a rock on which the waves of hatred beat in vain.

Corrie ten Boom

Beware that you are not swallowed up in books! An ounce of love is worth a pound of knowledge.

John Wesley

A TIMELY TIP

God loves you, and He wants you to reflect His love to those around you.

OBEDIENCE AND SERVICE

Whoever serves me must follow me. Then my servant will be with me everywhere I am. My Father will honor anyone who serves me.

John 12:26 NCV

As you seek to discover God's purpose for your life, you may rest assured that His plan for you is centered around service to your family, to your friends, to your church, to your community, and to the world. God intends that you work diligently on His behalf to serve His children and to share His Good News.

Whom will you choose to serve today? The needs are great and the workers are few. And God is doing His very best to enlist able-bodied believers—like you.

Let your fellowship with the Father and with the Lord Jesus Christ have as its one aim and object a life of quiet, determined, unquestioning obedience.

Andrew Murray

A prayerful heart and an obedient heart will learn, very slowly and not without sorrow, to stake everything on God Himself.

Elisabeth Elliot

A TIMELY TIP

If you're trying to mold your relationship with Jesus into something that fits comfortably into your own schedule and your own personal theology, you may be headed for trouble. A far better strategy is this: conform yourself to Jesus, not vice versa.

THE POWER OF CHRISTIAN FELLOWSHIP

How good and pleasant it is when brothers can live together!

Psalm 133:1 Holman CSB

It is almost impossible to underestimate the importance of Christian fellowship. When you join with fellow believers in worship and praise, you enrich their lives in the same way that they enrich yours.

Christ promised that wherever two or more are gathered together in His name, He is there also (Matthew 18:20). So let us gather together in the presence of Christ and worship Him with thanksgiving in our hearts, praise on our lips, and fellow believers by our sides.

I hope you will find a few folks who walk with God to also walk with you through the seasons of your life.

John Eldredge

Be united with other Christians. A wall with loose bricks is not good. The bricks must be cemented together.

Corrie ten Boom

A TIMELY TIP

The world has one agenda, and God has another. So you need to spend plenty of time with fellow Christians who can guide your steps and strengthen your faith.

PRACTICAL CHRISTIANITY

My counsel for you is simple and straightforward: Just go ahead with what you've been given. You received Christ Jesus, the Master; now live him. You're deeply rooted in him. You're well constructed upon him. You know your way around the faith. Now do what you've been taught. School's out; quit studying the subject and start living it! And let your living spill over into thanksgiving.

Colossians 2:6-7 MSG

As Christians, we must do our best to ensure that our actions are accurate reflections of our beliefs. Our theology must be demonstrated, not only by our words but, more importantly, by our actions. In short, we should be practical believers, quick to act whenever we see an opportunity to serve God.

Are you the kind of practical Christian who is willing to dig in and do what needs to be done when it needs to be done? If so, congratulations: God acknowledges your service and blesses it. But if you find yourself more interested in the fine points of theology than in the needs of your neighbors, it's time to rearrange your priorities. God needs believers who are willing to roll up their sleeves and go to work for Him. Count yourself among that number. Theology is a good thing unless it interferes with God's work. And it's up to you to make certain that your theology doesn't.

Had Jesus been the Word become word, He would have spun theories about life, but since he was the Word become flesh, he put shoes on all his theories and made them walk.

E. Stanley Jones

A TIMELY TIP

When Jesus endured His sacrifice on the cross, He paid a terrible price for you. What price are you willing to pay for Him?

WALKING IN THE LIGHT

I am the light of the world. Whoever follows me will never walk in darkness, but will have the light of life.

John 8:12 NIV

God's Holy Word instructs us that Jesus is, "the way, the truth, and the life" (John 14:6-7). Without Christ, we are as far removed from salvation as the east is removed from the west. And without Christ, we can never know the ultimate truth: God's truth.

Truth is God's way: He commands His believers live in truth, and He rewards those who do so. Jesus is the personification of God's liberating truth, a truth that offers salvation to mankind.

Do you seek to walk with God? Do you seek to feel His presence and His peace? Then you must walk in truth; you must walk in the light; you must walk with the Savior. There is simply no other way.

Jesus differs from all other teachers; they reach the ear, but he instructs the heart; they deal with the outward letter, but he imparts an inward taste for the truth.

C. H. Spurgeon

Those who walk in truth walk in liberty.

Beth Moore

A TIMELY TIP

Jesus offers you the Truth with a Capital T. How you respond to His Truth will determine the direction—and the destination—of your life.

THE HEALING TOUCH OF THE MASTER'S HAND

Those who sow in tears shall reap in joy.

Psalm 126:5 NKJV

Grief visits all of us who live long and love deeply. When we lose a loved one, or when we experience any other profound loss, darkness overwhelms us for a while, and it seems as if we cannot summon the strength to face another day—but, with God's help, we can.

When our friends or family members encounter life-shattering events, we struggle to find words that might offer them comfort and support. But finding the right words can be difficult, if not impossible. Sometimes, all that we can do is to be with our loved ones, offering them few words but much love.

Thankfully, God promises that He is "near to those who have a broken heart" (Psalm 34:18 NKJV). In times of intense sadness, we must turn to Him, and we must encourage our friends and family members to do likewise. When we do, our Father comforts us and, in time, He heals us.

Suffering doesn't teach me about myself from a textbook, it teaches me from my heart. It will always show me what I love—either the God of all comfort or the comfort that can become my god.

Joni Eareckson Tada

A TIMELY TIP

Whether you realize it or not, there are plenty of people who want to offer you encouragement, comfort, and support. Your job is to find them . . . and to let them help.

PROSPEROUS GENEROSITY

The one who blesses others is abundantly blessed; those who help others are helped.

Proverbs 11:25 MSG

God rewards generosity just as surely as He punishes sin. If we are generous, God blesses us in ways that we cannot fully understand. But if we allow ourselves to become closefisted and miserly, either with our possessions or with our love, we deprive ourselves of the spiritual abundance that would otherwise be ours.

Do you seek God's abundance and His peace? Then share the blessings that God has given you. Share your possessions, share your faith, share your testimony, and share your love. God expects no less, and He deserves no less. And neither, come to think of it, do your neighbors.

If you want to be truly happy, you won't find it on an endless quest for more stuff. You'll find it in receiving God's generosity and then passing that generosity along.

Bill Hybels

All the blessings we enjoy are divine deposits, committed to our trust on this condition: that they should be dispensed for the benefit of our neighbors.

John Calvin

A TIMELY TIP

There is a direct relationship between generosity and joy—the more you give to others, the more joy you will experience for yourself.

A STEADFAST FAITH IN A STEADFAST GOD

I have set the Lord always before me; because He is at my right hand I shall not be moved.

Psalm 16:8 NKJV

God is faithful to us even when we are not faithful to Him. God keeps His promises to us even when we stray far from His will. He continues to love us even when we disobey His commandments. But God does not force His blessings upon us. If we are to experience His love and His grace, we must claim them for ourselves.

Are you tired, discouraged, or fearful? Be comforted: God is with you. Are you confused? Listen to the quiet voice of your Heavenly Father. Are you bitter? Talk with God and seek His guidance. Are you celebrating a great victory? Thank God and praise Him. He is the Giver of all things good.

In whatever condition you find yourself, wherever you are, whether you are happy or sad, victorious or vanquished, troubled or triumphant, remember that God is faithful and that His love is eternal. And be comforted. God is not just near. He is here.

Let me encourage you to continue to wait with faith. God may not perform a miracle, but He is trustworthy to touch you and make you whole where there used to be a hole.

Lisa Whelchel

A TIMELY TIP

You cannot see the future, but God can . . . and you must have faith in His eternal plan for you.

USING YOUR GIFTS TO SERVE

There are different kinds of gifts, but they are all from the same Spirit. There are different ways to serve but the same Lord to serve.

1 Corinthians 12:4–5 NCV

God gives each of us a unique assortment of talents and opportunities. And our Heavenly Father instructs us to be faithful stewards of the gifts that He bestows upon us. But we live in a world that encourages us to do otherwise.

Ours is a society that is filled to the brim with countless opportunities to squander our time, our resources, and our talents. So we must be watchful for distractions and temptations that might lead us astray.

God has blessed you with unique opportunities to serve Him, and He has given you every tool that you need to do so. Today, accept this challenge: value the talent that God has given you, nourish it, make it grow, and share it with the world. After all, the best way to say "Thank You" for God's gifts is to use them.

If the attitude of servanthood is learned, by attending to God as Lord. Then, serving others will develop as a very natural way of life.

Eugene Peterson

God will open up places of service for you as He sees you are ready. Meanwhile, study the Bible and give yourself a chance to grow.

Warren Wiersbe

A TIMELY TIP

It is important to treat everybody with respect and kindness. And that means everybody!

FORGIVENESS IS A FORM OF WISDOM

The discretion of a man makes him slow to anger, and his glory is to overlook a transgression.

Proverbs 19:11 NCV

Bitterness is a form of self-punishment; forgiveness is a means of self-liberation. Bitterness focuses on the injustices of the past; forgiveness focuses on the blessings of the present and the opportunities of the future. Bitterness is an emotion that destroys you; forgiveness is a decision that empowers you. Bitterness is folly; forgiveness is wisdom.

Sometimes, amid the demands of daily life, we lose perspective. Life seems out of balance, and the pressures of everyday living seem overwhelming. What's needed is a fresh perspective, a restored sense of balance . . . and God's wisdom.

If we call upon the Lord and seek to see the world through His eyes, He will give us guidance, wisdom and perspective. When we make God's priorities our priorities, He will lead us according to His plan and according to His commandments. When we study God's Word, we are reminded that God's reality is the ultimate reality. May we live—and forgive—accordingly.

There is no use in talking as if forgiveness were easy. I could say of a certain man, "Have I forgiven him more times than I can count?" For we find that the work of forgiveness has to be done over and over again.

C. S. Lewis

A TIMELY TIP

When it comes to the task of forgiving others, God wants you to be relentless. He wants you to start forgiving now and keep forgiving until it sticks.

CELEBRATING GOD'S HANDIWORK

The heavens declare the glory of God, and the sky proclaims the work of His hands.

Psalm 19:1 Holman CSB

When we consider God's glorious universe, we marvel at the miracle of nature. The smallest seedlings and grandest stars are all part of God's infinite creation. God has placed His handiwork on display for all to see, and if we are wise, we will make time each day to celebrate the world that surrounds us.

Today, as you fulfill the demands of everyday life, pause to consider the majesty of heaven and earth. It is as miraculous as it is beautiful, as incomprehensible as it is breathtaking.

The Psalmist reminds us that the heavens are a declaration of God's glory. May we never cease to praise the Father for a universe that stands as an awesome testimony to His presence and His power.

It is impossible for me to look at the heavens at night without realizing there had to be a Creator.

Ruth Bell Graham

God made the country and man made the town—and you can certainly see the difference!

Vance Havner

A TIMELY TIP

Every day can be a celebration of God's creation. And every day should be.

TAPPING INTO GOD'S STRENGTH

Because the eyes of the Lord are on the righteous and His ears are open to their request. But the face of the Lord is against those who do evil.

1 Peter 3:12 Holman CSB

Have you made God the cornerstone of your life, or is He relegated to a few hours on Sunday morning? Have you genuinely allowed God to reign over every corner of your heart, or have you attempted to place Him in a spiritual compartment? The answer to these questions will determine the direction of your day and your life.

God loves you. In times of trouble, He will comfort you; in times of sorrow, He will dry your tears. When you are weak or sorrowful, God is as near as your next breath. He stands at the door of your heart and waits. Welcome Him in and allow Him to rule. And then, accept the peace, and the strength, and the protection, and the abundance that only God can give.

In God's faithfulness lies eternal security.

Corrie ten Boom

The God we seek is a God who is intrinsically righteous and who will be so forever. With His example and His strength, we can share in that righteousness.

Bill Hybels

A TIMELY TIP

When you invite the love of God into your heart, everything changes . . . including you.

WALKING WITH THE WISE

Whoever walks with the wise will become wise; whoever walks with fools will suffer harm.

Proverbs 13:20 NLT

D o you wish to become wise? Then you must walk with people who, by their words and their presence, make you wiser. And, to the best of your ability, you must avoid those people who encourage you to think foolish thoughts or do foolish things.

Today, as a gift to yourself, select, from your friends and family members, a mentor whose judgement you trust. Then listen carefully to your mentor's advice and be willing to accept that advice, even if accepting it requires effort, or pain, or both. Consider your mentor to be God's gift to you. Thank God for that gift, and use it.

Knowledge can be found in books or in school. Wisdom, on the other hand, starts with God . . . and ends there.

Marie T. Freeman

When you persevere through a trial, God gives you a special measure of insight.

Charles Swindoll

A TIMELY TIP

God makes His wisdom available to you. Your job is to acknowledge, to understand, and (above all) to use that wisdom.

DAILY DISTRACTIONS

If you decide for God, living a life of God-worship, it follows that you don't fuss about what's on the table at mealtimes or whether the clothes in your closet are in fashion. There is far more to your life than the food you put in your stomach, more to your outer appearance than the clothes you hang on your body.

Matthew 6:25 MSG

All of us must live through those days when the traffic jams, the computer crashes, and the dog makes a main course out of our homework. But, when we find ourselves distracted by the minor frustrations of life, we must catch ourselves, take a deep breath, and lift our thoughts upward.

Although we may, at times, struggle mightily to rise above the distractions of everyday living, we need never struggle alone. God is here—eternal and faithful, with infinite patience and love—and, if we reach out to Him, He will restore our sense of perspective and give peace to our souls.

Whatever we focus on determines what we become.

E. Stanley Jones

If the glories of heaven were more real to us, if we lived less for material things and more for things eternal and spiritual, we would be less easily disturbed in this present life.

Billy Graham

A TIMELY TIP

Take a few minutes to consider the everyday distractions that are interfering with your life and your faith. Then, jot down at least three ideas for minimizing those distractions or eliminating them altogether.

A FUTURE SO BRIGHT . . .

Wisdom is pleasing to you. If you find it, you have hope for the future.

Proverbs 24:14 NCV

L et's talk for a minute about the future . . . your future. How bright do you believe your future to be? Well, if you're a faithful believer, God has plans for you that are so bright that you'd better pack several pairs of sunglasses and a lifetime supply of sunblock!

The way that you think about your future will play a powerful role in determining how things turn out (it's called the "self-fulfilling prophecy," and it applies to everybody, including you). So here's another question: Are you expecting a terrific tomorrow, or are you dreading a terrible one? The answer to that question will have a powerful impact on the way tomorrow unfolds.

Today, as you live in the present and look to the future, remember that God has an amazing plan for you. Act—and believe—accordingly. And one more thing: don't forget the sunblock.

The Christian believes in a fabulous future.

Billy Graham

Every experience God gives us, every person he brings into our lives, is the perfect preparation for the future that only he can see.

Corrie ten Boom

A TIMELY TIP

Even when the world seems dark, the future is bright for those who look to the Son.

OUR INTENTIONS ARE IMPORTANT TO GOD

We justify our actions by appearances; God examines our motives.

Proverbs 21:2 MSG

The world sees you as you appear to be; God sees you as you really are . . . He sees your heart, and He understands your intentions. The opinions of others should be relatively unimportant to you; however, God's view of you—His understanding of your actions, your thoughts, and your motivations—should be vitally important.

Few things in life are more futile than "keeping up appearances" for the sake of neighbors. What is important, of course, is pleasing your Father in heaven. You please Him when your intentions are pure and your actions are just.

The more wisdom enters our hearts, the more we will be able to trust our hearts in difficult situations.

John Eldredge

Make God's will the focus of your life day by day. If you seek to please Him and Him alone, you'll find yourself satisfied with life.

Kay Arthur

A TIMELY TIP

The world wants you to pay attention to its distractions and temptations. God wants you to pay attention to His Son. Trust God.

COURAGE FOR TODAY . . . AND FOREVER

Don't be afraid, because I am your God. I will make you strong and will help you; I will support you with my right hand that saves you.

Isaiah 41:10 NCV

Christians have every reason to live courageously. After all, the ultimate battle has already been won on the cross at Calvary. But even dedicated followers of Christ may find their courage tested by the inevitable disappointments and fears that visit the lives of believers and non-believers alike.

When you find yourself worried about the challenges of today or the uncertainties of tomorrow, you must ask yourself whether or not you are ready to place your concerns and your life in God's all-powerful, all-knowing, all-loving hands. If the answer to that question is yes—as it should be—then you can draw courage today from the source of strength that never fails: your Heavenly Father.

If a person fears God, he or she has no reason to fear anything else. On the other hand, if a person does not fear God, then fear becomes a way of life.

Beth Moore

The Lord Jesus by His Holy Spirit is with me, and the knowledge of His presence dispels the darkness and allays any fears.

Bill Bright

A TIMELY TIP

Are you feeling anxious or fearful? If so, trust God more. Entrust the future—your future—to God.

STRENGTH FOR TOUGH TIMES

If you do nothing in a difficult time, your strength is limited.

Proverbs 24:10 Holman CSB

From time to time, all of us face adversity, hardship, disappointment, and loss. Old Man Trouble pays periodic visits to each of us; none of us are exempt. When we are troubled, God stands ready and willing to protect us. Our responsibility, of course, is to ask Him for protection. When we call upon Him in heartfelt prayer, He will answer—in His own time and in accordance with His own perfect plan.

Our world continues to change, but God's love remains constant. And, He remains ready to comfort us and strengthen us whenever we turn to Him. Psalm 145 promises, "The Lord is near to all who call on him, to all who call on him in truth. He fulfills the desires of those who fear him; he hears their cry and saves them" (vv. 18-20 NIV).

Life is often challenging, but as Christians, we must not be afraid. God loves us, and He will protect us. In times of hardship, He will comfort us; in times of sorrow, He will dry our tears. When we are troubled, or weak, or sorrowful, God is always with us. We must build our lives on the rock that cannot be shaken . . . we must trust in God. Always.

As sure as God puts his children in the furnace, he will be in the furnace with them.

C. H. Spurgeon

A TIMELY TIP

Remember that ultimately you and you alone are responsible for controlling your appetites. Others may warn you, help you, or encourage you, but in the end, the habits that rule your life are the very same habits that you yourself have formed. Thankfully, since you formed these habits, you can also break them—if you decide to do so.

EXPECTING GREAT THINGS

When a believing person prays, great things happen.

James 5:16 NCV

J ames 5:16 makes a promise that God intends to keep: when you pray earnestly, fervently, and often, great things will happen. Too many people, however, are too timid or too pessimistic to ask God to do big things. Don't count yourself among their number.

God can and will do great things through you if you have the courage to ask Him and the determination to keep asking Him. Honor God by making big requests. But don't expect Him to do all the work. When you do your part, He will do His part. And when He does, expect a miracle . . . a big miracle.

We honor God by asking for great things when they are a part of His promise. We dishonor Him and cheat ourselves when we ask for molehills where He has promised mountains.

Vance Havner

A prayerful heart and an obedient heart will learn, very slowly and not without sorrow, to stake everything on God Himself.

Elisabeth Elliot

A TIMELY TIP

There's no corner of your life that's too unimportant to pray about, so pray about everything.

WASTED WORDS

A useless person causes trouble, and a gossip ruins friendships.

Proverbs 16:28 NCV

Face it: gossip is bad—and the Bible clearly tells us that gossip is wrong. When we say things that we don't want other people to know we said, we're being somewhat dishonest, but if the things we say aren't true, we're being very dishonest. Either way, we have done something that we may regret later, especially when the other person finds out.

So do yourself a big favor: don't gossip. It's a waste of words, and it's the wrong thing to do. You'll feel better about yourself if you don't gossip (and other people will feel better about you, too). So don't do it!

To belittle is to be little.

Anonymous

The cost of gossip always exceeds its worth.

Jim Gallery

A TIMELY TIP

Don't wait. The best time to do a good deed is as soon as you can do it.

PLANNING AND DILIGENCE

The plans of hard-working people earn a profit, but those who act too quickly become poor.

Proverbs 21:5 NCV

Are you willing to plan for the future—and are you willing to work diligently to accomplish the plans that you've made? The Book of Proverbs teaches that the plans of hardworking people (like you) are rewarded.

If you desire to reap a bountiful harvest from life, you must plan for the future while entrusting the final outcome to God. Then, you must do your part to make the future better (by working dutifully), while acknowledging the sovereignty of God's hands over all affairs, including your own.

Are you in a hurry for success to arrive at your doorstep? Don't be. Instead, work carefully, plan thoughtfully, and wait patiently. Remember that you're not the only one working on your behalf: God, too, is at work. And with Him as your partner, your ultimate success is guaranteed.

Success and happiness are not destinations. They are exciting, never-ending journeys.

Zig Ziglar

You can't climb the ladder of life with your hands in your pockets.

Barbara Johnson

A TIMELY TIP

Don't let the world define success for you. Only God can do that.

ROOM TO GROW

*So let us stop going over the basics of Christianity again and again. Let us go on
instead and become mature in our understanding.*

Hebrews 6:1 NLT

Are you a fully-grown person? Physically: maybe so. But spiritually? No way! And thank goodness that you're not! Even if you're very mature for your age, you've still got lots of room to grow.

The 19th-century writer Hannah Whitall Smith observed, "The maturity of a Christian experience cannot be reached in a moment." No kidding. In truth, the search for spiritual growth lasts a lifetime.

When we cease to grow, either emotionally or spiritually, we do ourselves and our families a profound disservice. But, if we study God's Word, if we obey His commandments, and if we live in the center of His will, we will not be "stagnant" believers; we will, instead, be growing Christians . . . and that's exactly what God wants for our lives. Come to think of it, that's exactly what you should want, too.

I've never met anyone who became instantly mature. It's a painstaking process that God takes us through, and it includes such things as waiting, failing, losing, and being misunderstood—each calling for extra doses of perseverance.

Charles Swindoll

A TIMELY TIP

Change is inevitable; growth is not. God will come to your doorstep on countless occasions with opportunities to learn and to grow. And He will knock. Your challenge, of course, is to open the door.

PLANTING THE SEEDS OF FAITH

Without wavering, let us hold tightly to the hope we say we have, for God can be trusted to keep his promise.

Hebrews 10:23 NLT

L ife, like a garden is a leap of faith. We plant our seeds in God's good earth, and we expect Him to bring forth a plentiful harvest. And so it is when we plant the seeds of faith in our hearts: When we trust God completely, He brings forth a bountiful harvest in our lives, a harvest of abundance, joy, and peace.

Jesus Christ is the ultimate Savior of humanity and the personal Savior of those who believe in Him. As His servants, we must place Him at the very center of our lives, not on the periphery. When we form a personal bond with our Savior, the seeds of our faith will multiply and flourish not only for today, but also for eternity.

Relying on God has to begin all over again every day as if nothing had yet been done.

C. S. Lewis

If God chooses to remain silent, faith is content.

Ruth Bell Graham

A TIMELY TIP

Today, dare to place your hopes, your dreams, and your future in God's hands.

MAY 10

TODAY'S BIBLE READING
Old Testament: 2 Kings 9-11
New Testament: John 2

DON'T COMPROMISE

If you're not welcomed, not listened to, quietly withdraw. Don't make a scene. Shrug your shoulders and be on your way.

Mark 6:11 MSG

Sometimes, you may feel pressured to compromise yourself, and you may be afraid of what will happen if you firmly say "No." You may be afraid that you'll be rejected. But here's a tip: don't worry too much about rejection, especially when you're rejected for doing the right thing.

Pleasing other people is a good thing . . . up to a point. But you must never allow your "willingness to please" to interfere with your own good judgement or with God's commandments.

Instead of being afraid of rejection, focus on pleasing your Creator first and always. And when it comes to the world and all its inhabitants, don't worry too much about the folks you can't please. Focus, instead, on doing the right thing—and leave the rest up to God

You must never sacrifice your relationship with God for the sake of a relationship with another person.

Charles Stanley

When we are set free from the bondage of pleasing others, when we are free from currying others' favor and others' approval—then no one will be able to make us miserable or dissatisfied. And then, if we know we have pleased God, contentment will be our consolation.

Kay Arthur

A TIMELY TIP

If people put you down because you're willing to stand up for the things you believe in, don't let it get you down. A little rejection is a very good thing when you're rejected for the right reasons.

GUARDING OUR HEARTS AND MINDS

Summing it all up, friends, I'd say you'll do best by filling your minds and meditating on things true, noble, reputable, authentic, compelling, gracious, the best, not the worst; the beautiful, not the ugly; things to praise, not things to curse. Put into practice what you learned from me, what you heard and saw and realized. Do that, and God, who makes everything work together, will work you into his most excellent harmonies.

Philippians 4:8-9 MSG

You are near and dear to God. He loves you more than you can imagine, and He wants the very best for you. And one more thing: God wants you to guard your heart.

Every day, you are faced with choices . . . lots of them. You can do the right thing, or not. You can tell the truth, or not. You can be kind, and generous, and obedient. Or not.

Your mind and your heart will usually tell you the right thing to do. And if you listen to your parents and grandparents, they will help you, too, by teaching you God's rules. Then, you will learn that doing the right thing is always better than doing the wrong thing. And, by obeying God's rules, you will guard your heart by giving it to His Son Jesus.

Christ alone can bring lasting peace—peace with God—peace among men and nations—and peace within our hearts.

Billy Graham

A TIMELY TIP

God offers peace that passes human understanding . . . and He wants you to make His peace your peace.

UNIQUELY YOU

For you made us only a little lower than God, and you crowned us with glory and honor.

Psalm 8:5 NLT

How many people in the world are exactly like you? The only person in the world who's exactly like you . . . IS YOU! And that means you're special: special to God, special to your family, special to your friends, and a special addition to God's wonderful world!

But sometimes, when you're tired, angry, dejected, or depressed, you may not feel very special. In fact, you may decide that you're the ugliest duckling in the pond, a not-very-special person . . . but whenever you think like that, you're mistaken.

The Bible says that God made you in "an amazing and wonderful way." So the next time that you start feeling like you don't measure up, remember this: when God made all the people of the earth, He only made one you. You're incredibly valuable to God, and that means that you should think of yourself as a V.I.P. (a Very Important Person). God wants you to have the best, and you deserve the best . . . you're worth it!

Your core identity—and particularly your perception of it—plays a vital role in determining how you carry yourself in daily life, how much joy you experience, how you treat other people, and how you respond to God.

Josh McDowell

A TIMELY TIP

If you hang with people who bring you down, you'll make bad choices and before you know it, you'll find yourself in the wrong place at the wrong time.

WHEN GOD SPEAKS QUIETLY

Speak, Lord. I am your servant and I am listening.

1 Samuel 3:10 NCV

Sometimes God speaks loudly and clearly. More often, He speaks in a quiet voice—and if you are wise, you will be listening carefully when He does. To do so, you must carve out quiet moments each day to study His Word and sense His direction.

Can you quiet yourself long enough to listen to your conscience? Are you attuned to the subtle guidance of your intuition? Are you willing to pray sincerely and then to wait quietly for God's response. Hopefully so. Usually God refrains from sending His messages on stone tablets or city billboards. More often, He communicates in subtler ways. If you sincerely desire to hear His voice, you must listen carefully, and you must do so in the silent corners of your quiet, willing heart.

If you, too, will learn to wait upon God, to get alone with Him, and remain silent so that you can hear His voice when He is ready to speak to you, what a difference it will make in your life!

Kay Arthur

Growth takes place in quietness, in hidden ways, in silence and solitude. The process is not accessible to observation.

Eugene Peterson

A TIMELY TIP

Be still and listen to God. He has something important to say to you.

RIGHTEOUSNESS AND RIGHTNESS

Christ ended the law so that everyone who believes in him may be right with God.
Romans 10:4 NCV

How do we live a life that is "right with God"? By accepting God's Son and obeying His commandments. Accepting Christ is a decision that we make one time; following in His footsteps requires thousands of decisions each day.

Whose steps will you follow today? Will you honor God as you strive to follow His Son? Or will you join the lockstep legion that seeks to discover happiness and fulfillment through worldly means? If you are righteous and wise, you will follow Christ. You will follow Him today and every day. You will seek to walk in His footsteps without reservation or doubt. When you do so, you will be "right with God" precisely because you are walking aright with His only begotten Son.

For nourishment, comfort, exhilaration, and refreshment, no wine can rival the love of Jesus. Drink deeply.

C. H. Spurgeon

The crucial question for each of us is this: What do you think of Jesus, and do you yet have a personal acquaintance with Him?

Hannah Whitall Smith

A TIMELY TIP

Jesus loves you. Period. His love is amazing, it's wonderful, and it's meant for you.

HOPE NOW!

When dreams come true, there is life and joy.

Proverbs 13:12 NLT

The hope that the world offers is fleeting and imperfect. The hope that God offers is unchanging, unshakable, and unending. It is no wonder, then, that when we seek security from worldly sources, our are hopes are often dashed. Thankfully, God has no such record of failure.

Where will you place your hopes today? Will you entrust your future to man or to God? Will you seek solace exclusively from fallible human beings, or will you place your hopes, first and foremost, in the trusting hands of your Creator? The decision is yours, and you must live with the results of the choice you make.

For thoughtful believers, hope begins with God. Period. So today, as you embark upon the next stage of your life's journey, consider the words of the Psalmist: "You are my hope; O Lord GOD, You are my confidence" (71:5 NASB). Then, place your trust in the One who cannot be shaken.

Oh, remember this: There is never a time when we may not hope in God. Whatever our necessities, however great our difficulties, and though to all appearance help is impossible, yet our business is to hope in God, and it will be found that it is not in vain.

George Mueller

A TIMELY TIP

As you plan for your future, be aware that attitudes have a way of transforming themselves into reality. In other words, how you think will help determine what you become. So think realistically about yourself and your situation while making a conscious effort to focus on hopes, not fears. When you do, you'll put the self-fulfilling prophecy to work for you.

HE'S NUMBER ONE

Do not worship any other gods besides me.

Exodus 20:3 NLT

W ho is in charge of your heart? Is it God, or is it something else? Have you given Christ your heart, your soul, your talents, your time, and your testimony? Or are you giving Him little more than a few hours each Sunday morning?

In the book of Exodus, God warns that we should place no gods before Him. Yet all too often, we place our Lord in second, third, or fourth place as we worship other things. When we unwittingly place possessions or relationships above our love for the Creator, we create big problems for ourselves.

Does God rule your heart? Make certain that the honest answer to this question is a resounding yes. In the life of every radical believer, God comes first. And that's precisely the place that He deserves in your heart.

Give God what's right—not what's left!

Anonymous

Experience has taught me that the Shepherd is far more willing to show His sheep the path than the sheep are to follow. He is endlessly merciful, patient, tender, and loving. If we, His stupid and wayward sheep, really want to be led, we will without fail be led. Of that I am sure.

Elisabeth Elliot

A TIMELY TIP

You must guard your heart by putting God in His rightful place—first place.

BEING TRUE TO YOURSELF . . . AND TO GOD

The righteous man leads a blameless life; blessed are his children after him.

Proverbs 20:7 NIV

When God made you, He equipped you with an array of talents and abilities that are uniquely yours. It's up to you to discover those talents and to use them, but sometimes the world will encourage you to do otherwise. At times, our society will attempt to cubbyhole you, to standardize you, and to make you fit into particular, preformed mold. Perhaps God has other plans.

Have you found something in this life that you're passionate about? Something that inspires you to jump out of bed in the morning and hit the ground running? And does your work honor the Creator by making His world a better place? If so, congratulations: you're using your gifts well.

Sometimes, because you're a fallible human being, you may become so wrapped up in meeting society's expectations that you fail to focus on God's expectations. To do so is a mistake of major proportions—don't make it. Instead, seek God's guidance as you focus your energies on becoming the best "you" that you can possibly be.

What's the best way to thank God for the gifts that He has given you? By using them. And you might as well start using them today.

Maintaining your integrity in a world of sham is no small accomplishment.

Wayne Oates

A TIMELY TIP

Integrity pays big dividends. Deception creates massive headaches. Behave accordingly.

THE FUTILITY OF FOOLISH ARGUMENTS

But stay away from those who have foolish arguments and talk about useless family histories and argue and quarrel about the law. Those things are worth nothing and will not help anyone.

Titus 3:9 NCV

Arguments are seldom won but often lost. When we engage in petty squabbles, our losses usually outpace our gains. When we acquire the unfortunate habit of habitual bickering, we do harm to our friends, to our families, to our coworkers, and to ourselves.

Time and again, God's Word warns us that most arguments are a monumental waste of time, of energy, of life. In Titus, we are warned to refrain from "foolish arguments," and with good reason. Such arguments usually do more for the devil than they do for God.

So the next time you're tempted to engage in a silly squabble, whether inside the church or outside it, refrain. When you do, you'll put a smile on God's face, and you'll send the devil packing.

Whatever you do when conflicts arise, be wise. Fight against jumping to quick conclusions and seeing only your side. There are always two sides on the streets of conflict. Look both ways.

Charles Swindoll

A TIMELY TIP

If you're invited to an argument, you don't have to attend: If someone is ranting, raving, or worse, you have the right to get up and leave. Remember: emotions are highly contagious. So if someone is angry, you should feel free to excuse yourself from the argument before you become incensed, too.

DUTY TO GOD AND MANKIND

His master said to him, "Well done, good and faithful slave! You were faithful over a few things; I will put you in charge of many things. Enter your master's joy!"

Matthew 25:21 Holman CSB

God has promised us this: when we do our duties in small matters, He will give us additional responsibilities. When we do our work dutifully, and when we behave responsibly, God rewards us—in a time and in a manner of His choosing, not our own.

Sometimes, God rewards us by giving us additional burdens to bear, or by changing the course of our lives so that we may better serve Him. Sometimes, our rewards come in the form of temporary setbacks that lead, in turn, to greater victories. Sometimes, God rewards us by answering "no" to our prayers so that He can say "yes" to a far grander request that we, with our limited understanding, would never have thought to ask for.

If you seek to be God's servant in great matters, be faithful, be patient, and be dutiful in smaller matters. Then step back and watch as God surprises you with the spectacular creativity of His infinite wisdom and His perfect plan.

The secret of a happy life is to delight in duty. When duty becomes delight, then burdens become blessings.

Warren Wiersbe

When the law of God is written on our hearts, our duty will be our delight.

Matthew Henry

A TIMELY TIP

When you accept your duties and fulfill them, you'll feel good about yourself. When you avoid your obligations, you won't. Act accordingly.

A THIRST FOR GOD

My soul thirsts for God, for the living God.

Psalm 42:2 NKJV

Where is God? He is everywhere you have ever been and everywhere you will ever go. He is with you throughout the night and all through the day; He knows your every thought; He hears your every heartbeat.

When you earnestly seek Him, you will find Him because He is here, waiting patiently for you to reach out to Him . . . right here . . . right now. And make no mistake: your soul does indeed thirst for God. That thirst is planted in your heart, and it is a thirst that only God can quench. Let Him . . . right here . . . right now.

We may ignore, but we can nowhere evade, the presence of God. The world is crowded with Him. He walks everywhere incognito. And the incognito is not always hard to penetrate. The real labour is to remember, to attend. In fact, to come awake. Still more, to remain awake.

C. S. Lewis

God has never turned away the questions of a sincere searcher.

Max Lucado

A TIMELY TIP

Nobody can find Him for you. God is searching for you; it's up to you—and you alone—to open your heart to Him.

LIVING SIMPLY IN
A COMPLICATED WORLD

Do not conform any longer to the pattern of this world, but be transformed by the renewing of your mind. Then you will be able to test and approve what God's will is—his good, pleasing and perfect will.

Romans 12:2 NIV

I s yours a life of moderation or accumulation? Are you more interested in the possessions you can acquire or in the person you can become? The answers to these questions will determine the direction of your day and, in time, the direction of your life.

Ours is a highly complicated society, a place where people and corporations vie for your attention, for your time, and for your dollars. Don't let them succeed in complicating your life! Keep your eyes focused instead upon God.

If your material possessions are somehow distancing you from God, discard them. If your outside interests leave you too little time for your family or your God, slow down the merry-go-round, or better yet, get off completely. Remember: God wants your full attention, and He wants it today, so don't let anybody or anything get in His way.

The most powerful life is the most simple life. The most powerful life is the life that knows where it's going, that knows where the source of strength is; it is the life that stays free of clutter and happenstance and hurriedness.

Max Lucado

A TIMELY TIP

Simplicity and peace are two concepts that are closely related. Complexity and peace are not.

CHEERFUL CHRISTIANITY

A cheerful heart has a continual feast.

Proverbs 15:15 Holman CSB

Few things in life are more sad, or, for that matter, more absurd, than a grumpy Christian. Christ promises us lives of abundance and joy, but He does not force His joy upon us. We must claim His joy for ourselves, and when we do, Jesus, in turn, fills our spirits with His power and His love.

How can we receive from Christ the joy that is rightfully ours? By giving Him what is rightfully His: our hearts and our souls.

When we earnestly commit ourselves to the Savior of mankind, when we place Jesus at the center of our lives and trust Him as our personal Savior, He will transform us, not just for today, but for all eternity. Then we, as God's children, can share Christ's joy and His message with a world that needs both.

The people whom I have seen succeed best in life have always been cheerful and hopeful people who went about their business with a smile on their faces.

Charles Kingsley

When we bring sunshine into the lives of others, we're warmed by it ourselves. When we spill a little happiness, it splashes on us.

Barbara Johnson

A TIMELY TIP

Cheerfulness is its own reward—but not its only reward.

REMEMBERING GOD'S LOVE

For the Lord is good; His mercy is everlasting, and His truth endures to all generations.

Psalm 100:5 NKJV

How much does God love you? As long as you're alive, you'll never be able to figure it out because God's love is just too big to comprehend. But this much we know: God loves you so much that He sent His Son Jesus to come to this earth and to die for you! And, when you accepted Jesus into your heart, God gave you a gift that is more precious than gold: the gift of eternal life.

God's love is bigger and more powerful than anybody can imagine, but His love is very real. So do yourself a favor right now: accept God's love with open arms and welcome His Son Jesus into your heart. When you do, your life will be changed today, tomorrow, and forever.

Love, for instance, is not something God has which may grow or diminish or cease to be. His love is the way God is, and when He loves He is simply being Himself.

A. W. Tozer

Life in God is a great big hug that lasts forever!

Barbara Johnson

A TIMELY TIP

When all else fails, God's love does not. You can always depend upon God's love . . . and He is always your ultimate protection.

SHINING LIKE STARS

The wise people will shine like the brightness of the sky. Those who teach others to live right will shine like stars forever and ever.

Daniel 12:3 NCV

Our world needs Christian leaders who "will shine like stars forever and ever." Our world needs leaders who willingly honor God with their words and their deeds—with the emphasis on deeds.

If you seek to be a godly leader, then you must begin by being a worthy example to your family, to your friends, to your church, and to your community. After all, your words of instruction will never ring true unless you yourself are willing to follow them.

Are you the kind of leader whom you would want to follow? If so, congratulations. But if the answer to that question is no, then it's time to improve your leadership skills, beginning with the words that you speak and the example that you set. And the greatest of these, not surprisingly, is example.

The test of a leader is taking the vision from me to we.

John Maxwell

Integrity and maturity are two character traits vital to the heart of a leader.

Charles Stanley

A TIMELY TIP

Our world needs all the good leaders it can get, so don't be afraid to take a leadership role . . . now.

DISCOVERING GOD'S PURPOSE . . . AND DOING IT

If we live by the Spirit, we must also follow the Spirit.

Galatians 5:25 Holman CSB

God has plans for your life, wonderful, surprising plans . . . but He won't force those plans upon you. To the contrary, He has given you free will, the ability to make decisions on your own. Now, it's up to you to make those decisions wisely.

If you seek to live in accordance with God's plan for your life, you will study His Word, you will be attentive to His instructions, and you will be watchful for His signs. You will associate with fellow believers who, by their words and actions, will encourage your spiritual growth. You will assiduously avoid those two terrible temptations: the temptation to sin and the temptation to squander time. And finally, you will listen carefully, even reverently, to the conscience that God has placed in your heart.

God intends to use you in wonderful, unexpected ways if you let Him. Let Him. When you do, you'll be thoroughly surprised by the creativity and the beauty of His plans.

You cannot stay where you are and go with God. You cannot continue doing things your way and accomplish God's purposes in His ways. Your thinking cannot come close to God's thoughts. For you to do the will of God, you must adjust your life to Him, His purposes, and His ways.

Henry Blackaby

A TIMELY TIP

When you gain a clear vision of your purpose for life here on earth—and for life everlasting—your steps will be sure.

CONCERNING THE STUFF

Prosperity is as short-lived as a wildflower, so don't ever count on it.

James 1:10 MSG

Are you someone who's overly concerned with the stuff that money can buy? Hopefully not. On the grand stage of a well-lived life, material possessions should play a rather small role. Of course, we all need the basic necessities of life, but once we meet those needs for ourselves and for our families, the piling up of possessions creates more problems than it solves. Our real riches, of course, are not of this world. We are never really rich until we are rich in spirit.

Our society is in love with money and the things that money can buy. God is not. God cares about people, not possessions, and so must we. We must, to the best of our abilities, love our neighbors as ourselves, and we must, to the best of our abilities, resist the mighty temptation to place possessions ahead of people.

Money, in and of itself, is not evil; worshipping money is. So today, as you prioritize matters of importance in your life, remember that God is almighty, but the dollar is not.

The Scriptures also reveal warnings that if we are consumed with greed, not only do we disobey God, but we will miss the opportunity to allow Him to use us as instruments for others.

Charles Stanley

A TIMELY TIP

Material possessions may seem important at first, but they're nothing compared to the spiritual rewards that God gives to people (like you) who put Him first.

WORKING WITH HEART AND SOUL

He was diligent in every deed that he began in the service of God's temple, in the law and in the commandment, in order to seek his God, and he prospered.

2 Chronicles 31:21 Holman CSB

How does God intend for us to work? Does He intend for us to work diligently or does He, instead, reward mediocrity? The answer is obvious. God has created a world in which hard work is rewarded and sloppy work is not. Yet sometimes, we may seek ease over excellence, or we may be tempted to take shortcuts when God intends that we walk the straight and narrow path.

Today, heed God's Word by doing good work. Wherever you find yourself, whatever your job description, do your work, and do it with all your heart. When you do, you will most certainly win the recognition of your peers. But more importantly, God will bless your efforts and use you in ways that only He can understand. So do your work with focus and dedication. And leave the rest up to God.

Am I ignitable? God deliver me from the dread asbestos of "other things." Saturate me with the oil of the Spirit that I may be aflame.

Jim Elliot

Wouldn't it make astounding difference, not only in the quality of the work we do, but also in the satisfaction, even our joy, if we recognized God's gracious gift in every single task?

Elisabeth Elliot

A TIMELY TIP

Involve yourself in activities that you can support wholeheartedly and enthusiastically. It's easier to celebrate life when you're passionately involved in life.

THE POWER OF POSITIVE FRIENDSHIPS

Light shines on those who do right; joy belongs to those who are honest. Rejoice in the Lord, you who do right. Praise his holy name.

Psalm 97:11-12 NCV

If you'd like to build a positive life, find positive friends. If you'd like to live a godly life, seek the fellowship of godly friends. If you'd like to live passionately, prayerfully, and purposefully, spend time with people who are already living passionate, prayerful, purposeful lives. Soon, you'll discover that you will inevitably become more and more like the people who surround you day in and day out.

In choosing your friends, you set your course for the future. So choose carefully . . . very carefully.

For better or worse, you will eventually become more and more like the people you associate with. So why not associate with people who make you better, not worse?

Marie T. Freeman

One of the marks of Spiritual maturity is a consistent, Spirit-controlled life.

Vonette Bright

A TIMELY TIP

When the devil himself tried to tempt Jesus, Jesus used the Word of God as a defense against evil. So can you.

WHO RULES?

Do not worship any other gods besides me.

Exodus 20:3 NLT

Who rules your heart? Is it God, or is it something else? Do you give God your firstfruits or your last? Have you given Christ your heart, your soul, your talents, your time, and your testimony? Or are you giving Him little more than a few hours each Sunday morning?

In the book of Exodus, God warns that we should place no gods before Him. Yet all too often, we place our Lord in second, third, or fourth place as we worship the gods of pride, greed, power, or personal gratification. When we unwittingly place possessions or relationships above our love for the Creator, we must seek His forgiveness and repent from our disobedience.

Does God rule your heart? Make certain that the honest answer to this question is a resounding yes. In the life of every righteous believer, God comes first. And that's precisely the place that He deserves in your heart.

A sense of deity is inscribed on every heart.

John Calvin

God's all-sufficiency is a major. Your inability is a minor. Major in majors, not in minors.

Corrie ten Boom

A TIMELY TIP

Because God is infinite and eternal, you cannot comprehend Him. But you can understand your need to praise Him, to love Him, and to obey His Word.

FACING OUR RESPONSIBILITIES

We want each of you to go on with the same hard work all your lives so you will surely get what you hope for. We do not want you to become lazy. Be like those who through faith and patience will receive what God has promised.

Hebrews 6:11–12 NCV

These words from the sixth chapter of Hebrews remind us that as Christians we must labor diligently, patiently, and faithfully. Do you want to be a worthy example for your family and friends? If so, you must preach the gospel of responsible behavior not only with your words, but also by your actions.

Every time you refuse to face up to life and its problems, you weaken your character.

E. Stanley Jones

If, in your working hours, you make the work your end, you will presently find yourself all unawares inside the only circle in your profession that really matters. You will be one of the sound craftsmen, and other sound craftsmen will know it.

C. S. Lewis

A TIMELY TIP

When you accept responsibilities and fulfill them, you'll feel better about yourself. When you avoid your obligations, you won't. Act accordingly.

THANKING GOD FOR HIS GIFTS

Thanks be to God for his indescribable gift!

2 Corinthians 9:15 NIV

How do we thank God for the gifts He has given us? By using those gifts for the glory of His kingdom.

God has given you talents and opportunities that are uniquely yours. Are you willing to use your gifts in the way that God intends? And are you willing to summon the discipline that is required to develop your talents and to hone your skills? That's precisely what God wants you to do, and that's precisely what you should desire for yourself.

As you seek to expand your talents, you will undoubtedly encounter stumbling blocks along the way, such as the fear of rejection or the fear of failure. When you do, don't stumble! Just continue to refine your skills, and offer your services to God. And when the time is right, He will use you—but it's up to you to be thoroughly prepared when He does.

What we are is God's gift to us. What we become is our gift to God.

Anonymous

There's a unique sense of fulfillment that comes when we submit our gifts to God's use and ask him to energize them in a supernatural way—and then step back to watch what he does.

Lee Strobel

A TIMELY TIP

It's both stressful and futile to squander God's blessings. You possess a unique set of talents. These gifts are from the Creator—use them while you can.

THE CHEERFUL GIVER

God loves the person who gives cheerfully.

2 Corinthians 9:7 NLT

A re you a cheerful giver? If you intend to obey God's commandments, you must be. When you give, God looks not only at the quality of your gift, but also at the condition of your heart. If you give generously, joyfully, and without complaint, you obey God's Word. But, if you make your gifts grudgingly, or if the motivation for your gift is selfish, you disobey your Creator, even if you have tithed in accordance with Biblical principles.

Today, take God's commandments to heart and make this pledge: Be a cheerful, generous, courageous giver. The world needs your help, and you need the spiritual rewards that will be yours when you give faithfully, prayerfully, and cheerfully.

A happy spirit takes the grind out of giving. The grease of gusto frees the gears of generosity.

Charles Swindoll

The happiest and most joyful people are those who give money and serve.

Dave Ramsey

A TIMELY TIP

Would you like to be a little happier? Try sharing a few more of the blessings that God has bestowed upon you. In other words, if you want to be happy, be generous. And if you want to be unhappy, be greedy.

THE WISDOM OF MODERATION

Watch out! Don't let me find you living in careless ease and drunkenness, and filled with the worries of this life. Don't let that day catch you unaware.

Luke 21:34 NLT

Moderation and wisdom are traveling companions. If we are wise, we must learn to temper our appetites, our desires, and our impulses. When we do, we are blessed, in part, because God has created a world in which temperance is rewarded and intemperance is inevitably punished.

Would you like to improve your life? Then harness your appetites and restrain your impulses. Moderation is difficult, of course; it is especially difficult in a prosperous society such as ours. But the rewards of moderation are numerous and long-lasting. Claim those rewards today.

No one can force you to moderate your appetites. The decision to live temperately (and wisely) is yours and yours alone. And so are the consequences.

To many, total abstinence is easier than perfect moderation.

St. Augustine

A TIMELY TIP

God's Word instructs us to be moderate and disciplined as we guard our bodies, our minds, and our hearts.

LIVING IN THE SPIRIT OF TRUTH

But when the Spirit of truth comes, he will lead you into all truth.

John 16:13 NCV

God is vitally concerned with truth. His Word teaches the truth; His Spirit reveals the truth; His Son leads us to the truth. When we open our hearts to God, and when we allow His Son to rule over our thoughts and our lives, God reveals Himself, and we come to understand the truth about ourselves and the truth about God's gift of grace.

The familiar words of John 8:32 remind us that "you shall know the truth, and the truth shall make you free" (NKJV). May we, as believers, seek God's truth and live by it, this day and forever.

Those who walk in truth walk in liberty.

Beth Moore

Truth will triumph. The Father of truth will win, and the followers of truth will be saved.

Max Lucado

A TIMELY TIP

God is vitally concerned with the truth . . . and you should be, too.

THE WISDOM OF THANKSGIVING

It is good to give thanks to the Lord, to sing praises to the Most High. It is good to proclaim your unfailing love in the morning, your faithfulness in the evening.

Psalm 92:1-2 NLT

God's Word makes it clear: a wise heart is a thankful heart. Period. We are to worship God, in part, by the genuine gratitude we feel in our hearts for the marvelous blessings that our Creator has bestowed upon us. Yet even the most saintly among us must endure periods of bitterness, fear, doubt, and regret. Why? Because we are imperfect human beings who are incapable of perfect gratitude. Still, even on life's darker days, we must seek to cleanse our hearts of negative emotions and fill them, instead, with praise, with love, with hope, and with thanksgiving. To do otherwise is to be unfair to ourselves, to our loved ones, and to our God.

Thanksgiving or complaining—these words express two contrastive attitudes of the souls of God's children in regard to His dealings with them. The soul that gives thanks can find comfort in everything; the soul that complains can find comfort in nothing.

Hannah Whitall Smith

The devil moves in when a Christian starts to complain, but thanksgiving in the Spirit defeats the devil and glorifies the Lord.

Warren Wiersbe

A TIMELY TIP

If you need a little cheering up, start counting your blessings . . . and keep counting until you feel better.

LEARNING LIFE'S LESSONS . . . THE EASY WAY

Whoever is stubborn after being corrected many times will suddenly be hurt beyond cure.

Proverbs 29:1 NCV

When it comes to learning life's lessons, we can either do things the easy way or the hard way. The easy way can be summed up as follows: when God teaches us a lesson, we learn it . . . the first time! Unfortunately, too many of us learn much more slowly than that.

When we resist God's instruction, He continues to teach, whether we like it or not. Our challenge, then, is to discern God's lessons from the experiences of everyday life. Hopefully, we learn those lessons sooner rather than later because the sooner we do, the sooner He can move on to the next lesson and the next, and the next . . .

Any patch of sunlight in a wood will show you something about the sun which you could never get from reading books on astronomy. These pure and spontaneous pleasures are "patches of Godlight" in the woods of our experience.

C. S. Lewis

While it is wise to learn from experience, it is wiser to learn from the experience of others.

Rick Warren

A TIMELY TIP

Use your experiences—both good and bad—to learn, to grow, to share, and to teach.

THE POSITIVE PATH

But the path of the just is like the shining sun, that shines ever brighter unto the perfect day. The way of the wicked is like darkness; they do not know what makes them stumble.

Proverbs 4:18-19 NKJV

When Jesus addressed His disciples, He warned that each one must, "take up his cross and follow Me." The disciples must have known exactly what the Master meant. In Jesus' day, prisoners were forced to carry their own crosses to the location where they would be put to death. Thus, Christ's message was clear: in order to follow Him, Christ's disciples must deny themselves and, instead, trust Him completely. Nothing has changed since then.

If we are to be dutiful disciples of the One from Galilee, we must trust Him and we must follow Him. Jesus never comes "next." He is always first. He shows us the path of life.

Do you seek to be a worthy disciple of Jesus? Then pick up His cross today and follow in His footsteps. When you do, you can walk with confidence: He will never lead you astray.

There is but one good; that is God. Everything else is good when it looks to Him and bad when it turns from Him.

C. S. Lewis

What is God looking for? He is looking for men and women whose hearts are completely His.

Charles Swindoll

A TIMELY TIP

If you really want to follow Jesus, you must walk as He walked—you must strive to lead a righteous life, despite your imperfections.

JUNE 7

CELEBRATING LIFE

Rejoice in the Lord, you righteous ones; praise from the upright is beautiful.

Psalm 33:1 Holman CSB

What is the best day to celebrate life? This one! Today and every day should be a time for celebration as we consider the Good News of God's gift: salvation through Jesus Christ.

What do you expect from the day ahead? Are you expecting God to do wonderful things, or are you living beneath a cloud of worry and doubt?

The familiar words of Psalm 118:24 remind us of a profound yet simple truth: "This is the day which the LORD has made." Our duty, as believers, is to rejoice in God's marvelous creation. For Christians, every day begins and ends with God and His Son. Christ came to this earth to give us abundant life and eternal salvation. We give thanks to our Maker when we treasure each day. So with no further ado, let the celebration begin!

We will never be happy until we make God the source of our fulfillment and the answer to our longings.

Stormie Omartian

The people whom I have seen succeed best in life have always been cheerful and hopeful people who went about their business with smiles on their faces.

Charles Kingsley

A TIMELY TIP

God has given you the gift of life (here on earth) and the promise of eternal life (in heaven). Now, He wants you to celebrate those gifts.

COMMENDING OURSELVES TO OTHERS

Therefore, since we have this ministry, as we have received mercy, we do not give up. Instead, we have renounced shameful secret things, not walking in deceit or distorting God's message, but in God's sight we commend ourselves to every person's conscience by an open display of the truth.

2 Corinthians 4:1-2 Holman CSB

God has given us a guidebook for righteous living called the Holy Bible. It contains thorough instructions which, if followed, lead to fulfillment, righteousness, and salvation. But, if we choose to ignore God's commandments, the results are as predictable as they are tragic.

A righteous life has many components: faith, honesty, generosity, love, kindness, humility, gratitude, and worship, to name but a few. If we seek to follow the steps of our Savior, Jesus Christ, we must seek to live according to His commandments. In short, we must, to the best of our abilities, live according to the principles contained in God's Holy Word.

So today and every day of your life, study God's Word and live by it. Make your life a shining example for those who have not yet found Christ. Embrace righteousness.

And for further instructions, read the manual.

Learning God's truth and getting it into our heads is one thing, but living God's truth and getting it into our characters is quite something else.

Warren Wiersbe

A TIMELY TIP

Today, consider the value of living a life that is pleasing to God. And while you're at it, think about the rewards that are likely to be yours when you do the right thing day in and day out.

RETURNING GOD'S LOVE . . . BY SHARING IT

My dear, dear friends, if God loved us like this, we certainly ought to love each other.

1 John 4:11 MSG

God loves you. How will you respond to His love? The Bible clearly defines what your response should be: "You shall love the Lord your God with all your heart, with all your soul, and with all your strength" (Deuteronomy 6:5 NKJV). But you must not stop there. You must also love your neighbor as yourself. Jesus teaches that "On these two commandments hang all the Law and the Prophets" (Matthew 22:40).

Today, as you meet the demands of everyday living, will you pause long enough to return God's love? And then will you share it? Prayerfully, you will. When you embrace God's love, you are forever changed. When you embrace God's love, you feel differently about yourself, your family, your friends, and your world. When you embrace God's love, you have enough love to keep and enough love to share: enough love for a day, enough love for a lifetime, enough love for all eternity.

He who is filled with love is filled with God Himself.

St. Augustine

In souls filled with love, the desire to please God is continual prayer.

John Wesley

A TIMELY TIP

God is love, and He expects us to share His love.

BEYOND SELF-DECEPTION

If we claim that we're free of sin, we're only fooling ourselves. A claim like that is errant nonsense. On the other hand, if we admit our sins—make a clean breast of them—he won't let us down; he'll be true to himself. He'll forgive our sins and purge us of all wrongdoing.

1 John 1:8-9 MSG

If we deny our sins, we allow those sins to flourish. And if we allow sinful behaviors to become habits, we invite hardships into our own lives and into the lives of our loved ones. When we yield to the distractions and temptations of this troubled world, we suffer. But God has other intentions, and His plans for our lives do not include sin or denial.

When we allow ourselves to encounter God's presence, He will lead us away from temptation, away from confusion, and away from the self-deception. God is the champion of truth and the enemy of denial. May we see ourselves through His eyes and conduct ourselves accordingly.

God has a plan and the devil has a plan, and you will have to decide which plan you are going to fit into.

Billy Graham

Self is the root, the branches, and the tree of all the evil of our fallen state.

Andrew Murray

A TIMELY TIP

Every day of your life, you will be tempted to rebel against God's teachings. Your job, simply put, is to guard your heart against the darkness as you focus on the light.

COURAGE IS CONTAGIOUS

I will lift up my eyes to the hills—From whence comes my help? My help comes from the Lord, Who made heaven and earth.

Psalm 121:1-2 NKJV

The more we trust God, the more courageously we live. And the more we trust God, the more we can encourage others.

Courage is contagious, and courage inspired by a steadfast trust in a loving Heavenly Father is highly contagious. Today, as you interact with friends, family members, or coworkers, share your courage, your hopes, your dreams, and your enthusiasm. Your positive outlook will be almost as big a blessing to them as it is to you.

Our Lord is searching for people who will make a difference. Christians dare not dissolve into the background or blend into the neutral scenery of the world.

Charles Swindoll

If you are God's child, you are no longer bound to your past or to what you were. You are a brand new creature in Christ Jesus.

Kay Arthur

A TIMELY TIP

If you are a disciple of the risen Christ, you have every reason on earth—and in heaven—to live courageously. And that's precisely what you should do.

WHAT GOD REQUIRES

But he's already made it plain how to live, what to do, what God is looking for in men and women. It's quite simple: Do what is fair and just to your neighbor, be compassionate and loyal in your love, and don't take yourself too seriously—take God seriously.

Micah 6:8 MSG

What does God require of us? That we worship Him only, that we welcome His Son into our hearts, and that we walk humbly with our Creator.

When Jesus was tempted by Satan, the Master's response was unambiguous. Jesus chose to worship the Lord and serve Him only. We, as followers of Christ, must follow in His footsteps.

When we place God in a position of secondary importance, we do ourselves great harm and we put ourselves at great risk. But when we place God squarely in the center of our lives—when we walk humbly and obediently with Him—we are blessed and we are protected.

In the great orchestra we call life, you have an instrument and a song, and you owe it to God to play them both sublimely.

Max Lucado

Opportunities for service abound, and you will be surprised that when you seek God's direction, a place of suitable service will emerge where you can express your love through service.

Charles Stanley

A TIMELY TIP

Whether you realize it or not, God has called you to a life of service. Your job is to find a place to serve and to get busy.

THE LOVE OF MONEY . . .

Pursue righteousness, godliness, faith, love, endurance, and gentleness. Fight the good fight for the faith; take hold of eternal life, to which you were called and have made a good confession before many witnesses.

1 Timothy 6:11-12 Holman CSB

Our society is in love with money and the things that money can buy. God is not. God cares about people, not possessions, and so must we. We must, to the best of our abilities, love our neighbors as ourselves, and we must, to the best of our abilities, resist the mighty temptation to place possessions ahead of people.

Money, in and of itself, is not evil; worshipping money is. So today, as you prioritize matters of importance for you and yours, remember that God is almighty, but the dollar is not. If we worship God, we are blessed. But if we worship "the almighty dollar," we are inevitably punished because of our misplaced priorities—and our punishment inevitably comes sooner rather than later.

If you want to be truly happy, you won't find it on an endless quest for more stuff. You'll find it in receiving God's generosity and in passing that generosity along.

Bill Hybels

A TIMELY TIP

If you find yourself focusing too much on stuff, try spending a little less time at the mall and a little more time talking to God. And remember this fact: Too much stuff doesn't eliminate stress. In fact, having too much stuff can actually create stress.

SHARE THE GOOD NEWS

Christ did not send me to baptize people but to preach the Good News. And he sent me to preach the Good News without using words of human wisdom so that the cross of Christ would not lose its power.

1 Corinthians 1:17 NCV

A good way to build your faith is by talking about it—and that's precisely what God wants you to do.

In his second letter to Timothy, Paul shares a message to believers of every generation when he writes, "God has not given us a spirit of timidity" (1:7). Paul's meaning is clear: When sharing your testimony, you must be courageous and unashamed.

Let's face facts: You live in a world that desperately needs the healing message of Jesus Christ. Every believer, including you, bears responsibility for sharing the Good News. And it is important to remember that you give your testimony through your words and your actions.

So today, preach the Gospel through your words and your deeds . . . but not necessarily in that order.

To stand in an uncaring world and say, "See, here is the Christ" is a daring act of courage.

Calvin Miller

Let God have perfect liberty when you speak. Before God's message can liberate other souls, the liberation must be real in you.

Oswald Chambers

A TIMELY TIP

Whether you realize it or not, you have a profound responsibility to tell as many people as you can about the eternal life that Christ offers to those who believe in Him.

GODLY THOUGHTS, GODLY ACTIONS

Commit your activities to the Lord and your plans will be achieved.

Proverbs 16:3 Holman CSB

Our thoughts have the power to lift us up or drag us down; they have the power to energize us or deplete us, to inspire us to greater accomplishments or to make those accomplishments impossible.

God intends that you experience joy and abundance, but He will not impose His joy upon you; you must accept it for yourself. It's up to you to celebrate the life that God has given you by focusing your mind upon "whatever is of good repute" (Philippians 4:8) Today, spend more time thinking about God's blessings, and less time fretting about the minor inconveniences of life. Then, take time to thank the Giver of all things good for gifts that are glorious, miraculous, and eternal.

It is the thoughts and intents of the heart that shape a person's life.

John Eldredge

As we have by faith said no to sin, so we should by faith say yes to God and set our minds on things above, where Christ is seated in the heavenlies.

Vonette Bright

A TIMELY TIP

Unless you're willing to guard your thoughts, you'll never be able to guard your heart.

THE POWER OF WILLING HANDS

A lazy person will end up poor, but a hard worker will become rich.

Proverbs 10:4 NCV

God's Word teaches us the value of hard work. In his second letter to the Thessalonians, Paul warns, ". . . if anyone will not work, neither shall he eat" (3:10 NKJV). And the Book of Proverbs proclaims, "A person who doesn't work hard is just like someone who destroys things" (18:9 NCV). In short, God has created a world in which diligence is rewarded but sloth is not. So, whatever it is that you choose to do, do it with enthusiasm and dedication.

Hard work is not simply a proven way to get ahead, it's also part of God's plan for you. God did not create you for a life of mediocrity; He created you for far greater things. Reaching for greater things usually requires work and lots of it, which is perfectly fine with God. After all, He knows that you're up to the task, and He has big plans for you if you possess a loving heart and willing hands.

We must trust as if it all depended on God and work as if it all depended on us.

C. H. Spurgeon

All work, if offered to Him, is transformed. It is not secular but sacred, sanctified in the glad offering.

Elisabeth Elliot

A TIMELY TIP

Here's a time-tested formula for success: have faith in God and do the work. It has been said that there are no shortcuts to any place worth going. Hard work is not simply a proven way to get ahead, it's also part of God's plan for His children, including you.

FAITHFULNESS AND FOCUS

But if from there you seek the LORD your God, you will find him if you look for him with all your heart and with all your soul.

Deuteronomy 4:29 NIV

God deserves your best. Is He getting it? Do you make an appointment with your Heavenly Father each day? Do you carve out moments when He receives your undivided attention? Or is your devotion to Him fleeting, distracted, and sporadic?

When you acquire the habit of focusing your heart and mind squarely upon God's intentions for your life, He will guide your steps and bless your endeavors. But if you allow distractions to take priority over your relationship with God, they will—and you will pay a price for your mistaken priorities.

Today, focus upon God's Word and upon His will for your life. When you do, you'll be amazed at how quickly everything else comes into focus, too.

It is important to set goals because if you do not have a plan, a goal, a direction, a purpose, and a focus, you are not going to accomplish anything for the glory of God.

Bill Bright

When Jesus is in our midst, He brings His limitless power along as well. But, Jesus must be in the middle, all eyes and hearts focused on Him.

Shirley Dobson

A TIMELY TIP

Whether you are talking to someone or working at your job, focus your attention on the task at hand. There is an important difference between "investing yourself" and "going through the motions."

UNDERSTANDING THE GREATNESS OF CHRIST'S LOVE

And I pray that you and all God's holy people will have the power to understand the greatness of Christ's love—how wide and how long and how high and how deep that love is. Christ's love is greater than anyone can ever know, but I pray that you will be able to know that love. Then you can be filled with the fullness of God.

Ephesians 3:18–19 NCV

Christ's love for you is personal. He loves you so much that He gave His life in order that you might spend all eternity with Him. Christ loves you individually and intimately; His is a love unbounded by time or circumstance. Are you willing to experience an intimate relationship with Him? Your Savior is waiting patiently; don't make Him wait a single minute longer. Embrace His love today. Fill yourself with the fullness of God.

Christ is like a river that is continually flowing. There are always fresh supplies of water coming from the fountain-head, so that a man may live by it and be supplied with water all his life. They who live upon Christ may have fresh supplies from him for all eternity.

Jonathan Edwards

Spiritual growth is the process of replacing lies with truth.

Rick Warren

A TIMELY TIP

One way to guard your heart is by continuing to grow in your faith.

TODAY'S BIBLE READING
Old Testament: Nehemiah 11-13
New Testament: Acts 6

THE TIME IS NOW

Hard work means prosperity; only fools idle away their time.

Proverbs 12:11 NLT

Time is a nonrenewable gift from God. But sometimes, we treat our time here on earth as if it were not a gift at all: We may be tempted to invest our lives in trivial pursuits and mindless diversions. But our Father in heaven wants us to do more . . . much more.

Are you one of those people who puts things off until the last minute? Do you waste time doing things that don't matter very much while putting off the important things until it's too late to do the job right? If so, it's now time to start making better choices.

It may seem like you've got all the time in the world to do the things you need to do, but time is shorter than you think. Time here on earth is limited . . . use it or lose it!

Our time is short! The time we can invest for God, in creative things, in receiving our fellowmen for Christ, is short!

Billy Graham

Overcommitment and time pressures are the greatest destroyers of marriages and families. It takes time to develop any friendship, whether with a loved one or with God himself.

James Dobson

A TIMELY TIP

If you don't value your time . . . neither will anybody else.

FAITH ON FIRE

I tell you the truth, whoever believes in me will do the same things that I do. Those who believe will do even greater things than these, because I am going to the Father.

John 14:12 NCV

John Wesley advised, "Catch on fire with enthusiasm and people will come for miles to watch you burn." His words still ring true. When we fan the flames of enthusiasm for Christ, our faith serves as a beacon to others.

Our world desperately needs faithful believers who share the Good News of Jesus with joyful exuberance. Be such a believer. The world desperately needs your enthusiasm, and just as importantly, you need the experience of sharing it.

One of the great needs in the church today is for every Christian to become enthusiastic about his faith in Jesus Christ.

Billy Graham

We must go out and live among them, manifesting the gentle, loving spirit of our Lord. We need to make friends before we can hope to make converts.

Lottie Moon

A TIMELY TIP

Don't wait for enthusiasm to find you . . . go looking for it. Look at your life and your relationships as exciting adventures. Don't wait for life to spice itself; spice things up yourself.

BEYOND BLAME

When they continued to ask Jesus their question, he raised up and said, "Anyone here who has never sinned can throw the first stone at her."

John 8:7 NCV

To blame others for our own problems is the height of futility. Yet blaming others is so easy to do and improving ourselves is so much harder. So instead of solving problems ourselves, we are tempted to do otherwise; we are tempted to fret over the perceived unfairness of life while doing precious little else.

Are you looking for an ironclad formula for problem-solving that will leave you happier, healthier, wealthier, and wiser? Here it is: don't play the blame game—because to play it is to lose it.

The main thing is this: we should never blame anyone or anything for our defeats. No matter how evil their intentions may be, they are altogether unable to harm us until we begin to blame them and use them as excuses for our own unbelief.

A. W. Tozer

Bitterness only makes suffering worse and closes the spiritual channels through which God can pour His grace.

Warren Wiersbe

A TIMELY TIP

If you take responsibility for your actions, you're headed in the right direction. If you try to blame others, you're headed down a dead-end street.

FAIRNESS AND HONEST DEALINGS

The Lord hates dishonest scales, but he is pleased with honest weights.

Proverbs 11:1 NCV

It has been said on many occasions and in many ways that honesty is the best policy. For believers, it is far more important to note that honesty is God's policy. And if we are to be servants worthy of our Savior, Jesus Christ, we must be honest and forthright in our communications with others.

Sometimes, honesty is difficult; sometimes, honesty is painful; always, honesty is God's commandment. In the Book of Exodus, God did not command, "Thou shalt not bear false witness when it is convenient." And He didn't say, "Thou shalt not bear false witness most of the time." God said, "Thou shalt not bear false witness against thy neighbor." Period.

Sometime soon, perhaps even today, you will be tempted to bend the truth or perhaps even to break it. Resist that temptation. Truth is God's way . . . and it must also be yours. Period.

The single most important element in any human relationship is honesty—with oneself, with God, and with others.

Catherine Marshall

Much guilt arises in the life of the believer from practicing the chameleon life of environmental adaptation.

Beth Moore

A TIMELY TIP

Beware of "white" lies. Sometimes, we're tempted to "shade" the truth. Unfortunately, little white lies have a tendency to turn black . . . and they grow. The best strategy is to avoid untruths of all sizes and colors.

THE POWER OF EXPECTANT PRAYER

Therefore I say to you, whatever things you ask when you pray, believe that you receive them, and you will have them.

Mark 11:24 NKJV

In case you've been wondering, wonder no more—God does answer your prayers. What God does not do is this: He does not always answer your prayers as soon as you might like, and He does not always answer your prayers by saying "Yes."

God isn't an order-taker, and He's not some sort of cosmic vending machine. Sometimes—even when we want something very badly—our loving Heavenly Father responds to our requests by saying "No," and we must accept His answer, even if we don't understand it.

God answers prayers not only according to our wishes but also according to His master plan. We cannot know that plan, but we can know the Planner . . . and we must trust His wisdom, His righteousness, and His love.

Of this you can be sure: God is listening, and He wants to hear from you now. So what are you waiting for?

Whatever may be our circumstances in life, may each one of us really believe that by way of the Throne we have unlimited power.

Annie Armstrong

A TIMELY TIP

Today, ask yourself if your prayer life is all that it should be. If the answer is yes, keep up the good work. But if the answer is no, set aside a specific time each morning to talk to God. And then, when you've set aside a time for prayer, don't allow yourself to become sidetracked.

WHEN IN DOUBT . . .

Don't depend on your own wisdom. Respect the Lord and refuse to do wrong.

Proverbs 3:7 NCV

If you're like most young people, you're busy . . . very busy. And sometimes, because so much is expected of you, you may lose perspective. Your life may seem to be spinning out of control, and the pressures of everyday living seem overwhelming. What's needed is a fresh perspective, a restored sense of balance . . . and God's wisdom.

Would you really like to become wise? If so, learning about wisdom isn't enough. You must also behave wisely. Wisdom is as wisdom does. Wisdom is determined not by words, but by deeds.

Do you wish to walk among the wise? If so, you must walk wisely. There is simply no other way.

Mark it down. God never turns away the honest seeker. Go to God with your questions. You may not find all the answers, but in finding God, you know the One who does.

Max Lucado

Wisdom is the God-given ability to see life with rare objectivity and to handle life with rare stability.

Charles Swindoll

A TIMELY TIP

Need wisdom? God's got it. If you want it, then study God's Word and associate with godly people.

PUTTING OFF TILL TOMORROW

If you make a promise to God, don't be slow to keep it. God is not happy with fools, so give God what you promised.

Ecclesiastes 5:4 NCV

The habit of procrastination takes a two-fold toll on its victims. First, important work goes unfinished; second, valuable energy is wasted in the process of putting off the things that remain undone. Procrastination results from an individual's short-sighted attempt to postpone temporary discomfort. What results is a senseless cycle of 1. delay, followed by 2. worry followed by 3. a panicky and often futile attempt to "catch up." Procrastination is, at its core, a struggle against oneself; the only antidote is action.

Once you acquire the habit of doing what needs to be done when it needs to be done, you will avoid untold trouble, worry, and stress. So learn to defeat procrastination by paying less attention to your fears and more attention to your responsibilities. God has created a world that punishes procrastinators and rewards people who "do it now." In other words, life doesn't procrastinate. Neither should you.

Not now becomes never.

Martin Luther

Every time you refuse to face up to life and its problems, you weaken your character.

E. Stanley Jones

A TIMELY TIP

It's easy to put off unpleasant tasks until "later." A far better strategy is this: Do the unpleasant work first so you can enjoy the rest of the day.

DISCOVERING GOD'S PURPOSE IN TIMES OF ADVERSITY

In this world you will have trouble. But take heart! I have overcome the world.

John 16:33 NIV

The Bible promises this: tough times are temporary but God's love is not—God's love lasts forever. So what does that mean to you? Just this: From time to time, everybody faces tough times, and so will you. And when tough times arrive, God will always stand ready to protect you and heal you.

Psalm 147 promises, "He heals the brokenhearted" (v. 3, NIV), but Psalm 147 doesn't say that He heals them instantly. Usually, it takes time (and maybe even a little help from you) for God to fix things. So if you're facing tough times, face them with God by your side. If you find yourself in any kind of trouble, pray about it and ask God for help. And be patient. God will work things out, just as He has promised, but He will do it in His own way and in His own time.

If your every human plan and calculation has miscarried, if, one by one, human props have been knocked out . . . take heart. God is trying to get a message through to you, and the message is: "Stop depending on inadequate human resources. Let me handle the matter."

Catherine Marshall

A TIMELY TIP

Remember that ultimately you and you alone are responsible for controlling your appetites. Others may warn you, help you, or encourage you, but in the end, the habits that rule your life are the very same habits that you yourself have formed. Thankfully, since you formed these habits, you can also break them—if you decide to do so.

PRAISING GOD'S GLORIOUS CREATION

The heavens declare the glory of God, and the sky proclaims the work of His hands.

Psalm 19:1 Holman CSB

Each morning, the sun rises upon a glorious world that is a physical manifestation of God's infinite power and His infinite love. And yet we're sometimes too busy to notice.

We live in a society filled with more distractions than we can possibly count and more obligations than we can possibly meet. Is it any wonder, then, that we often overlook God's handiwork as we rush from place to place, giving scarcely a single thought to the beauty that surrounds us?

Today, take time to really observe the world around you. Take time to offer a pray of thanks for the sky above and the beauty that lies beneath it. And take time to ponder the miracle of God's creation. The time you spend celebrating God's wonderful world is always time well spent.

Today, you will encounter God's creation. When you see the beauty around you, let each detail remind you to lift your head in praise.

Max Lucado

No philosophical theory which I have yet come across is a radical improvement on the words of Genesis, that "in the beginning God made Heaven and Earth."

C. S. Lewis

A TIMELY TIP

Don't miss out on God's glorious creation. Take time today, and every day, to observe and celebrate nature.

GOD'S TIMETABLE

There is an occasion for everything, and a time for every activity under heaven.

Ecclesiastes 3:1 Holman CSB

Most of us are impatient for God to grant us the desires of our heart. Usually, we know what we want, and we know precisely when we want it: right now, if not sooner. But God may have other plans. And when God's plans differ from our own, we must trust in His infinite wisdom and in His infinite love.

As busy guys living in a fast-paced world, many of us find that waiting quietly for God is difficult. Why? Because we are imperfect human beings seeking to live according to our own timetables, not God's. In our better moments, we realize that patience is not only a virtue, but it is also a commandment from the Creator.

God instructs us to be patient in all things. We must be patient with our families, with our friends, and with our acquaintances. We must also be patient with our Heavenly Father as He unfolds His plan for our lives. And that's as it should be. After all, think how patient God has been with us.

It is wise to wait because God gives clear direction only when we are willing to wait.

Charles Stanley

God is in no hurry. Compared to the works of mankind, He is extremely deliberate. God is not a slave to the human clock.

Charles Swindoll

A TIMELY TIP

God's timing is best, so don't allow yourself to become discouraged if things don't work out exactly as you wish. Instead of worrying about your future, entrust it to God.

STRENGTH FOR TODAY

The LORD is my strength and my song; he has become my victory. He is my God, and I will praise him.

Exodus 15:2 NLT

Where do you go to find strength? The gym? The health food store? The espresso bar? There's a better source of strength, of course, and that source is God. He is a never-ending source of strength and courage if you call upon Him.

Have you "tapped in" to the power of God? Have you turned your life and your heart over to Him, or are you muddling along under your own power? The answer to this question will determine the quality of your life here on earth and the destiny of your life throughout all eternity. So start tapping in—and remember that when it comes to strength, God is the Ultimate Source.

God is the One who provides our strength, not only to cope with the demands of the day, but also to rise above them. May we look to Him for the strength to soar.

Jim Gallery

Worry does not empty tomorrow of its sorrow; it empties today of its strength.

Corrie ten Boom

A TIMELY TIP

Need strength? Slow down, get more rest, engage in sensible exercise, and turn your troubles over to God . . . . but not necessarily in that order.

THIS IS THE DAY

This is the day the Lord has made; let us rejoice and be glad in it.

Psalm 118:24 Holman CSB

Are you basically a thankful person? Do you appreciate the stuff you've got and the life that you're privileged to live? You most certainly should be thankful. After all, when you stop to think about it, God has given you more blessings than you can count. So the question of the day is this: will you slow down long enough to thank your Heavenly Father . . . or not?

Sometimes, life here on earth can be complicated, demanding, and frustrating. When the demands of life leave you rushing from place to place with scarcely a moment to spare, you may fail to pause and thank your Creator for the countless blessings He has given you. Failing to thank God is understandable . . . but it's wrong.

God's Word makes it clear: a wise heart is a thankful heart. Period. You Heavenly Father has blessed you beyond measure, and you owe Him everything, including your thanks. God is always listening—are you willing to say thanks? It's up to you, and the next move is yours.

Why wait until the fourth Thursday in November? Why wait until the morning of December twenty-fifth? Thanksgiving to God should be an everyday affair. The time to be thankful is now!

Jim Gallery

A TIMELY TIP

Don't overlook God's gifts. Every sunrise represents yet another beautifully wrapped gift from God. Unwrap it; treasure it; use it; and give thanks to the Giver.

THE POWER OF OUR THOUGHTS

Set your minds on what is above, not on what is on the earth.

Colossians 3:2 Holman CSB

Our thoughts have the power to shape our lives—for better or worse. Thoughts have the power to lift our spirits, to improve our circumstances, and to strengthen our relationship with the Creator. But, our thoughts also have the power to cause us great harm if we focus too intently upon those things that distance us from God.

Today, make your thoughts an offering to God. Seek—by the things you think and the actions you take—to honor Him and serve Him. He deserves no less. And neither, for that matter, do you.

The things we think are the things that feed our souls. If we think on pure and lovely things, we shall grow pure and lovely like them; and the converse is equally true.

Hannah Whitall Smith

Every major spiritual battle is in the mind.

Charles Stanley

A TIMELY TIP

Watch what you think. If your inner voice is like a broken record that keeps repeating negative thoughts, you must guard your heart more carefully. And while you're at it, you should train yourself to begin thinking thoughts that are more rational, more positive, more forgiving, and less destructive.

FINDING THE PURPOSE BENEATH THE PROBLEM

Be joyful because you have hope. Be patient when trouble comes, and pray at all times.

Romans 12:12 NCV

Hidden beneath every problem is the seed of a solution—God's solution. Your challenge, as a faithful believer, is to trust God's providence and seek His solutions. When you do, you will eventually discover that God does nothing without a very good reason: His reason.

Are you willing to faithfully trust God on good days and bad ones? Hopefully so, because an important part of walking with God is finding His purpose in the midst of your problems.

Looking back, I can see that the most exciting events of my life have all risen out of trouble.

Catherine Marshall

Life is literally filled with God-appointed storms. These squalls surge across everyone's horizon. We all need them.

Charles Swindoll

A TIMELY TIP

If it weren't for trouble . . . we might think we could handle our lives by ourselves. Jim Cymbala writes, "Trouble is one of God's great servants because it reminds us how much we continually need the Lord." We should thank the Lord for challenges that bring us closer to Him.

LIVING IN AN ANXIOUS WORLD

Don't fret or worry. Instead of worrying, pray. Let petitions and praises shape your worries into prayers, letting God know your concerns. Before you know it, a sense of God's wholeness, everything coming together for good, will come and settle you down. It's wonderful what happens when Christ displaces worry at the center of your life.

Philippians 4:6-7 MSG

We live in a world that often breeds anxiety and fear. When we come face-to-face with tough times, we may fall prey to discouragement, doubt, or depression. But our Father in heaven has other plans. God has promised that we may lead lives of abundance, not anxiety. In fact, His Word instructs us to "be anxious for nothing." But how can we put our fears to rest? By taking those fears to God and leaving them there.

As you face the challenges of everyday living, do you find yourself becoming anxious, troubled, discouraged, or fearful? If so, turn every one of your concerns over to your Heavenly Father. The same God who created the universe will comfort you if you ask Him . . . so ask Him and trust Him. And then watch in amazement as your anxieties melt into the warmth of His loving hands.

Worry and anxiety are sand in the machinery of life; faith is the oil.

E. Stanley Jones

A TIMELY TIP

Divide your areas of concern into two categories: those you can control and those you cannot. Resolve never to waste time or energy worrying about the latter.

HOLINESS BEFORE HAPPINESS

Blessed are those who hunger and thirst for righteousness, because they will be filled.

Matthew 5:6 Holman CSB

Because you are an imperfect human being, you are not "perfectly" happy—and that's perfectly okay with God. He is far less concerned with your happiness than He is with your holiness.

God continuously reveals Himself in everyday life, but He does not do so in order to make you contented; He does so in order to lead you to His Son. So don't be overly concerned with your current level of happiness: it will change. Be more concerned with the current state of your relationship with Christ: He does not change. And because your Savior transcends time and space, you can be comforted in the knowledge that in the end, His joy will become your joy . . . for all eternity.

Holiness isn't in a style of dress. It's not a matter of rules and regulations. It's a way of life that emanates quietness and rest, joy in family, shared pleasures with friends, the help of a neighbor—and the hope of a Savior.

Joni Eareckson Tada

God's glory is the result of his nature and his actions. He is glorious in his character, for he holds within him everything that is holy, good, and lovely.

C. H. Spurgeon

A TIMELY TIP

God is holy and wants you to be holy. Christ died to make you holy. Make sure that your response to Christ's sacrifice is worthy of Him.

HE IS HERE

Every morning he wakes me. He teaches me to listen like a student. The Lord God helps me learn . . .

Isaiah 50:4-5 NCV

Do you ever wonder if God is really here? If so, you're not the first person to think such thoughts. In fact, some of the biggest heroes in the Bible had their doubts—and so, perhaps, will you. But when questions arise and doubts begin to creep into your mind, remember this: God hasn't gone on vacation; He hasn't left town; and He doesn't have an unlisted number. You can talk with Him any time you feel like it. In fact, He's right here, right now, listening to your thoughts and prayers, watching over your every move.

Sometimes, you will allow yourself to become very busy, and that's when you may be tempted to ignore God. But, when you quiet yourself long enough to acknowledge His presence, God will touch your heart and restore your spirits. By the way, He's ready to talk right now. Are you?

God makes prayer as easy as possible for us. He's completely approachable and available, and He'll never mock or upbraid us for bringing our needs before Him.

Shirley Dobson

A TIMELY TIP

God is here, and He wants to establish an intimate relationship with you. When you sincerely reach out to Him, you will sense His presence.

LIVING ON PURPOSE

God chose you to be his people, so I urge you now to live the life to which God called you.

Ephesians 4:1 NCV

Life is best lived on purpose. And purpose, like everything else in the universe, begins with God. Whether you realize it or not, God has a plan for your life, a divine calling, a direction in which He is leading you. When you welcome God into your heart and establish a genuine relationship with Him, He will begin, in time, to make His purposes known.

Sometimes, God's intentions will be clear to you; other times, God's plan will seem uncertain at best. But even on those difficult days when you are unsure which way to turn, you must never lose sight of these overriding facts: God created you for a reason; He has important work for you to do; and He's waiting patiently for you to do it.

And the next step is up to you.

The really committed leave the safety of the harbor, accept the risk of the open seas of faith, and set their compasses for the place of total devotion to God and whatever life adventures He plans for them.

Bill Hybels

There is wonderful freedom and joy in coming to recognize that the fun is in the becoming.

Gloria Gaither

A TIMELY TIP

Before you make a big decision, think about the things you stand for. And be sure that what you're about to do is consistent with your values.

HELPING THE HELPLESS

I have shown you in every way, by laboring like this, that you must support the weak. And remember the words of the Lord Jesus, that He said, "It is more blessed to give than to receive."

Acts 20:35 NKJV

The words of Jesus are unambiguous: "Freely you have received, freely give" (Matthew 10:8 NIV). As followers of Christ, we are commanded to be generous with our friends, with our families, and especially with those in need. We must give freely of our time, our possessions, our love.

In 2 Corinthians 9, Paul reminds us "God loves a cheerful giver" (v. 7 NKJV). So take God's words to heart and make this pledge: Be a cheerful, generous, courageous giver. The world needs your help, and you need the spiritual rewards that will be yours when you do.

Nothing is really ours until we share it.

C. S. Lewis

Wise Christians will be generous with their neighbors and live peaceably with them.

Warren Wiersbe

A TIMELY TIP

God has given you countless blessings . . . and He wants you to share them.

CHRISTIANITY HERE AND NOW

Teach me to do Your will, for You are my God; Your Spirit is good. Lead me in the land of uprightness.

Psalm 143:10 NKJV

Jesus made an extreme sacrifice for you. Are you willing to make extreme changes in your life for Him? Can you honestly say that you're passionate about your faith and that you're really following Jesus? Hopefully so. But if you're preoccupied with other things—or if you're strictly a one-day-a-week Christian—then you're in need of an extreme spiritual makeover!

Jesus doesn't want you to be a run-of-the-mill, follow-the-crowd kind of guy. Jesus wants you to be a "new creation" through Him. And that's exactly what you should want for yourself, too. Nothing is more important than your wholehearted commitment to your Creator and to His only begotten Son. Your faith must never be an afterthought; it must be your ultimate priority, your ultimate possession, and your ultimate passion.

You are the recipient of Christ's love. Accept it enthusiastically and share it passionately. Jesus deserves your extreme enthusiasm; the world deserves it; and you deserve the experience of sharing it.

When Jesus put the little child in the midst of His disciples, He did not tell the little child to become like His disciples; He told the disciples to become like the little child.

Ruth Bell Graham

A TIMELY TIP

Talk is cheap. Real ministry has legs. When it comes to being a disciple, make sure that you back up your words with deeds.

EXPECTING GOD'S BLESSINGS

My cup runs over. Surely goodness and mercy shall follow me all the days of my life; and I will dwell in the house of the Lord forever.

Psalm 23:5-6 NKJV

Face facts: pessimism and Christianity don't mix. Why? Because Christians have every reason to be optimistic about life here on earth and life eternal. Mrs. Charles E. Cowman advised, "Never yield to gloomy anticipation. Place your hope and confidence in God. He has no record of failure."

Sometimes, despite our trust in God, we may fall into the spiritual traps of worry, frustration, anxiety, or sheer exhaustion, and our hearts become heavy. What's needed is plenty of rest, a large dose of perspective, and God's healing touch, but not necessarily in that order.

Today, make this promise to yourself and keep it: vow to be a hope-filled Christian. Think optimistically about your life, your education, your family, and your future. Trust your hopes, not your fears. Take time to celebrate God's glorious creation. And then, when you've filled your heart with hope, share your optimism with others. They'll be better for it, and so will you. But not necessarily in that order.

If our hearts have been attuned to God through an abiding faith in Christ, the result will be joyous optimism and good cheer.

Billy Graham

Our hope in Christ for the future is the mainstream of our joy.

C. H. Spurgeon

A TIMELY TIP

Today (and every day), it's time to count your blessings and to think optimistically about your future.

ANSWERED PRAYERS

God answered their prayers because they trusted him.

1 Chronicles 5:20 MSG

God answers our prayers. What God does not do is this: He does not answer our prayers in a time and fashion of our choosing, and He does not always answer our prayers in the affirmative. Sometimes our loving Heavenly Father responds to our requests by saying "No," and we must accept His answer, even though we may not understand it.

God answers prayers not according to our wishes but according to His master plan. We cannot know that plan, but we can know the Planner . . . and we must trust His wisdom, His righteousness, and His unending love.

What God gives in answer to our prayers will always be the thing we most urgently need, and it will always be sufficient.

Elisabeth Elliot

I firmly believe a great many prayers are not answered because we are not willing to forgive someone.

D. L. Moody

A TIMELY TIP

Give God your full attention by putting prayer at the very top of your daily to-do list.

BEYOND BITTERNESS

Those who show mercy to others are happy, because God will show mercy to them.

Matthew 5:7 NCV

A re you mired in the quicksand of bitterness or regret? If so, you are not only disobeying God's Word, you are also wasting your time. The world holds few if any rewards for those who remain angrily focused upon the past. Still, the act of forgiveness is difficult.

Being frail, fallible, imperfect human beings, most of us are quick to anger, quick to blame, slow to forgive, and even slower to forget. Yet as Christians, we are commanded to forgive others, just as we, too, have been forgiven.

If there exists even one person—alive or dead—against whom you hold bitter feelings, it's time to forgive. Or, if you are embittered against yourself for some past mistake or shortcoming, it's finally time to forgive yourself and move on. Hatred, bitterness, and regret are not part of God's plan for your life. Forgiveness is.

Give me such love for God and men as will blot out all hatred and bitterness.

Dietrich Bonhoeffer

Bitterness is the trap that snares the hunter.

Max Lucado

A TIMELY TIP

Holding a grudge? Drop it! Remember, holding a grudge is like letting somebody live rent-free in your brain . . . so don't do it!

LESSONS IN LEADERSHIP

Shepherd God's flock, for whom you are responsible. Watch over them because you want to, not because you are forced. That is how God wants it. Do it because you are happy to serve.

1 Peter 5:2 NCV

John Maxwell writes, "Great leaders understand that the right attitude will set the right atmosphere, which enables the right response from others." If you are in a position of leadership, whether at work, home, or at school, it's up to you to set the right tone by maintaining the right attitude.

What's your attitude today? Are you fearful, angry, bored, or worried? Are you confused, bitter, or pessimistic? If so, then you should ask yourself if you're the kind of leader whom you would want to follow. If the answer to that question is no, then it's time to improve your leadership skills.

Our world needs Christian leadership. You can become a trusted, competent, thoughtful leader if you learn to maintain the right attitude: one that is realistic, optimistic, forward looking, and Christ-centered.

When God wants to accomplish something, He calls dedicated men and women to challenge His people and lead the way.

Warren Wiersbe

People who inspire others are those who see invisible bridges at the end of dead-end streets.

Charles Swindoll

A TIMELY TIP

Leadership comes in many forms, and you can lead others in your own way using your own style.

TODAY'S BIBLE READING
Old Testament: Psalms 7-8
New Testament: Acts 20

TRUSTING THE QUIET VOICE

In quietness and trust is your strength.

Isaiah 30:15 NASB

Whenever you're about to make an important decision, you should listen carefully to the quiet voice inside. Sometimes, of course, it's tempting to do otherwise. From time to time you'll be tempted to abandon your better judgement by ignoring your conscience. Don't do it. Instead of ignoring that quiet little voice, pay careful attention to it. If you do, your conscience will lead you in the right direction—in fact, it's trying to lead you right now. So listen . . . and learn.

It is neither safe nor prudent to do anything against conscience.

Martin Luther

Whatever weakens your reason, impairs the tenderness of your conscience, obscures your sense of God, or removes your relish for spiritual things—that is sin to you.

Susanna Wesley

A TIMELY TIP

If your friends are telling you one thing and your conscience is telling you something else, trust your conscience.

BEYOND ANGER

Mockers can get a whole town agitated, but those who are wise will calm anger.

Proverbs 29:8 NLT

Your temper is either your master or your servant. Either you control it, or it controls you. And the extent to which you allow anger to rule your life will determine, to a surprising extent, the quality of your relationships with others and your relationship with God.

Anger and peace cannot coexist in the same mind. If you allow yourself to be chronically angry, you must forfeit, albeit temporarily, the peace that might otherwise be yours through Christ. So obey God's Word by turning away from anger today and every day. You'll be glad you did, and so will your family and friends.

Anger is the noise of the soul; the unseen irritant of the heart; the relentless invader of silence.

Max Lucado

Life is too short to spend it being angry, bored, or dull.

Barbara Johnson

A TIMELY TIP

When times are tough, you should guard your heart by turning it over to God.

THE POSSESSIONS WE OWN, AND VICE VERSA

We brought nothing into the world, so we can take nothing out. But, if we have food and clothes, we will be satisfied with that.

1 Timothy 6:7-8 NCV

How important are your material possessions? Not as important as you might think. In the life of a committed Christian, material possessions should play a rather small role. In fact, when we become overly enamored with the things we own, we needlessly distance ourselves from the peace that God offers to those who place Him at the center of their lives.

Of course, we all need the basic necessities of life, but once we meet those needs for ourselves and for our families, the piling up of possessions creates more problems than it solves. Our real riches, of course, are not of this world. We are never really rich until we are rich in spirit.

Do you find yourself wrapped up in the concerns of the material world? If so, it's time to reorder your priorities by turning your thoughts and your prayers to more important matters. And, it's time to begin storing up riches that will endure throughout eternity: the spiritual kind.

Order your soul; reduce your wants; associate in Christian community; obey the laws; trust in Providence

St. Augustine

A TIMELY TIP

Perhaps you think that the more stuff you acquire, the happier you'll be. If so, think again. Too much stuff means too many headaches, so start simplifying now.

DIRECTING OUR THOUGHTS

Finally, brothers, whatever is true, whatever is noble, whatever is right, whatever is pure, whatever is lovely, whatever is admirable—if anything is excellent or praiseworthy—think about such things.

Philippians 4:8 NIV

How will you direct your thoughts today? Will you obey the words of Philippians 4:8 by dwelling upon those things that are honorable, true, and worthy of praise? Or will you allow your thoughts to be hijacked by the negativity that seems to dominate our troubled world?

Are you fearful, angry, bored, or worried? Are you so preoccupied with the concerns of this day that you fail to thank God for the promise of eternity? Are you confused, bitter, or pessimistic? If so, God wants to have a little talk with you. He wants to remind you of His infinite love and His boundless grace. As you contemplate these things, and as you give thanks for God's blessings, negativity should no longer dominate your day or your life.

Your thoughts are the determining factor as to whose mold you are conformed to. Control your thoughts and you control the direction of your life.

Charles Stanley

Whether we think of, or speak to, God, whether we act or suffer for him, all is prayer when we have no other object than his love and the desire of pleasing him.

John Wesley

A TIMELY TIP

Good thoughts lead to good deeds and bad thoughts lead elsewhere. So guard your thoughts accordingly.

GIVING GOD OUR COMPLETE ATTENTION

Worship the Lord your God and . . . serve Him only.

Matthew 4:10 Holman CSB

Nineteenth-century clergyman Edwin Hubbel Chapin warned, "Neutral men are the devil's allies." His words were true then, and they're true now. Neutrality in the face of evil is a sin. Yet all too often, we fail to fight evil, not because we are neutral, but because we are shortsighted: we don't fight the devil because we don't recognize his handiwork.

If we are to recognize evil and fight it, we must pay careful attention. We must pay attention to God's Word, and we must pay attention to the realities of everyday life. When we observe life objectively, and when we do so with eyes and hearts that are attuned to God's Holy Word, we can no longer be neutral believers. And when we are no longer neutral, God rejoices while the devil despairs.

The greatest enemy of holiness is not passion; it is apathy.

John Eldredge

Be half a Christian, and you will have just enough religion to make you miserable.

C. H. Spurgeon

A TIMELY TIP

If you're having trouble staying motivated at school, start praying more about your life, your future, and your work. And while you're at it, ask God to help you discover His purpose for your life.

OUR PROBLEMS =
GOD'S OPPORTUNITIES

As for God, his way is perfect. All the LORD's promises prove true. He is a shield for all who look to him for protection.

Psalm 18:30 NLT

Here's a riddle: What is it that is too unimportant to pray about yet too big for God to handle? The answer, of course, is: "nothing." Yet sometimes, when the challenges of the day seem overwhelming, we may spend more time worrying about our troubles than praying about them. And, we may spend more time fretting about our problems than solving them. A far better strategy is to pray as if everything depended entirely upon God and to work as if everything depended entirely upon us.

What we see as problems God sees as opportunities. And if we are to trust Him completely, we must acknowledge that even when our own vision is dreadfully impaired, His vision is perfect. Today and every day, let us trust God by courageously confronting the things that we see as problems and He sees as possibilities.

We are all faced with a series of great opportunities, brilliantly disguised as unsolvable problems. Unsolvable without God's wisdom, that is.

Charles Swindoll

A TIMELY TIP

Everyone has problems, but not everyone deals with their problems in the same way. The way you address your problems—whether you choose to avoid them or address them—determines how successfully—and how quickly—you overcome them.

GRACE FOR TODAY

But He said to me, "My grace is sufficient for you, for power is perfected in weakness."

2 Corinthians 12:9 Holman CSB

God's grace is not earned . . . thank goodness! To earn God's love and His gift of eternal life would be far beyond the abilities of even the most righteous man or woman. Thankfully, God's grace is not an earthly reward for righteous behavior; it is a blessed spiritual gift that can be accepted by believers who dedicate themselves to God through Christ. When we accept Christ into our hearts, we are saved by His grace.

As you contemplate the day ahead, praise God for His blessings. He is the Giver of all things good. He is the Comforter, the Protector, the Teacher, and the Savior. Praise Him today and forever.

The grace of God is sufficient for all our needs, for every problem, and for every difficulty, for every broken heart, and for every human sorrow.

Peter Marshall

The realization that it was impossible to get into heaven on my own ticket became a tremendously liberating experience for me. I realized I had to catch a different train, and that's when I was run over by a locomotive called grace.

Bill Hybels

A TIMELY TIP

By God's grace we are saved, and by God's grace we live each day. Each new day is a gift from God—treasure it; use it; and give thanks!

SCATTERING SEEDS OF KINDNESS

Be devoted to one another in brotherly love. Honor one another above yourselves.
Romans 12:10 NIV

What is a friend? The dictionary defines the word *friend* as "a person who is attached to another by feelings of affection or personal regard." This definition is accurate, as far as it goes, but when we examine the deeper meaning of friendship, so many more descriptors come to mind: trustworthiness, loyalty, helpfulness, kindness, understanding, forgiveness, encouragement, humor, and cheerfulness, to mention but a few.

How wonderful are the joys of friendship. Today, as you consider the many blessings that God has given you, remember to thank Him for the friends He has chosen to place along your path. May you be a blessing to them, and may they richly bless you today, tomorrow, and every day that you live.

That's a good part of the good old days—to be genuinely interested in your neighbor, and if you hear a distress signal, go see about him and his problem.
Jerry Clower

A person who really cares about his or her neighbor, a person who genuinely loves others, is a person who bears witness to the truth.
Anne Graham Lotz

A TIMELY TIP

Here's a question worth asking yourself: are you the kind of neighbor you'd want to have living next door to you and your family?

FOLLOWING IN THE FOOTSTEPS

Whoever serves me must follow me. Then my servant will be with me everywhere I am. My Father will honor anyone who serves me.

John 12:26 NCV

If you genuinely want to make choices that are pleasing to God, you must ask yourself this question: "How does God want me to serve others?"

Whatever your age, wherever you happen to be, you may be certain of this: service to others is an integral part of God's plan for your life.

Every single day of your life, including this one, God will give you opportunities to serve Him by serving other people. Welcome those opportunities with open arms. They are God's gift to you, His way of allowing you to achieve greatness in His kingdom.

Opportunities for service abound, and you will be surprised that when you seek God's direction, a place of suitable service will emerge where you can express your love through service.

Charles Stanley

If you aren't serving, you're just existing, because life is meant for ministry.

Rick Warren

A TIMELY TIP

You can make a difference: If you choose to serve, you'll be doing the world (and yourself) a big favor.

LIVING ABOVE THE DAILY WHINE

Do everything readily and cheerfully—no bickering, no second-guessing allowed! Go out into the world uncorrupted, a breath of fresh air in this squalid and polluted society. Provide people with a glimpse of good living and of the living God. Carry the light-giving Message into the night.

Philippians 2:14-15 MSG

Because we are imperfect human beings, we often lose sight of our blessings. Ironically, most of us have more blessings than we can count, but we may still find reasons to complain about the minor frustrations of everyday life. To do so, of course, is not only wrong; it is also the pinnacle of shortsightedness and a serious roadblock on the path to spiritual abundance.

Are you tempted to complain about the inevitable minor frustrations of everyday living? Don't do it! Today and every day, make it a practice to count your blessings, not your hardships. It's the truly decent way to live.

Life goes on. Keep on smiling and the whole world smiles with you.

Dennis Swanberg

I may not be able to change the world I see around me, but I can change the way I see the world within me.

John Maxwell

A TIMELY TIP

If you're a Christian, you have every reason on earth—and in heaven—to have a positive attitude.

TRUSTING GOD'S WORD

But He answered, "It is written: Man must not live on bread alone, but on every word that comes from the mouth of God."

Matthew 4:4 Holman CSB

The Bible is unlike any other book. A. W. Tozer wrote, "The purpose of the Bible is to bring men to Christ, to make them holy and prepare them for heaven. In this it is unique among books, and it always fulfills its purpose."

As Christians, we are called upon to share God's Holy Word with a world in desperate need of His healing hand. The Bible is a priceless gift, a tool for Christians to use as they share the Good News of their Savior, Christ Jesus. Too many Christians, however, keep their spiritual tool kits tightly closed and out of sight.

Jonathan Edwards advised, "Be assiduous in reading the Holy Scriptures. This is the fountain whence all knowledge in divinity must be derived. Therefore let not this treasure lie by you neglected." God's Holy Word is, indeed, a priceless, one-of-a-kind treasure. Handle it with care, but more importantly, handle it every day.

Weave the unveiling fabric of God's word through your heart and mind. It will hold strong, even if the rest of life unravels.

Gigi Graham Tchividjian

The Gospel is not so much a demand as it is an offer, an offer of new life to man by the grace of God.

E. Stanley Jones

A TIMELY TIP

You're never too young—or too old—to become a big-time student of God's Word.

WHAT KIND OF EXAMPLE?

You should be an example to the believers in speech, in conduct, in love, in faith, in purity.

1 Timothy 4:12 Holman CSB

Whether we like it or not, all of us are examples. The question is not whether we will be examples to our families and friends; the question is simply what kind of examples will we be.

What kind of example are you? Are you the kind of person whose life serves as a powerful example of righteousness? Are you a young person whose behavior serves as a positive role model for younger folks? Are you the kind of person whose actions, day in and day out, are honorable, ethical, and admirable? If so, you are not only blessed by God, but you are also a powerful force for good in a world that desperately needs positive influences such as yours.

D. L. Moody advised, "A man ought to live so that everybody knows he is a Christian, and most of all, his family ought to know." And that's sound advice because our families and friends are watching . . . and so, for that matter, is God.

More depends on my walk than my talk.

D. L. Moody

A TIMELY TIP

As a Christian, the most important light you shine is the light that your own life shines on the lives of others. May your light shine brightly, righteously, obediently, and eternally!

JULY 25

EARTHLY PRESSURES AND THE SPIRITUAL PATH

We say they are happy because they did not give up. You have heard about Job's patience, and you know the Lord's purpose for him in the end. You know the Lord is full of mercy and is kind.

James 5:11 NCV

Some friends encourage us to obey God—these friends help us make wise choices. Other friends put us in situations where we are tempted to disobey God—these friends tempt us to make unwise choices.

Are you hanging out with people who make you a better Christian, or are you spending time with people who encourage you to stray from your faith? The answer to this question will help determine the condition of your spiritual health. One of the best ways to ensure that you follow Christ is to find fellow believers who are willing to follow Him with you.

Christians don't fail to live as they should because they are in the world; they fail because the world has gotten into them.

Billy Graham

Because the world is deceptive, it is dangerous. The world can even deceive God's own people and lead them into trouble.

Warren Wiersbe

A TIMELY TIP

The friends you choose will determine the kind of person you become.

DEFEATING THOSE EVERYDAY FRUSTRATIONS

Foolish people are always fighting, but avoiding quarrels will bring you honor.

Proverbs 20:3 NCV

Anger is a natural human emotion that is sometimes necessary and appropriate. Even Jesus became angry when confronted the moneychangers in the temple (Matthew 21). Righteous indignation is an appropriate response to evil, but God does not intend that anger should rule our lives. Far from it. God intends that we turn away from anger whenever possible and forgive our neighbors just as we seek forgiveness for ourselves.

Life is full of frustrations: some great and some small. On occasion, you, like Jesus, will confront evil, and when you do, you may respond as He did: vigorously and without reservation. But, more often your frustrations will be of the more mundane variety. As long as you live here on earth, you will face countless opportunities to lose your temper over small, relatively insignificant events: a traffic jam, a spilled cup of coffee, an inconsiderate comment, a broken promise. When you are tempted to lose your temper over the minor inconveniences of life, don't. Turn away from anger, hatred, bitterness, and regret. Turn instead to God. When you do, you'll be following His commandments and giving yourself a priceless gift . . . the gift of peace.

Anger breeds remorse in the heart, discord in the home, bitterness in the community, and confusion in the state.

Billy Graham

A TIMELY TIP

No more angry outbursts! If you think you're about to explode in anger, slow down, catch your breath, and walk away if you must. It's better to walk away—and keep walking—than it is to blurt out angry words that can't be un-blurted.

ENOUGH IS ENOUGH

Your life should be free from the love of money. Be satisfied with what you have, for He Himself has said, I will never leave you or forsake you.

Hebrews 13:5 Holman CSB

Ours is a world that glorifies material possessions. Christians, of course, should not. As believers who have been touched and transformed by the grace of a risen Savior, we must never allow the things of this earth to distance us from our sense of God's presence and the direction of God's hand. If we are to enjoy the peace and abundance that God has promised us, we must reign in our desire for more and more; we must acknowledge that when it comes to earthly possessions, enough is always enough.

Contentment is something we learn by adhering to the basics—cultivating a growing relationship with Jesus Christ, living daily, and knowing that Christ strengthens us for every challenge.

Charles Stanley

The happiness which brings enduring worth to life is not the superficial happiness that is dependent on circumstances. It is the happiness and contentment that fills the soul in the midst of the most distressing of circumstances.

Billy Graham

A TIMELY TIP

God offers you His peace, His protection, and His promises. If you accept these gifts, you will be content.

FINDING PURPOSE THROUGH SERVICE

But he who is greatest among you shall be your servant. And whoever exalts himself will be humbled, and he who humbles himself will be exalted.

Matthew 23:11-12 NLT

The words of Jesus are clear: the most esteemed men and women in this world are not the big-shots who jump up on stage and hog the spotlight; the greatest among us are those who are willing to become humble servants.

Are you willing to become a servant for Christ? Are you willing to pitch in and make the world a better place, or are you determined to keep all your blessings to yourself? Hopefully, you are determined to follow Christ's example by making yourself an unselfish servant to those who need your help.

Today, you may be tempted to take more than you give. But if you feel the urge to be selfish, resist that urge with all your might. Don't be stingy, selfish, or self-absorbed. Instead, serve your friends quietly and without fanfare. Find a need and fill it . . . humbly. Lend a helping hand . . . anonymously. Share a word of kindness . . . with quiet sincerity. As you go about your daily activities, remember that the Savior of all humanity made Himself a servant, and we, as His followers, must do no less.

Service is the pathway to real significance.

Rick Warren

You get the most out of your work when you view yourself as a servant.

Charles Stanley

A TIMELY TIP

Jesus was a servant, and if you want to follow Him, you must be a servant, too—even when service requires sacrifice.

LOOKING AHEAD

Do not remember the past events, pay no attention to things of old. Look, I am about to do something new; even now it is coming. Do you not see it? Indeed, I will make a way in the wilderness, rivers in the desert.

Isaiah 43:18-19 Holman CSB

For busy people living in a fast-paced 21st-century world, life may seem like a merry-go-round that never stops turning. If that description seems to fit your life, then you may find yourself running short of patience, or strength, or both. If you're feeling tired or discouraged, there is a source from which you can draw the power needed to renew your spirit and your strength. That source is God.

God can make all things new, including you. Your job is to let Him.

God is not running an antique shop! He is making all things new!

Vance Havner

God is great and God is powerful, but we must invite him to be powerful in our lives. His strength is always there, but it's up to us to provide a channel through which that power can flow.

Bill Hybels

A TIMELY TIP

God wants to give you peace, and He wants to renew your spirit. It's up to you to slow down and give Him a chance to do so.

LOVING GOD AND OTHERS

He said to him, "You shall love the Lord your God with all your heart, with all your soul, and with all your mind. This is the greatest and most important commandment. The second is like it: You shall love your neighbor as yourself. All the Law and the Prophets depend on these two commandments."

Matthew 22:37-40 Holman CSB

Christ's words leave no room for interpretation: He instructs us to love the Lord with all our hearts and to love our neighbors as we love ourselves. But sometimes, despite our best intentions, we fall short. When we become embittered with ourselves, with our neighbors, or most especially with God, we disobey the One who gave His life for us. And we bring inevitable, needless suffering into our lives.

If we are to please God, we must cleanse ourselves of the negative feelings that separate us from others and from Him. In 1 Corinthians 13, we are told that love is the foundation upon which all our relationships are to be built—our relationships with others and our relationship with our Creator. May we fill our hearts with love; may we never yield to bitterness. And may we praise the Son of God who, in His infinite wisdom, made love His greatest commandment.

Our commission is quite specific. We are told to be His witness to all nations. For us, as His disciples, to refuse any part of this commission frustrates the love of Jesus Christ, the Son of God.

Catherine Marshall

A TIMELY TIP

The best day to respond to Christ's Great Commission is this day.

WORSHIPPING THE RISEN CHRIST

He is not here, but He has been resurrected!

Luke 24:6 Holman CSB

G od has a wonderful plan for your life, and an important part of that plan includes worship. We should never deceive ourselves: every life is based upon some form of worship. The question is not whether we worship, but what we worship.

Some of us choose to worship God. The result is a plentiful harvest of joy, peace, and abundance. Others distance themselves from God by foolishly worshipping earthly possessions and personal gratification. To do so is a mistake of profound proportions.

Have you accepted the grace of God's only begotten Son? Then worship Him. Worship Him today and every day. Worship Him with sincerity and thanksgiving. Write His name on your heart and rest assured that He, too, has written your name on His.

Abide in Jesus, the sinless one—which means, give up all of self and its life, and dwell in God's will and rest in His strength. This is what brings the power that does not commit sin.

Andrew Murray

The dearest friend on earth is but a mere shadow compared with Jesus Christ.

Oswald Chambers

A TIMELY TIP

Jesus loves you. His love can—and should—be the cornerstone and the touchstone of your life.

NEW BEGINNINGS

Give your entire attention to what God is doing right now, and don't get worked up about what may or may not happen tomorrow. God will help you deal with whatever hard things come up when the time comes.

Matthew 6:34 MSG

Today, like every other day, is literally brimming with possibilities. Whether we realize it or not, God is always working in us and through us; our job is to let Him do His work without undo interference. Yet we are imperfect beings who, because of limited vision, often resist God's will. We want life to unfold according to our own desires, not God's. But our Heavenly Father may have other plans.

As you begin the new day, think carefully about the work that God can do through you. And then, welcome the coming day with a renewed sense of purpose and hope. God has the power to make all things new, including you. Your task is to let Him do it.

Today is mine. Tomorrow is none of my business. If I peer anxiously into the fog of the future, I will strain my spiritual eyes so that I will not see clearly what is required of me now.

Elisabeth Elliot

When your life comes to a close, you will remember not days but moments. Treasure each one.

Barbara Johnson

A TIMELY TIP

This is the day! Remember the beautiful words found in the 118th Psalm: "This is the day which the LORD has made; let us rejoice and be glad in it" (v. 24). The present moment is a priceless gift. Treasure it; savor it; and use it.

FIRST THINGS FIRST

Happy is the person who finds wisdom, the one who gets understanding.

Proverbs 3:13 NCV

When something important needs to be done, the best time to do it is sooner rather than later. But sometimes, instead of doing the smart thing (which, by the way, is choosing "sooner"), we may choose "later." When we do, we may pay a heavy price for our shortsightedness.

Are you one of those people who puts things off till the last minute? If so, it's time to change your ways. Your procrastination is probably the result of your shortsighted attempt to postpone (or avoid altogether) the discomfort that you associate with a particular activity. Get over it!

Whatever "it" is, do it now. When you do, you won't have to worry about "it" later.

You can't get second things by putting them first; you can get second things only by putting first things first.

C. S. Lewis

A bird does not know it can fly before it uses its wings. We learn God's love in our hearts as soon as we act upon it.

Corrie ten Boom

A TIMELY TIP

Your Heavenly Father wants you to prioritize your day and your life. And the best place to start is by putting God first.

ON GUARD AGAINST EVIL

Your love must be real. Hate what is evil, and hold on to what is good.

Romans 12:9 NCV

Face facts: this world is inhabited by quite a few people who are very determined to do evil things. The devil and his human helpers are working 24/7 to cause pain and heartbreak in every corner of the globe . . . including your corner. So you'd better beware.

Your job, if you choose to accept it, is to recognize evil and fight it. The moment that you decide to fight evil whenever you see it, you can no longer be a lukewarm, halfhearted Christian. And, when you are no longer a lukewarm Christian, God rejoices while the devil despairs.

When will you choose to get serious about fighting the evils of our world? Before you answer that question, consider this: in the battle of good versus evil, the devil never takes a day off . . . and neither should you.

We are in a continual battle with the spiritual forces of evil, but we will triumph when we yield to God's leading and call on His powerful presence in prayer.

Shirley Dobson

Holiness has never been the driving force of the majority. It is, however, mandatory for anyone who wants to enter the kingdom.

Elisabeth Elliot

A TIMELY TIP

Evil exists, and it exists someplace not too far from you. You must guard your steps and your heart accordingly.

IN SEARCH OF A QUIET CONSCIENCE

My child, if sinners try to lead you into sin, do not follow them.

Proverbs 1:10 NCV

American humorist Josh Billings observed, "Reason often makes mistakes, but conscience never does." How true. Even when we deceive our neighbors, and even when we attempt to deceive ourselves, God has given each of us a conscience, a small, quiet voice that tells us right from wrong. We must listen to that inner voice . . . or else we must accept the consequences that inevitably befall those who choose to rebel against God.

Arm yourself with the Word of God, and your conscience will sound off loud and clear when you're headed in the wrong direction.

Charles Stanley

Guilt is a healthy regret for telling God one thing and doing another.

Max Lucado

A TIMELY TIP

If you're not sure what to do . . . slow down and listen to your conscience. That little voice inside your head is remarkably dependable, but you can't depend upon it if you never listen to it. So stop, listen, and learn—your conscience is almost always right!

TRUSTING GOD'S LOVE

Do you think anyone is going to be able to drive a wedge between us and Christ's love for us? There is no way! Not trouble, not hard times, not hatred, not hunger, not homelessness, not bullying threats, not backstabbing, not even the worst sins listed in Scripture . . . I'm absolutely convinced that nothing, nothing living or dead, angelic or demonic, today or tomorrow, high or low, thinkable or unthinkable, absolutely nothing can get between us and God's love because of the way that Jesus our Master has embraced us.

Romans 8:35,38-39 MSG

The Bible makes it clear: God's got a plan—a very big plan—and you're an important part of that plan. But here's the catch: God won't force His plans upon you; you've got to figure things out for yourself . . . or not.

As a follower of Christ, you should ask yourself this question: "How closely can I make my plans match God's plans?" The more closely you manage to follow the path that God intends for your life, the better.

Do you have questions or concerns about the future? Take them to God in prayer. Do you have hopes and expectations? Talk to God about your dreams. Are you carefully planning for the days and weeks ahead? Consult God as you establish your priorities. Turn every concern over to your Heavenly Father, and sincerely seek His guidance—prayerfully, earnestly, and often. Then, listen for His answers . . . and trust the answers that He gives.

The greatest love of all is God's love for us, a love that showed itself in action.

Billy Graham

A TIMELY TIP

God's love for you is too big to understand, but it's not too big to share.

ABUNDANCE IN THE YEAR AHEAD

My purpose is to give life in all its fullness.

John 10:10 Holman CSB

Have you made the choice to rejoice? Hopefully so. After all, if you're a believer, you have plenty of reasons to be joyful. Yet sometimes, amid the inevitable hustle and bustle of life here on earth, you may lose sight of your blessings as you wrestle with the challenges of everyday life.

Christ made it clear to His followers: He intended that His joy would become their joy. And it still holds true today: Christ intends that His believers share His love with His joy in their hearts.

What does life have in store for you? A world full of possibilities (of course it's up to you to seize them) and God's promise of abundance (of course it's up to you to accept it). So, as you embark upon the next phase of your journey, remember to celebrate the life that God has given you. Your Creator has blessed you beyond measure. Honor Him with your prayers, your words, your deeds, and your joy.

God has promised us abundance, peace, and eternal life. These treasures are ours for the asking; all we must do is claim them. One of the great mysteries of life is why on earth do so many of us wait so very long to lay claim to God's gifts?

Marie T. Freeman

The Bible says that being a Christian is not only a great way to die, but it's also the best way to live.

Bill Hybels

A TIMELY TIP

God offers you His abundance—the rest is up to you.

GOLDEN RULE

Here is a simple, rule-of-thumb for behavior: Ask yourself what you want people to do for you, then grab the initiative and do it for them. Add up God's Law and Prophets and this is what you get.

Matthew 7:12 MSG

Would you like to make the world a better place? If so, you can start by practicing the Golden Rule.

Is the Golden Rule your rule, or is it just another Bible verse that goes in one ear and out the other? Jesus made Himself perfectly clear: He instructed you to treat other people in the same way that you want to be treated. But sometimes, especially when you're feeling pressure from friends, or when you're tired or upset, obeying the Golden Rule can seem like an impossible task—but it's not. So if you want to know how to treat other people, ask the person you see every time you look into the mirror. The answer you receive will tell you exactly what to do.

The mark of a Christian is that he will walk the second mile and turn the other cheek. A wise man or woman gives the extra effort, all for the glory of the Lord Jesus Christ.

John Maxwell

A TIMELY TIP

What's good for you is good for them, too. If you want others to treat you according to the Golden Rule, then you should be quick to treat them in the same way. In other words, always play by the rule: the Golden Rule.

LESSONS IN PATIENCE

Give all your worries and cares to God, for he cares about what happens to you.

1 Peter 5:6 NLT

Are you anxious for God to work out His plan for your life? Who isn't? As believers, we all want God to do great things for us and through us, and we want Him to do those things now. But sometimes, God has other plans. Sometimes, God's timetable does not coincide with our own. It's worth noting, however, that God's timetable is always perfect.

The next time you find your patience tested to the limit, remember that the world unfolds according to God's plan, not ours. Sometimes, we must wait patiently, and that's as it should be. After all, think how patient God has been with us.

To wait upon God is the perfection of activity.

Oswald Chambers

When we read of the great Biblical leaders, we see that it was not uncommon for God to ask them to wait, not just a day or two, but for years, until God was ready for them to act.

Gloria Gaither

A TIMELY TIP

You don't know precisely what you need—or when you need it—but God does. So trust His timing.

ASKING GOD

Your Father knows exactly what you need even before you ask him!

Matthew 6:8 NLT

Sometimes, amid the demands and the frustrations of everyday life, we forget to slow ourselves down long enough to talk with God. Instead of turning our thoughts and prayers to Him, we rely instead upon our own resources. Instead of praying for strength and courage, we seek to manufacture it within ourselves. Instead of asking God for guidance, we depend only upon our own limited wisdom. The results of such behaviors are unfortunate and, on occasion, tragic.

Are you in need? Ask God to sustain you. Are you troubled? Take your worries to Him in prayer. Are you weary? Seek God's strength. In all things great and small, seek God's wisdom and His grace. He hears your prayers, and He will answer. All you must do is ask.

There is a communion with God that asks for nothing, yet asks for everything . . . He who seeks the Father more than anything he can give is likely to have what he asks, for he is not likely to ask amiss.

George MacDonald

God makes prayer as easy as possible for us. He's completely approachable and available, and He'll never mock or upbraid us for bringing our needs before Him.

Shirley Dobson

A TIMELY TIP

Today, think of a specific need that is weighing heavily on your heart. Then, spend a few quiet moments asking God for His guidance and for His help.

ALONE WITH GOD

Step out of the traffic! Take a long, loving look at me, your High God, above politics, above everything.

Psalm 46:10 MSG

As you organize your day and your life, where does God fit in? Do you "squeeze Him in" on Sundays and at mealtimes? Or do you consult Him more often than that?

This book asks that you give your undivided attention to God for at least two minutes each day. And make no mistake about it: the emphasis in the previous sentence should be placed on the words "at least." In truth, you should give God lots more time than a couple of minutes a day, but hey, it's a start.

Even if you're the busiest person on the planet, you can still carve out a little time for God. And when you think about it, isn't that the very least you should do?

Knowing God involves an intimate, personal relationship that is developed over time through prayer and getting answers to prayer, through Bible study and applying its teaching to our lives, through obedience and experiencing the power of God, through moment-by-moment submission to Him that results in a moment-by-moment filling of the Holy Spirit.

Anne Graham Lotz

A TIMELY TIP

How much time can you spare? Decide how much of your time God deserves, and then give it to Him. Don't organize your day so that God gets "what's left." Give Him what you honestly believe He deserves.

RENEWAL DAY BY DAY

So we're not giving up. How could we! Even though on the outside it often looks like things are falling apart on us, on the inside, where God is making new life, not a day goes by without his unfolding grace.

2 Corinthians 4:16 MSG

Each day, we should spend time alone with God. But the demands of everyday living often conspire to rob us of those precious moments with our Creator. The cycle is predictable: we become so busy with the inevitable distractions of life that we fail to carve out quiet moments with our Creator. And when we do, we suffer because of our misuse of time.

We live in a world filled to overflowing with distractions, temptations, frustrations, and obligations. Our need for God is great. We must consult Him often, and we should consult Him in solitude. No time is more valuable than the quiet time we spend with God.

Walking with God leads to receiving his intimate counsel, and counseling leads to deep restoration.

John Eldredge

In those desperate times when we feel like we don't have an ounce of strength, He will gently pick up our heads so that our eyes can behold something—something that will keep His hope alive in us.

Kathy Troccoli

A TIMELY TIP

God is in the business of making all things new: Vance Havner correctly observed, "God is not running an antique shop! He is making all things new!" And that includes you.

THE HEART OF A THANKFUL CHRISTIAN

In everything give thanks; for this is the will of God in Christ Jesus for you.

2 Thessalonians 5:18 NKJV

As believing Christians, we are blessed beyond measure. God sent His only Son to die for our sins. And, God has given us the price-less gifts of eternal love and eternal life. We, in turn, are instruct-ed to approach our Heavenly Father with reverence and thanksgiving. But sometimes, in the crush of everyday living, we simply don't stop long enough to pause and thank our Creator for the countless blessings He has bestowed upon us.

When we slow down and express our gratitude to the One who made us, we enrich our own lives and the lives of those around us. Thanksgiving should become a habit, a regular part of our daily routines. God has blessed us beyond measure, and we owe Him everything, including our eternal praise. To paraphrase the familiar children's blessing, "God is great, God is good, let us thank Him for . . . everything!"

Do we not continually pass by blessings innumerable without notice, and instead fix our eyes on what we feel to be our trials and our losses, and think and talk about these until our whole horizon is filled with them, and we almost begin to think we have no blessings at all?

Hannah Whitall Smith

A TIMELY TIP

Of course you are thankful to the Creator for all His blessings. Tell Him so.

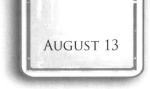

WISDOM FROM ABOVE

The Lord says, "I will make you wise and show you where to go. I will guide you and watch over you."

Psalm 32:8 NCV

Your head is undoubtedly filled with valuable information. But, there is much yet to learn. Wisdom is like a savings account: If you add to it consistently, then eventually you'll have a great sum. The secret to success is consistency.

Would you like to be wise? Then keep learning. Seek wisdom every day, and seek it in the right place. That place, of course, is, first and foremost, the Word of God. And remember this: it's not enough to simply read God's Word; you've also got to live by it.

If we neglect the Bible, we cannot expect to benefit from the wisdom and direction that result from knowing God's Word.

Vonette Bright

Wisdom is the right use of knowledge. To know is not to be wise. Many men know a great deal, and are all the greater fools for it. But to know how to use knowledge is to have wisdom.

C. H. Spurgeon

A TIMELY TIP

Need wisdom? Study God's Word and hang out with wise people.

TODAY'S BIBLE READING
Old Testament: Psalms 89
New Testament: Romans 15:14-21

CONTAGIOUS CHRISTIANITY

All those who stand before others and say they believe in me, I will say before my Father in heaven that they belong to me.

Matthew 10:32 NCV

Genuine, heartfelt Christianity is contagious. If you enjoy a life-altering relationship with God, that relationship will have an impact on others—perhaps a profound impact.

Are you genuinely excited about your faith? And do you make your enthusiasm known to those around you? Or are you a "silent ambassador" for Christ? God's preference is clear: He intends that you stand before others and proclaim your faith.

Does Christ reign over your life? Then share your testimony and your excitement. The world needs both.

In their heart of hearts, I think all true followers of Christ long to become contagious Christians. Though unsure about how to do so or the risks involved, deep down they sense that there isn't anything as rewarding as opening a person up to God's love and truth.

Bill Hybels

Has he taken over your heart? Perhaps he resides there, but does he preside there?

Vance Havner

A TIMELY TIP

Where is your focus today? Remember that it's important to focus your thoughts on Jesus first.

ABANDONING THE STATUS QUO

I have come as a light into the world, so that everyone who believes in Me would not remain in darkness.

John 12:46 Holman CSB

Okay, answer this question honestly: Do you behave differently because of your relationship with Jesus? Or do you behave in pretty much the same way that you would if you weren't a believer? Hopefully, the fact that you've invited Christ to reign over your heart means that you've made BIG changes in your thoughts and your actions.

Doing the right thing is not always easy, especially when you're tired or frustrated. But, doing the wrong thing almost always leads to trouble. And sometimes, it leads to big trouble.

If you're determined to follow "the crowd," you may soon find yourself headed in the wrong direction. So here's some advice: Don't follow the crowd—follow Jesus. And keep following Him every day of your life.

Christianity says we were created by a righteous God to flourish and be exhilarated in a righteous environment. God has "wired" us in such a way that the more righteous we are, the more we'll actually enjoy life.

Bill Hybels

Although God causes all things to work together for good for His children, He still holds us accountable for our behavior.

Kay Arthur

A TIMELY TIP

When it comes to telling the world about your relationship with God . . . your actions speak much more loudly than your words . . . so behave accordingly.

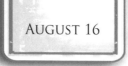

BARNABAS, THE ENCOURAGING FRIEND

Now Joseph, a Levite of Cyprian birth, who was also called Barnabas by the apostles (which translated means Son of Encouragement) . . .

Acts 4:36 NASB

Barnabas, a man whose name meant "Son of Encouragement," was a leader in the early Christian church. He was known for his kindness and for his ability to encourage others. Because of Barnabas, many people were introduced to Christ. And today, as believers living in a difficult world, we must seek to imitate the "Son of Encouragement."

We imitate Barnabas when we speak kind words to our families and to our friends. We imitate Barnabas when our actions give credence to our beliefs. We imitate Barnabas when we are generous with our possessions and with our praise. We imitate Barnabas when we give hope to the hopeless and encouragement to the downtrodden.

Today, be like Barnabas: become a source of encouragement to those who cross your path. When you do so, you will quite literally change the world, one person—and one moment—at a time.

You can't light another's path without casting light on your own.

John Maxwell

We urgently need people who encourage and inspire us to move toward God and away from the world's enticing pleasures.

Jim Cymbala

A TIMELY TIP

To find golden words, use the Golden Rule. When choosing the right words to say to someone else, think about the words that you would want to hear if you were in standing in that person's shoes.

VIGILANT CHRISTIANITY

Be careful! Watch out for attacks from the Devil, your great enemy. He prowls around like a roaring lion, looking for some victim to devour. Take a firm stand against him, and be strong in your faith.

1 Peter 5:8-9 NLT

I f you stop to think about it, the cold, hard evidence is right in front of your eyes: you live in a temptation-filled world. The devil is out on the street, hard at work, causing pain and heartache in more ways than ever before. Yep, you live in a temptation nation, a place where the bad guys are working 24/7 to lead you astray. That's why you must remain vigilant. Not only must you resist Satan when he confronts you, but you must also avoid those places where Satan can most easily tempt you.

In a letter to believers, Peter offers a stern warning: "Your adversary, the devil, prowls around like a roaring lion, seeking someone to devour" (1 Peter 5:8 NASB). What was true in New Testament times is equally true in our own. Satan tempts his prey and then devours them (and it's up to you—and only you—to make sure that you're not one of the ones being devoured!).

As believing Christians, we must beware because temptations are everywhere. Satan is determined to win; we must be equally determined that he does not.

Temptation is not a sin. Even Jesus was tempted. The Lord Jesus gives you the strength needed to resist temptation.

Corrie ten Boom

A TIMELY TIP

If life's inevitable temptations seem to be getting the best of you, try praying more often, even if many of those prayers are simply brief, "open-eyed" requests to your Father in heaven.

A WORLD OF PROMISES

Whatever has been born of God conquers the world. This is the victory that has conquered the world: our faith.

1 John 5:4 Holman CSB

The world makes promises that it simply cannot fulfill. It promises happiness, contentment, prosperity, and abundance. But genuine, lasting abundance is not a function of worldly possessions, it is a function of our thoughts, our actions, and the relationship we choose to create with our God. The world's promises are incomplete and illusory; God's promises are unfailing.

We must build our lives on the firm foundation of God's promises . . . nothing else will suffice.

The true Christian, though he is in revolt against the world's efforts to brainwash him, is no mere rebel for rebellion's sake. He dissents from the world because he knows that it cannot make good on its promises.

A. W. Tozer

Aim at heaven and you will get earth thrown in; aim at earth and you will get neither.

C. S. Lewis

A TIMELY TIP

The world makes plenty of promises that it can't keep. God, on the other hand, keeps every single one of His promises.

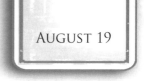
OBEDIENCE TO THE ULTIMATE AUTHORITY

We must obey God rather than men.

Acts 5:29 Holman CSB

Obedience to God is determined not by words, but by deeds. Talking about righteousness is easy; living righteously is far more difficult, especially in today's fast-paced, temptation-filled world.

Since God created Adam and Eve, we human beings have been rebelling against our Creator. Why? Because we are unwilling to trust God's Word, and we are unwilling to follow His commandments. God has given us a guidebook for righteous living called the Holy Bible. It contains thorough instructions which, if followed, lead to fulfillment, righteousness, and salvation. But, if we choose to ignore God's commandments, the results are as predictable as they are tragic.

Unless we are willing to abide by God's laws, all of our righteous proclamations ring hollow. How can we best proclaim our love for the Lord? By obeying Him. And, for further instructions, read the manual.

Perfect obedience would be perfect happiness, if only we had perfect confidence in the power we were obeying.

Corrie ten Boom

When we choose deliberately to obey Him, then He will tax the remotest star and the last grain of sand to assist us with all His almighty power.

Oswald Chambers

A TIMELY TIP

Because God first loved you, you should love Him. And one way that you demonstrate your love is by obeying Him.

GOD MAKES ALL THINGS POSSIBLE

You are the God who does wonders; You have declared Your strength among the peoples.

Psalm 77:14 NKJV

Sometimes, because we are imperfect human beings with limited understanding and limited faith, we place limitations on God. But, God's power has no limitations. God will work miracles in our lives if we trust Him with everything we have and everything we are. When we do, we experience the miraculous results of His endless love and His awesome power.

Do you lack the faith that God can work miracles in your own life? If so, it's time to reconsider. Are you a "Doubting Thomas" or a "Negative Nancy"? If so, you are attempting to place limitations on a God who has none. Instead, you must trust in God and trust in His power. Then, you must wait patiently . . . because something miraculous is just about to happen.

There is Someone who makes possible what seems completely impossible.

Catherine Marshall

Only God can move mountains, but faith and prayer can move God.

E. M. Bounds

A TIMELY TIP

God is in the business of doing miraculous things. You should never be afraid to ask Him for a miracle.

IMITATING OUR SAVIOR

If you love Me, you will keep My commandments.

John 14:15 Holman CSB

Imitating Christ is impossible, but attempting to imitate Him is both possible and advisable. By attempting to imitate Jesus, we seek, to the best of our abilities, to walk in His footsteps. To the extent we succeed in following Him, we receive the spiritual abundance that is the rightful possession of those who love Christ and keep His commandments.

Do you seek God's blessings for the day ahead? Then, to the best of your abilities, imitate His Son. You will fall short, of course. But if your heart is right and your intentions are pure, God will bless your efforts, your day, and your life.

Every Christian is to become a little Christ. The whole purpose of becoming a Christian is simply nothing else.

C. S. Lewis

Prayer makes a godly man and puts within him "the mind of Christ," the mind of humility, of self-surrender, of service, and of piety. If we really pray, we will become more like God, or else we will quit praying.

E. M. Bounds

A TIMELY TIP

The world wants to capture your attention and your time. But if you are a Christian, you should focus on Jesus, not the world.

THE WISDOM OF SILENCE

My soul, wait silently for God alone, For my expectation is from Him.

Psalm 62:5 NKJV

Do you take time each day for an extended period of silence? And during those precious moments, do you sincerely open your heart to your Creator? If so, you are wise and you are blessed.

The world can be a noisy place, a place filled to the brim with distractions, interruptions, and frustrations. And if you're not careful, the struggles and stresses of everyday living can rob you of the peace that should rightfully be yours because of your personal relationship with Christ. So take time each day to quietly commune with your Savior. When you do, those moments of silence will enable you to participate more fully in the only source of peace that endures: God's peace.

Instead of waiting for the feeling, wait upon God. You can do this by growing still and quiet, then expressing in prayer what your mind knows is true about Him, even if your heart doesn't feel it at this moment.

Shirley Dobson

If the pace and the push, the noise and the crowds are getting to you, it's time to stop the nonsense and find a place of solace to refresh your spirit.

Charles Swindoll

A TIMELY TIP

You live in a noisy world filled with distractions, a world where silence is in short supply. But God wants you to carve out quiet moments with Him. Silence is, indeed, golden.

A PLAN FOR TODAY

Depend on the Lord in whatever you do, and your plans will succeed.

Proverbs 16:3 NCV

Would you like a formula for successful living that never fails? Here it is: Include God in every aspect of your life's journey, including the plans that you make and the steps that you take. But beware: as you make plans for the days and weeks ahead, you may become sidetracked by the demands of everyday living.

If you allow the world to establish your priorities, you will eventually become discouraged, or disappointed, or both. But if you genuinely seek God's will for every important decision that you make, your loving Heavenly Father will guide your steps and enrich your life. So as you plan your work, remember that every good plan should start with God, including yours.

God has a course mapped out for your life, and all the inadequacies in the world will not change His mind. He will be with you every step of the way. And though it may take time, He has a celebration planned for when you cross over the "Red Seas" of your life.

Charles Swindoll

Allow your dreams a place in your prayers and plans. God-given dreams can help you move into the future He is preparing for you.

Barbara Johnson

A TIMELY TIP

It isn't that complicated: If you plan your steps carefully, and if you follow your plan conscientiously, you will probably succeed. If you don't, you probably won't.

PUTTING POSSESSIONS IN PROPER PERSPECTIVE

No one can serve two masters. The person will hate one master and love the other, or will follow one master and refuse to follow the other. You cannot serve both God and worldly riches.

Matthew 6:24 NCV

"So much stuff to shop for, and so little time . . ." These words seem to describe the priorities of our 21st-century world. Hopefully, you're not building your life around your next visit to the local mall—but you can be sure that many people are!

Our society is in love with money and the things that money can buy. God is not. God cares about people, not possessions, and so must we. We must, to the best of our abilities, love our neighbors as ourselves, and we must, to the best of our abilities, resist the mighty temptation to place possessions ahead of people.

Money, in and of itself, is not evil; worshipping money is. So today, as you prioritize matters of importance for you and yours, remember that God is almighty, but the dollar is not.

If we worship God, we are blessed. But if we worship "the almighty dollar," we are inevitably punished because of our misplaced priorities—and our punishment inevitably comes sooner rather than later.

When possessions become our god, we become materialistic and greedy . . . and we forfeit our contentment and our joy.

Charles Swindoll

A TIMELY TIP

God's Word warns against the spiritual trap of materialism. Material possessions may seem appealing at first, but they pale in comparison to the spiritual gifts that God gives to those who put Him first. Count yourself among that number.

FEARS IN PERSPECTIVE

They won't be afraid of bad news; their hearts are steady because they trust the Lord.

Psalm 112:7 NCV

His adoring fans called him the "Sultan of Swat." He was Babe Ruth, the baseball player who set records for home runs and strikeouts. Babe's philosophy was simple. He said, "Never let the fear of striking out get in your way." That's smart advice on the diamond or off.

Of course it's never wise to take foolish risks (so buckle up, slow down, and don't do anything silly). But when it comes to the game of life, you should not let the fear of failure keep you from taking your swings.

Today, ask God for the courage to step beyond the boundaries of your self-doubts. Ask Him to guide you to a place where you can realize your full potential—a place where you are freed from the fear of failure. Ask Him to do His part, and promise Him that you will do your part. Don't ask Him to lead you to a "safe" place; ask Him to lead you to the "right" place . . . and remember: those two places are seldom the same.

Earthly fears are no fears at all. Answer the big question of eternity, and the little questions of life fall into perspective.

Max Lucado

When we submit difficult and alarming situations to God, he promises that his peace will be like a military garrison to guard our hearts from fear.

Dennis Swanberg

A TIMELY TIP

Everybody faces obstacles. Don't overestimate the size of yours.

THE JOYS OF FELLOWSHIP

Then all the people went away to eat and drink, to send some of their food to others, and to celebrate with great joy. They finally understood what they had been taught.

Nehemiah 8:12 NCV

Fellowship with other believers should be an integral part of your everyday life. Your association with fellow Christians should be uplifting, enlightening, encouraging, and consistent.

Are you an active member of your own fellowship? Are you a builder of bridges inside the four walls of your church and outside it? Do you contribute to God's glory by contributing your time and your talents to a close-knit band of believers? Hopefully so. The fellowship of believers is intended to be a powerful tool for spreading God's Good News and uplifting His children. And God intends that you be a fully contributing member of that fellowship. Your intentions should be the same.

One of the ways God refills us after failure is through the blessing of Christian fellowship. Just experiencing the joy of simple activities shared with other children of God can have a healing effect on us.

Anne Graham Lotz

Every person in the church is either a help or a hindrance.

C. H. Spurgeon

A TIMELY TIP

God intends for you to be an active member of your fellowship. Your intentions should be the same.

OBEDIENCE TO THE FATHER

But prove yourselves doers of the word, and not merely hearers.

James 1:22 NASB

God's commandments are not "suggestions," and they are not "helpful hints." They are, instead, immutable laws which, if followed, lead to repentance, salvation, and abundance. But if you choose to disobey the commandments of your Heavenly Father or the teachings of His Son, you will most surely reap a harvest of regret.

The formula for a successful life is surprisingly straightforward: Study God's Word and obey it. Does this sound too simple? Perhaps it is simple, but it is also the only way to reap the marvelous riches that God has in store for you.

Let me tell you—there is no "high" like the elation and joy that come from a sacrificial act of obedience.

Bill Hybels

Believe and do what God says. The life-changing consequences will be limitless, and the results will be confidence and peace of mind.

Franklin Graham

A TIMELY TIP

Obey God or face the consequences. God rewards obedience and punishes disobedience. It's not enough to understand God's rules; you must also live by them . . . or else.

PRAYING FOR PURPOSE

One day Jesus told his disciples a story to illustrate their need for constant prayer and to show them that they must never give up.

Luke 18:1 NLT

A re you faced with a difficult choice or an important decision? Then pray about it. If you talk to God sincerely and often, He won't lead you astray. Instead, God will guide you and help you make more intelligent choices . . . if you take the time to talk with Him.

If you have questions about whether you should do something or not, pray about it. If there is something you're worried about, ask God to comfort you. If you're having trouble with your relationships, ask God to help you sort things out. As you pray more, you'll discover that God is always near and that He's always ready to hear from you. So don't worry about things; pray about them. God is waiting . . . and listening!

When we pray, we have linked ourselves with Divine purposes, and we therefore have Divine power at our disposal for human living.

E. Stanley Jones

We sometimes fear to bring our troubles to God because we think they must seem small to Him. But, if they are large enough to vex and endanger our welfare, they are large enough to touch His heart of love.

R. A. Torrey

A TIMELY TIP

Prayer changes things and it changes you. So pray.

IN SEARCH OF PEACE

Peace I leave with you. My peace I give to you. I do not give to you as the world gives. Your heart must not be troubled or fearful.

John 14:27 Holman CSB

The beautiful words of John 14:27 give us hope: "Peace I leave with you, my peace I give unto you . . . ." Jesus offers us peace, not as the world gives, but as He alone gives. We, as believers, can accept His peace or ignore it.

When we accept the peace of Jesus Christ into our hearts, our lives are transformed. And then, because we possess the gift of peace, we can share that gift with fellow Christians, family members, friends, and associates. If, on the other hand, we choose to ignore the gift of peace—for whatever reason—we simply cannot share what we do not possess.

Today, as a gift to yourself, to your family, and to your friends, claim the inner peace that is your spiritual birthright: the peace of Jesus Christ. It is offered freely; it has been paid for in full; it is yours for the asking. So ask. And then share.

The better you become acquainted with God, the less tensions you feel and the more peace you possess.

Charles L. Allen

God loves you and wants you to experience peace and life—abundant and eternal.

Billy Graham

A TIMELY TIP

God's peace surpasses human understanding. When you accept His peace, it will revolutionize your life.

MOUNTAIN-MOVING FAITH

For I assure you: If you have faith the size of a mustard seed, you will tell this mountain, "Move from here to there," and it will move. Nothing will be impossible for you.

Matthew 17:20 Holman CSB

Have you ever felt your faith in God slipping away? If so, you are not alone. Every life—including yours—is a series of successes and failures, celebrations and disappointments, joys and sorrows. But even when we feel very distant from God, God is never distant from us.

Jesus taught His disciples that if they had faith, they could move mountains. You can too. When you place your faith, your trust, indeed your life in the hands of Christ Jesus, you'll be amazed at the marvelous things He can do with you and through you. So strengthen your faith through praise, through worship, through Bible study, and through prayer. And trust God's plans. With Him, all things are possible, and He stands ready to open a world of possibilities to you if you have faith.

Faith in faith is pointless. Faith in a living, active God moves mountains.

Beth Moore

It is faith that saves us, not works, but the faith that saves us always produces works.

C. H. Spurgeon

A TIMELY TIP

Faith should be practiced more than studied. Vance Havner said, "Nothing is more disastrous than to study faith, analyze faith, make noble resolves of faith, but never actually to make the leap of faith." How true!

PRAISE FOR THE FATHER

From the rising of the sun to its setting, the name of the LORD is to be praised.

Psalm 113:3 NASB

O kay, from the looks of things, you're an extremely busy person. And perhaps, because of your demanding schedule, you've neglected to pay sufficient attention to a particularly important part of your life: the spiritual part. If so, today is the day to change, and one way to make that change is simply to spend a little more time talking with God.

God is trying to get His message through to you. Are you listening?

Perhaps, on occasion, you may find yourself overwhelmed by the press of everyday life. Perhaps you may forget to slow yourself down long enough to talk with God. Instead of turning your thoughts and prayers to Him, you may rely upon our own resources. Instead of asking God for guidance, you may depend only upon your own limited wisdom. A far better course of action is this: simply stop what you're doing long enough to open your heart to God; then listen carefully for His directions.

In all things great and small, seek God's wisdom and His grace. He hears your prayers, and He will answer. All you must do is ask.

Be not afraid of saying too much in the praises of God; all the danger is of saying too little.

Matthew Henry

Praise Him! Praise Him! / Tell of His excellent greatness. / Praise Him! Praise Him! / Ever in joyful song!

Fanny Crosby

A TIMELY TIP

Thoughtful believers (like you) make it a habit to carve out quiet moments throughout the day to praise God.

A THANKFUL HEART

Enter his gates with thanksgiving; go into his courts with praise. Give thanks to him and bless his name. For the Lord is good. His unfailing love continues forever, and his faithfulness continues to each generation.

Psalm 100:4-5 NLT

If you're like most people on the planet, you're very busy. Your life is probably hectic, demanding, and complicated. When the demands of life leave you rushing from place to place with scarcely a moment to spare, you may fail to pause and thank your Creator for the blessings He has bestowed upon you. Big mistake.

No matter how busy you are, you should never be too busy to thank God for His gifts. Your task, as a follower of the living Christ, is to praise God many times each day. Then, with gratitude in your heart, you can face your daily duties with the perspective and power that only He can provide.

When you slow down and express your gratitude to your Heavenly Father, you enrich your own life and the lives of those around you. That's why thanksgiving should become a habit, a regular part of your daily routine. Yes, God has blessed you beyond measure, and you owe Him everything, including your eternal praise.

The ability to rejoice in any situation is a sign of spiritual maturity.

Billy Graham

A TIMELY TIP

When is the best time to say "thanks" to God? Any time. God never takes a vacation, and He's always ready to hear from you. So what are you waiting for?

THE OPTIMISTIC CHRISTIAN

Make me hear joy and gladness.

Psalm 51:8 NKJV

A s you take the next step in your life's journey, you should do so with feelings of hope and anticipation. After all, as a Christian, you have every reason to be optimistic about life. As John Calvin observed, "There is not one blade of grass, there is no color in this world that is not intended to make us rejoice." But, sometimes, rejoicing may be the last thing on your mind. Sometimes, you may fall prey to worry, frustration, anxiety, or sheer exhaustion. What's needed is plenty of rest, a large dose of perspective, and God's healing touch, but not necessarily in that order.

A. W. Tozer writes, "Attitude is all-important. Let the soul take a quiet attitude of faith and love toward God, and from there on, the responsibility is God's. He will make good on His commitments." These words remind us that even when the challenges of the day seem daunting, God remains steadfast. And, so must we.

Christ can put a spring in your step and a thrill in your heart. Optimism and cheerfulness are products of knowing Christ.

Billy Graham

A TIMELY TIP

Focus on possibilities, not stumbling blocks. Of course you will encounter occasional disappointments, and, from time to time, you will encounter failure. But, don't invest large quantities of your life focusing on past misfortunes. Instead, look to the future with optimism and hope . . . and encourage your friends and family members to do the same.

FINDING TIME FOR GOD

I am always praising you; all day long I honor you.

Psalm 71:8 NCV

Each new day is a gift from God, and if we are wise, we spend a few quiet moments each morning thanking the Giver. Daily life is a tapestry of habits, and no habit is more important to our spiritual health than the discipline of daily prayer and devotion to the Creator. When we begin each day with heads bowed and hearts lifted, we remind ourselves of God's love, His protection, and His commandments. And if we are wise, we take time throughout the day to align our priorities with the teachings and commandments that God has given us through His Holy Word.

Are you thankful for God's blessings? Then give Him a gift that demonstrates your gratitude: the gift of time.

Meditating upon His Word will inevitably bring peace of mind, strength of purpose, and power for living.

Bill Bright

A person with no devotional life generally struggles with faith and obedience.

Charles Stanley

A TIMELY TIP

Find the best time of the day to spend with God: Hudson Taylor, an English missionary, wrote, "Whatever is your best time in the day, give that to communion with God." That's powerful advice that leads to a powerful faith.

FAITH WITHOUT WORKS

Dear friends, do you think you'll get anywhere in this if you learn all the right words but never do anything? Does merely talking about faith indicate that a person really has it? For instance, you come upon an old friend dressed in rags and half-starved and say, "Good morning, friend! Be clothed in Christ! Be filled with the Holy Spirit!" and walk off without providing so much as a coat or a cup of soup—where does that get you? Isn't it obvious that God-talk without God-acts is outrageous nonsense?

James 2:14-17 MSG

The central message of James' letter is the need for believers to act upon their beliefs. James' instruction is clear: "faith without works is dead." We are saved by our faith in Christ, but salvation does not signal the end of our earthly responsibilities; it marks the true beginning of our work for the Lord.

If your faith in God is strong, you will find yourself drawn toward God's work. You will serve Him, not just with words or prayers, but also with deeds. Because of your faith, you will feel compelled to do God's work—to do it gladly, faithfully, joyfully, and consistently.

Today, redouble your efforts to do God's bidding here on earth. Never have the needs—or the opportunities—been greater.

It is faith that saves us, not works, but the faith that saves us always produces works.

C. H. Spurgeon

A TIMELY TIP

Whether you realize it or not, your work always speaks for itself. So make sure that your work speaks well of your efforts.

KEEPING LIFE IN PERSPECTIVE

All I'm doing right now, friends, is showing how these things pertain to Apollos and me so that you will learn restraint and not rush into making judgments without knowing all the facts. It is important to look at things from God's point of view. I would rather not see you inflating or deflating reputations based on mere hearsay.

1 Corinthians 4:6 MSG

Sometimes, amid the demands of daily life, we lose perspective. Life seems out of balance, and the pressures of everyday living seem overwhelming. What's needed is a fresh perspective, a restored sense of balance . . . and God. If we call upon the Lord and seek to see the world through His eyes, He will give us guidance and wisdom and perspective. When we make God's priorities our priorities, He will lead us according to His plan and according to His commandments. God's reality is the ultimate reality. May we live accordingly.

Like a shadow declining swiftly . . . away . . . like the dew of the morning gone with the heat of the day; like the wind in the treetops, like a wave of the sea, so are our lives on earth when seen in light of eternity.

Ruth Bell Graham

What you see and hear depends a good deal on where you are standing; it also depends on what sort of person you are.

C. S. Lewis

A TIMELY TIP

When you focus on the world, you lose perspective. When you focus on God's promises, you gain clearer perspective.

COURAGE FOR EVERYDAY LIVING

God doesn't want us to be shy with his gifts, but bold and loving and sensible.

2 Timothy 1:7 MSG

L ife-here-on-earth can be difficult and discouraging at times. During our darkest moments, God offers us strength and courage if we turn our hearts and our prayers to Him.

As believing Christians, we have every reason to live courageously. After all, the ultimate battle has already been fought and won on the cross at Calvary. But sometimes, because we are imperfect human beings who possess imperfect faith, we fall prey to fear and doubt. The answer to our fears, of course, is God.

The next time you find your courage tested to the limit, remember that God is as near as your next breath. He is your shield and your strength; He is your protector and your deliverer. Call upon Him in your hour of need and then be comforted. Whatever your challenge, whatever your trouble, God can handle it . . . and will!

When once we are assured that God is good, then there can be nothing left to fear.

Hannah Whitall Smith

Down through the centuries, in times of trouble and trial, God has brought courage to the hearts of those who love Him. The Bible is filled with assurances of God's help and comfort in every kind of trouble.

Billy Graham

A TIMELY TIP

If you trust God completely and without reservation, you have every reason on earth—and in heaven—to live courageously. And that's precisely what you should do.

FINDING GOD'S PURPOSE IN EVERYDAY LIFE

Do not be afraid or discouraged. For the LORD your God is with you wherever you go.

Joshua 1:9 NLT

Each morning, as the sun rises in the east, you welcome a new day, one that is filled to the brim with opportunities, with possibilities, and with God. As you contemplate God's blessings in your own life, you should prayerfully seek His guidance for the day ahead.

Discovering God's unfolding purpose for your life is a daily journey, a journey guided by the teachings of God's Holy Word. As you reflect upon God's promises and upon the meaning that those promises hold for you, ask God to lead you throughout the coming day. Let your Heavenly Father direct your steps; concentrate on what God wants you to do now, and leave the distant future in hands that are far more capable than your own: His hands.

If we are ever going to be or do anything for our Lord, now is the time.

Vance Havner

We may run, walk, stumble, drive, or fly, but let us never lose sight of the reason for the journey, or miss a chance to see a rainbow on the way.

Gloria Gaither

A TIMELY TIP

Perhaps you're in a hurry to understand God's unfolding plan for your life. If so, remember that God operates according to a perfect timetable. That timetable is His, not yours. So be patient. God has big things in store for you, but He may have quite a few lessons to teach you before you are fully prepared to do His will and fulfill His purpose.

THE BREAD OF LIFE

Then Jesus said, "I am the bread that gives life. Whoever comes to me will never be hungry, and whoever believes in me will never be thirsty."

John 6:35 NCV

He was the Son of God, but He wore a crown of thorns. He was the Savior of mankind, yet He was put to death on a roughhewn cross made of wood. He offered His healing touch to an unsaved world, and yet the same hands that had healed the sick and raised the dead were pierced with nails.

Jesus Christ, the Son of God, was born into humble circumstances. He walked this earth, not as a ruler of men, but as the Savior of mankind. His crucifixion, a torturous punishment that was intended to end His life and His reign, instead became the pivotal event in the history of all humanity.

Jesus is the bread of life. Accept His grace. Share His love. And follow His footsteps.

Jesus was the Savior Who would deliver them not only from the bondage of sin but also from meaningless wandering through life.

Anne Graham Lotz

Our Lord is the Bread of Life. His proportions are perfect. There never was too much or too little of anything about Him. Feed on Him for a well-balanced ration. All the vitamins and calories are there.

Vance Havner

A TIMELY TIP

Jesus is the light of the world. Make sure that you are capturing and reflecting His light.

MORE OPPORTUNITIES THAN WE CAN COUNT

Everything is possible to the one who believes.

Mark 9:23 Holman CSB

Whether you realize it or not, opportunities are whirling around you like stars crossing the night sky: beautiful to observe but too numerous to count. Yet you may be too wrapped up in the daily grind to notice.

Take time to step back from the challenges of everyday living so that you can focus your thoughts on two things: the talents God has given you and the opportunities that He has placed before you. God is leading you in the direction of those opportunities. Your task is to watch carefully, to pray fervently, and to act accordingly.

Be careful what you pray for—because everything and anything is possible through the power of prayer!

Barbara Johnson

The most profane word we use is "hopeless." When you say a situation or person is hopeless, you are slamming the door in the face of God.

Kathy Troccoli

A TIMELY TIP

You have potential . . . lots of it. And the rest is up to you.

ABOVE AND BEYOND OUR WORRIES

So don't worry about tomorrow, because tomorrow will have its own worries. Each day has enough trouble of its own.

Matthew 6:34 NCV

When we're worried, there are two places we should take our concerns: to the people who love us and to God.

When troubles arise, it helps to talk about them with parents, grandparents, concerned adults, and trusted friends. But we shouldn't stop there: we should also talk to God through our prayers.

If you're worried about something, pray about it. Remember that God is always listening, and He always wants to hear from you.

So when you're upset about something, try this simple plan: talk and pray. Talk openly to the people who love you, and pray to the Heavenly Father who made you. The more you talk and the more you pray, the better you'll feel.

Worry does not empty tomorrow of its sorrow; it empties today of its strength.

Corrie ten Boom

When worry is present, trust cannot crowd its way in.

Billy Graham

A TIMELY TIP

If you're worried about the future . . . stop worrying and start working. The more time you spend working, the less time you'll have to spend worrying. Don't fret about your problems; fix them!

PRAYER: MORE IS BETTER

Rejoice always! Pray constantly. Give thanks in everything, for this is God's will for you in Christ Jesus.

1 Thessalonians 5:16-18 Holman CSB

Genuine, heartfelt prayer changes things and it changes us. When we lift our hearts to our Father in heaven, we open ourselves to a never-ending source of divine wisdom and infinite love.

Do you have questions that you simply can't answer? Ask for the guidance of your Father in heaven. Whatever your need, no matter how great or small, pray about it. Instead of waiting for mealtimes or bedtimes, follow the instruction of your Savior: pray always and never lose heart. And remember: God is not just near; He is here, and He's ready to talk with you. Now!

Prayer succeeds when all else fails.

E. M. Bounds

So often we pray and then fret anxiously, waiting for God to hurry up and do something. All the while God is waiting for us to calm down, so He can do something through us.

Corrie ten Boom

A TIMELY TIP

Pray specifically. If you need something, don't ask for God's help in general terms; ask specifically for the things you need.

WHEN THE PATH IS DARK

Though I sit in darkness, the Lord will be my light.

Micah 7:8 Holman CSB

Doubts come in several shapes and sizes: doubts about God, doubts about the future, and doubts about our own abilities, for starters. But when doubts creep in, as they will from time to time, we need not despair. As Sheila Walsh observed, "To wrestle with God does not mean that we have lost faith, but that we are fighting for it."

God never leaves our side, not for an instant. He is always with us, always willing to calm the storms of life. When we sincerely seek His presence—and when we genuinely seek to establish a deeper, more meaningful relationship Him—God is prepared to touch our hearts, to calm our fears, to answer our doubts, and to restore our confidence.

Doubting may temporarily disturb, but will not permanently destroy, your faith in Christ.

Charles Swindoll

Resisting His will for your life will cause you to doubt.

Anne Graham Lotz

A TIMELY TIP

Doubts creeping in? Increase the amount of time you spend in Bible study, prayer, and worship.

TRUSTING YOUR CONSCIENCE

Don't let evil get the best of you; get the best of evil by doing good.

Romans 12:21 MSG

Billy Graham correctly observed, "Most of us follow our conscience as we follow a wheelbarrow. We push it in front of us in the direction we want to go." To do so, of course, is a profound mistake. Yet all of us, on occasion, have failed to listen to the voice that God planted in our hearts, and all of us have suffered the consequences.

God gave you a conscience for a very good reason: to make your path conform to His will. Wise believers make it a practice to listen carefully to that quiet internal voice. Count yourself among that number. When your conscience speaks, listen and learn. In all likelihood, God is trying to get His message through. And in all likelihood, it is a message that you desperately need to hear.

To go against one's conscience is neither safe nor right. Here I stand. I cannot do otherwise.

Martin Luther

God desires that we become spiritually healthy enough through faith to have a conscience that rightly interprets the work of the Holy Spirit.

Beth Moore

A TIMELY TIP

Being popular isn't all it's cracked up to be. So please don't ever compromise yourself in an attempt to be popular because it's never worth it.

LIVING AND WORKING PASSIONATELY

In all the work you are doing, work the best you can. Work as if you were doing it for the Lord, not for people.

Colossians 3:23 NCV

Are you passionate about your life, your loved ones, your work, and your faith? As a believer who has been saved by a risen Christ, you should be.

As a thoughtful Christian, you have every reason to be enthusiastic about life, but sometimes the struggles of everyday living may cause you to feel decidedly unenthusiastic. If you feel that your zest for life is slowly fading away, it's time to slow down, to rest, to count your blessings, and to pray. When you feel worried or weary, you must pray fervently for God to renew your sense of wonderment and excitement.

Life with God is a glorious adventure; revel in it. When you do, God will most certainly smile upon your work and your life.

When we wholeheartedly commit ourselves to God, there is nothing mediocre or run-of-the-mill about us. To live for Christ is to be passionate about our Lord and about our lives.

Jim Gallery

I do not want merely to possess a faith; I want a faith that possesses me.

Charles Kingsley

A TIMELY TIP

Feeling a little lazy? That means that you're not excited about your work. So here's your challenge: find things that you're passionate about. When you do, you'll discover that work becomes easier when you're working on the things you enjoy.

HOW THEY KNOW THAT WE KNOW

Here's how we can be sure that we know God in the right way: Keep his commandments. If someone claims, "I know him well!" but doesn't keep his commandments, he's obviously a liar. His life doesn't match his words. But the one who keeps God's word is the person in whom we see God's mature love. This is the only way to be sure we're in God. Anyone who claims to be intimate with God ought to live the same kind of life Jesus lived.

1 John 2:3-6 MSG

How do others know that we are followers of Christ? By our words and by our actions. And when it comes to proclaiming our faith, the actions we take are far more important than the proclamations we make.

Is your conduct a worthy example for believers and non-believers alike? Is your behavior a testimony to the spiritual abundance that is available to those who allow Christ to reign over their hearts? If so, you are wise: congratulations. But if you're like most of us, then you know that some important aspect of your life could stand improvement. If so, today is the perfect day to make yourself a living, breathing example of the wonderful changes that Christ can make in the lives of those who choose to walk with Him.

Let us remember therefore this lesson: That to worship our God sincerely we must evermore begin by hearkening to His voice, and by giving ear to what He commands us. For if every man goes after his own way, we shall wander. We may well run, but we shall never be a whit nearer to the right way, but rather farther away from it.

John Calvin

A TIMELY TIP

God has rules. When we follow them, we are blessed; when we ignore them, we are harmed.

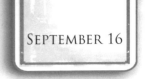

THE COMPANY YOU KEEP

Do not be deceived: "Bad company corrupts good morals."

1 Corinthians 15:33 Holman CSB

Our world is filled with pressures: some good, some bad. The pressures that we feel to follow God's will and to behave responsibly are positive pressures. God places them on our hearts, and He intends that we act accordingly. But we also face different pressures, ones that are definitely not from God. When we feel pressured to do things—or even to think thoughts—that lead us away from God, we must beware.

Society seeks to mold us into the cookie-cutter images that are the product of the modern media. God seeks to mold us into new beings, new creations through Christ, beings that are most certainly not conformed to this world. If we are to please God, we must resist the pressures that society seeks to impose upon us, and we must conform ourselves, instead, to His will, to His path, and to His Son.

Do you want to be wise? Choose wise friends.

Charles Swindoll

True friends will always lift you higher and challenge you to walk in a manner pleasing to our Lord.

Lisa Bevere

A TIMELY TIP

If you're hanging with the right people, peer pressure can be a positive thing, and when it is, your job is get more of it.

TODAY'S BIBLE READING
Old Testament: Proverbs 24-25
New Testament: 2 Corinthians 11:1-11

MARY, MARTHA, AND THE MASTER

You will teach me how to live a holy life. Being with you will fill me with joy; at your right hand I will find pleasure forever.

Psalm 16:11 NCV

Martha and Mary were sisters who both loved Jesus, but they showed their love in different ways. Mary sat at the Master's feet, taking in every word. Martha, meanwhile, busied herself with preparations for the meal to come. When Martha asked Jesus if He was concerned about Mary's failure to help, Jesus replied, "Mary has chosen the better thing, and it will never be taken away from her" (Luke 10:42 NCV). The implication is clear: as believers, we must spend time with Jesus before we spend time for him. But, once we have placed Christ where He belongs—at the center of our hearts—we must go about the business of serving the One who has saved us.

How can we serve Christ? By sharing His message, His mercy, and His love with those who cross our paths. Everywhere we look, it seems, the needs are great and so are the temptations. Still, our challenge is clear: we must love God, obey His commandments, trust His Son, and serve His children. When we do, we claim spiritual treasures that will endure forever.

The crucial question for each of us is this: What do you think of Jesus, and do you yet have a personal acquaintance with Him?

Hannah Whitall Smith

A TIMELY TIP

Today, think about your relationship with Jesus: what it is, what it should be, and what it will be today, tomorrow, and throughout all eternity.

DAY BY DAY WITH GOD

Uphold my steps in Your paths, that my footsteps may not slip.

Psalm 17:5 NKJV

Our world is in a state of constant change. God is not. At times, the world seems to be trembling beneath our feet. But we can be comforted in the knowledge that our Heavenly Father is the rock that cannot be shaken. His Word promises, "I am the Lord, I do not change" (Malachi 3:6 NKJV).

Every day that we live, we mortals encounter a multitude of changes—some good, some not so good. And on occasion, all of us must endure life-changing personal losses that leave us breathless. When we do, our loving Heavenly Father stands ready to protect us, to comfort us, to guide us, and, in time, to heal us.

Are you facing difficult circumstances or unwelcome changes? If so, please remember that God is far bigger than any problem you may face. So, instead of worrying about life's inevitable challenges, put your faith in the Father and His only begotten Son: Jesus Christ is the same yesterday, today, and forever (Hebrews 13:8). And rest assured: It is precisely because your Savior does not change that you can face your challenges with courage for this day and hope for the future.

When we truly walk with God throughout our day, life slowly starts to fall into place.

Bill Hybels

A TIMELY TIP

The world is constantly vying for your attention, and sometimes the noise can be deafening. Remember the words of Elisabeth Elliot; she said, "The world is full of noise. Let us learn the art of silence, stillness, and solitude."

REALLY LIVING MEANS REALLY LOVING

And may the Lord cause you to increase and overflow with love for one another and for everyone, just as we also do for you.

1 Thessalonians 3:12 Holman CSB

Christ's words are clear: we are to love God first, and secondly, we are to love others as we love ourselves (Matthew 22:37-40). These two commands are seldom easy, and because we are imperfect beings, we often fall short. But God's Holy Word commands us to try.

The Christian path is an exercise in love and forgiveness. If we are to walk in Christ's footsteps, we must forgive those who have done us harm, and we must accept Christ's love by sharing it freely with family, friends, neighbors, and strangers.

God is love, and He wants us to share that attribute with Him and with others.

Charles Stanley

Love is an attribute of God. To love others is evidence of a genuine faith.

Kay Arthur

A TIMELY TIP

Today, think about someone you know who, for whatever reason, is difficult to love. Then, think of a good way to express your love for that person, even if you'd rather express some other, less favorable, emotion.

PRAYERFUL PATIENCE

The Lord is good to those whose hope is in him, to the one who seeks him; it is good to wait quietly for the salvation of the Lord.

Lamentations 3:25-26 NIV

Lamentations 3:25-26 reminds us that it is good to wait quietly for God. But for most of us, waiting patiently for Him is difficult. Why? Because we are fallible human beings with a long list of earthly desires and a definite timetable for obtaining them.

The next time you find yourself impatiently waiting for God to reveal Himself, remember that the world unfolds according to His timetable, not ours. Sometimes, we must wait, and when we do, we should do so quietly and patiently. And, as we consider God's love for us and the perfection of His plans, we can be comforted in the certain knowledge that His timing is perfect, even if our patience is not.

To receive the blessing we need, we must believe and keep on believing, to wait and keep on waiting. We need to wait in prayer, wait with our Bibles open as we confess his promises, wait in joyful praise and worship of the God who will never forget our case, and wait as we continue serving others in his name.

Jim Cymbala

A TIMELY TIP

When you learn to be more patient with others, you'll make your world—and your heart—a more peaceful and less stressful place.

A HUMBLE SPIRIT

But he who is greatest among you shall be your servant. And whoever exalts himself will be humbled, and he who humbles himself will be exalted.

Matthew 23:11-12 NLT

Sometimes our faith is tested more by prosperity than by adversity. Why? Because in times of plenty, we are tempted to stick out our chests and say, "I did that." But nothing could be further from the truth. All of our blessings start and end with God; whatever "it" is, He did it. And He deserves the credit.

Who are the greatest among us? Are they the proud and the powerful? Hardly. The greatest among us are the humble servants who care less for their own glory and more for God's glory. If we seek greatness in God's eyes, we must forever praise His good works, not our own.

Nothing sets a person so much out of the devil's reach as humility.

Jonathan Edwards

The preoccupation with self is the enemy of humility.

Franklin Graham

A TIMELY TIP

God favors the humble just as surely as He disciplines the proud.

ASKING AND ACCEPTING

So I say to you, keep asking, and it will be given to you. Keep searching, and you will find. Keep knocking, and the door will be opened to you.

Luke 11:9 Holman CSB

God gives the gifts; we, as believers, should accept them—but oftentimes, we don't. Why? Because we fail to trust our Heavenly Father completely, and because we are, at times, surprisingly stubborn. Luke 11 teaches us that God does not withhold spiritual gifts from those who ask. Our obligation, quite simply, is to ask for them.

Are you asking God to move mountains in your life, or are you expecting Him to stumble over molehills? Whatever the size of your challenges, God is big enough to handle them. Ask for His help today, with faith and with fervor, and then watch in amazement as your mountains begin to move.

All we have to do is to acknowledge our need, move from self-sufficiency to dependence, and ask God to become our hiding place.

Bill Hybels

God uses our most stumbling, faltering faith-steps as the open door to His doing for us "more than we ask or think."

Catherine Marshall

A TIMELY TIP

If you're searching for peace and abundance, ask for God's help—and keep asking—until He answers your prayers.

QUESTIONS AND ANSWERS

Listen carefully to wisdom; set your mind on understanding.

Proverbs 2:2 NCV

Each day has 1,440 minutes—can you give God five of them? Of course you can . . . and of course you should!

This book asks that you give your undivided attention to God for at least five minutes each day. And make no mistake about it: the emphasis in the previous sentence should be placed on the words "at least." In truth, you should give God lots more time than a measly five minutes, but hey, it's a start.

Has the busy pace of life robbed you of time with God? If so, it's time to reorder your priorities and your life. Nothing is more important than the time you spend with your Heavenly Father, so slow down and have a word or two with Him. Then, claim the peace and abundance that can be yours when you regularly spend time with your Heavenly Father. His peace is offered freely; it has been paid for in full; it is yours for the asking. So ask. And then share.

If you are struggling to make some difficult decisions right now that aren't specifically addressed in the Bible, don't make a choice based on what's right for someone else. You are the Lord's and He will make sure you do what's right.

Lisa Whelchel

A TIMELY TIP

If you've got a decision to make, the first thing you should do is slow down and check it out with God.

BUILDING CHARACTER, MOMENT BY MOMENT

May integrity and uprightness protect me, because my hope is in you.

Psalm 25:21 NIV

It has been said that character is what we are when nobody is watching. How true. But, as Bill Hybels correctly observed, "Every secret act of character, conviction, and courage has been observed in living color by our omniscient God." And isn't that a sobering thought?

When we do things that we know aren't right, we try to hide our misdeeds from family members and friends. But even then, God is watching.

If you sincerely wish to walk with God, you must seek, to the best of your ability, to follow His commandments. When you do, your character will take care of itself . . . and you won't need to look over your shoulder to see who, besides God, is watching.

Your true character is something that no one can injure but yourself.

C. H. Spurgeon

If God can fashion the mountains, if God can keep the sun in its orbit, if God can split a sea and dry the ground beneath it so an entire nation can cross, do you doubt that he can transform your character?

Bill Hybels

A TIMELY TIP

Integrity is more important than popularity. Always has been, always will be.

LOVE GOD AND GET BUSY

So don't get tired of doing what is good. Don't get discouraged and give up, for we will reap a harvest of blessing at the appropriate time.

Galatians 6:9 NLT

The old saying is both familiar and true: actions speak louder than words. And as believers, we must beware: our actions should always give credence to the changes that Christ can make in the lives of those who walk with Him.

God calls upon each of us to act in accordance with His will and with respect for His commandments. If we are to be responsible believers, we must realize that it is never enough simply to hear the instructions of God; we must also live by them. And it is never enough to wait idly by while others do God's work here on earth; we, too, must act. Doing God's work is a responsibility that each of us must bear, and when we do, our loving Heavenly Father rewards our efforts with a bountiful harvest.

He who waits until circumstances completely favor his undertaking will never accomplish anything.

Martin Luther

Every time you refuse to face up to life and its problems, you weaken your character.

E. Stanley Jones

A TIMELY TIP

Because actions do speak louder than words, it's always a good time to let your actions speak for themselves.

GUIDED BY HONESTY

Good people will be guided by honesty; dishonesty will destroy those who are not trustworthy.

Proverbs 11:3 NCV

Charles Swindoll correctly observed, "Nothing speaks louder or more powerfully than a life of integrity." Godly men and women agree.

Integrity is built slowly over a lifetime. It is a precious thing—difficult to build but easy to tear down. As believers in Christ, we must seek to live each day with discipline, honesty, and faith. When we do, at least two things happen: integrity becomes a habit, and God blesses us because of our obedience to Him.

Living a life of integrity isn't always the easiest way, but it is always right way. And God clearly intends that it should be our way, too.

God never called us to naïveté. He called us to integrity . . . . The biblical concept of integrity emphasizes mature innocence not childlike ignorance.

Beth Moore

The commandment of absolute truthfulness is really only another name for the fullness of discipleship.

Dietrich Bonhoeffer

A TIMELY TIP

The real test of integrity is being willing to tell the truth when it's hard.

SINCE TOMORROW IS NOT PROMISED

We must do the works of Him who sent Me while it is day. Night is coming when no one can work.

John 9:4 Holman CSB

The words of John 9:4 remind us that "night is coming" for all of us. But until then, God gives us each day and fills it to the brim with possibilities. The day is presented to us fresh and clean at midnight, free of charge, but we must beware: Today is a non-renewable resource—once it's gone, it's gone forever. Our responsibility, of course, is to use this day in the service of God's will and in accordance with His commandments.

Today, treasure the time that God has given you. And search for the hidden possibilities that God has placed along your path. This day is a priceless gift from your Creator, so use it joyfully and productively. And encourage others to do likewise. After all, night is coming when no one can work . . .

Live in such a way that any day would make a suitable capstone for life. Live so that you need not change your mode of living, even if your sudden departure were immediately predicted to you.

C. H. Spurgeon

Do not so contemplate eternity that you waste today.

Vance Havner

A TIMELY TIP

Today is a wonderful, one-of-a-kind gift from God. Treat it that way.

THE RICH HARVEST

Remember this: the person who sows sparingly will also reap sparingly, and the person who sows generously will also reap generously.

2 Corinthians 9:6 Holman CSB

How can we serve God? By sharing His message, His mercy, and His love with those who cross our paths. Everywhere we look, or so it seems, the needs are great. And at every turn, it seems, so are the temptations. Still, our challenge is clear: we must love God, obey His commandments, trust His Son, and serve His children. When we place the Lord in His rightful place—at the center of our lives—we will reap a bountiful spiritual harvest that will endure forever.

That's what I love about serving God. In His eyes, there are no little people . . . because there are no big people. We are all on the same playing field.

Joni Eareckson Tada

Through our service to others, God wants to influence our world for Him.

Vonette Bright

A TIMELY TIP

With God on your side, you have every reason to be a confident person.

QUIET, PLEASE!

Truly my soul silently waits for God; from Him comes my salvation.

Psalm 62:1 NKJV

Face it: We live in a noisy world, a world filled with distractions, frustrations, and complications. But if we allow those distractions to separate us from God's peace, we do ourselves a profound disservice.

Are you one of those who rush through the day with scarcely a single moment for quiet contemplation and prayer? If so, it's time to reorder your priorities.

Nothing is more important than the time you spend with your Savior. So be still and claim the inner peace that is your spiritual birthright: the peace of Jesus Christ. It is offered freely; it has been paid for in full; it is yours for the asking. So ask. And then share.

The remedy for distractions is the same now as it was in earlier and simpler times: prayer, meditation, and the cultivation of the inner life.

A. W. Tozer

The world is full of noise. Might we not set ourselves to learn silence, stillness, solitude?

Elisabeth Elliot

A TIMELY TIP

Spend a few moments each day in silence. You owe it to your Creator . . . and to yourself.

NO SHORTCUTS

Take care of your own business, and do your own work as we have already told you. If you do, then people who are not believers will respect you, and you will not have to depend on others for what you need.

1 Thessalonians 4:11-12 NCV

The world often tempts us with instant gratification: get rich—today; lose weight—today; have everything you want—today. Yet life's experiences and God's Word tell us that the best things in life require heaping helpings of both time and work.

It has been said, quite correctly, that there are no shortcuts to any place worth going. For believers, it's important to remember that hard work is not simply a proven way to get ahead; it's also part of God's plan for His children.

So do yourself this favor: don't look for shortcuts . . . because there aren't any.

Ordinary work, which is what most of us do most of the time, is ordained by God every bit as much as is the extraordinary.

Elisabeth Elliot

God provides the ingredients for our daily bread but expects us to do the baking. With our own hands!

Barbara Johnson

A TIMELY TIP

When you find work that pleases God—and when you apply yourself conscientiously to the job at hand—you'll be rewarded.

FACING OUR FEARS

I, even I, am the LORD, and apart from me there is no Savior.

Isaiah 43:11 NIV

All of us may find our courage tested by the inevitable disappointments and tragedies of life. After all, ours is a world filled with uncertainty, hardship, sickness, and danger. Old Man Trouble, it seems, is never too far from the front door.

When we focus upon our fears and our doubts, we may find many reasons to lie awake at night and fret about the uncertainties of the coming day. A better strategy, of course, is to focus not upon our fears, but instead upon our God.

God is as near as your next breath, and He is in control. He offers salvation to all His children, including you. God is your shield and your strength; you are His forever. So don't focus your thoughts upon the fears of the day. Instead, trust God's plan and His eternal love for you. And remember: God is good, and He always has the last word.

Call upon God. Prayer itself can defuse fear.

Bill Hybels

God alone can give us songs in the night.

C. H. Spurgeon

A TIMELY TIP

If you're too afraid of failure, you may not live up to your potential. Remember that failing isn't nearly as bad as failing to try.

THE LIFE OF MODERATION

Do you want to be counted wise, to build a reputation for wisdom? Here's what you do: Live well, live wisely, live humbly. It's the way you live, not the way you talk, that counts.

James 3:13 MSG

When we allow our appetites to run wild, they usually do. When we abandon moderation and focus, instead, on accumulation, we forfeit the inner peace that God offers—but does not guarantee—to His children. When we live intemperate lives, we rob ourselves of countless blessings that would have otherwise been ours.

God's instructions are clear: if we seek to live wisely, we must be moderate in our appetites and disciplined in our behavior. To do otherwise is an affront to Him . . . and to ourselves.

Virtue—even attempted virtue—brings light; indulgence brings fog.

C. S. Lewis

To many, total abstinence is easier than perfect moderation.

St. Augustine

A TIMELY TIP

Remember that God's Word instructs you to be moderate and disciplined as you guard your body, your mind, and your heart. So when in doubt, be a little more moderate than necessary.

WHEN CHANGE IS PAINFUL

We are pressured in every way but not crushed; we are perplexed but not in despair.

2 Corinthians 4:8 Holman CSB

When life unfolds according to our wishes, or when we experience unexpected good fortune, we find it easy to praise God's plan. That's when we greet change with open arms. But sometimes the changes that we must endure are painful. When we struggle through the difficult days of life, as we must from time to time, we may ask ourselves, "Why me?" The answer, of course, is that God knows, but He isn't telling . . . yet.

Have you endured a difficult transition that has left your head spinning or your heart broken? If so, you have a clear choice to make: either you can cry and complain, or you can trust God and get busy fixing what's broken. The former is a formula for disaster; the latter is a formula for a well-lived life.

Pain is the fuel of passion—it energizes us with an intensity to change that we don't normally possess.

Rick Warren

When we are young, change is a treat, but as we grow older, change becomes a threat. But when Jesus Christ is in control of your life, you need never fear change or decay.

Warren Wiersbe

A TIMELY TIP

If a big change is called for . . . don't be afraid to make a big change—sometimes, one big leap is better than a thousand baby steps.

PROSPERITY, PROMISES, AND PEACE

The Lord's blessing brings wealth, and no sorrow comes with it.

Proverbs 10:22 NCV

We live in an era of prosperity, a time when many of us have been richly blessed with an assortment of material possessions that our forebears could have scarcely imagined. As believers living in these prosperous times, we must be cautious: we must keep prosperity in perspective.

The world stresses the importance of material possessions; God does not. The world offers the promise of happiness through wealth and public acclaim; God offers the promise of peace through His Son. When in doubt, we must distrust the world and trust God. The world often makes promises that it cannot keep, but when God makes a promise, He keeps it, not just for a day or a year or a lifetime, for all eternity.

There is nothing wrong with people possessing riches. The wrong comes when riches possess people.

Billy Graham

Saints are poor sometimes, but they do not know the poverty of the man who has no God.

C. H. Spurgeon

A TIMELY TIP

God wants to bless you abundantly and eternally. When you trust God completely and obey Him faithfully, you will be blessed.

NAVIGATING DEAD-END STREETS

He gives strength to the weary and strengthens the powerless.

Isaiah 40:29 Holman CSB

As we travel the roads of life, all of us are confronted with streets that seem to be dead ends. When we do, we may become discouraged. After all, we live in a society where expectations can be high and demands even higher.

If you find yourself enduring difficult circumstances, remember that God remains in His heaven. If you become discouraged with the direction of your day or your life, turn your thoughts and prayers to Him. He is a God of possibility, not negativity. He will guide you through your difficulties and beyond them. And then, with a renewed spirit of optimism and hope, you can thank the Giver of all things good for gifts that are simply too profound to fully understand and for treasures that are too numerous to count.

God never hurries. There are no deadlines against which He must work. To know this is to quiet our spirits and relax our nerves.

A. W. Tozer

We must leave it to God to answer our prayers in His own wisest way. Sometimes, we are so impatient and think that God does not answer. God always answers! He never fails! Be still. Abide in Him.

Mrs. Charles E. Cowman

A TIMELY TIP

You should always trust God, and you should wait patiently for His plans to unfold. God's timing is best.

TIME FOR REST

Are you tired? Worn out? Burned out on religion? Come to me. Get away with me and you'll recover your life. I'll show you how to take a real rest. Walk with me and work with me . . . watch how I do it. Learn the unforced rhythms of grace. I won't lay anything heavy or ill-fitting on you. Keep company with me and you'll learn to live freely and lightly.

Matthew 11:28-30 MSG

Even the most inspired Christians can, from time to time, find themselves "running out of steam." If you currently fit that description, remember that God expects you to do your work, but He also intends for you to rest. When you fail to take time for sufficient rest, you do a disservice to yourself, to your family, and to your friends.

Is your energy on the wane? Is your spiritual tank near empty? Are your emotions frayed? If so, it's time to turn your thoughts and your prayers to God. And when you're finished, it's time to treat yourself to a heaping helping of "R&R," which stands for "Rest and Renewal."

Life is strenuous. See that your clock does not run down.

Mrs. Charles E. Cowman

Satan does some of his worst work on exhausted Christians when nerves are frayed and their minds are faint.

Vance Havner

A TIMELY TIP

God wants you to get enough rest. The world wants you to burn the candle at both ends. Trust God.

A LIFE OF PRAYER

May the words of my mouth and the thoughts of my heart be pleasing to you, O Lord, my rock and my redeemer.

Psalm 19:14 NLT

I s prayer an integral part of your daily life, or is it a hit-or-miss habit? Do you "pray without ceasing," or is your prayer life an afterthought? Do you regularly pray in the solitude of the early morning darkness, or do you bow your head only when others are watching?

The quality of your spiritual life will be in direct proportion to the quality of your prayer life. Today, instead of turning things over in your mind, turn them over to God in prayer. Instead of worrying about your next decision, ask God to lead the way. Don't limit your prayers to the dinner table or the bedside table. Pray constantly about things great and small. God is always listening; it's up to you to do the rest.

The Christian on his knees sees more than the philosopher on tiptoe.

D. L. Moody

I need the spiritual revival that comes from spending quiet time alone with Jesus in prayer and in thoughtful meditation on His Word.

Anne Graham Lotz

A TIMELY TIP

Avoid people and places that might tempt you to disobey God's commandments.

PUTTING FAITH TO THE TEST

Even though good people may be bothered by trouble seven times, they are never defeated.

Proverbs 24:16 NCV

Life is a tapestry of good days and difficult days, with good days predominating. During the good days, we are tempted to take our blessings for granted (a temptation that we must resist with all our might). But, during life's difficult days, we discover precisely what we're made of. And more importantly, we discover what our faith is made of.

Has your faith been put to the test yet? If so, then you know that with God's help, you can endure life's darker days. But if you have not yet faced the inevitable trials and tragedies of life-here-on-earth, don't worry: you will. And when your faith is put to the test, rest assured that God is perfectly willing—and always ready—to give you strength for the struggle.

A faith that hasn't been tested can't be trusted.

Adrian Rogers

He wants us to have a faith that does not complain while waiting, but rejoices because we know our times are in His hands—nail-scarred hands that labor for our highest good.

Kay Arthur

A TIMELY TIP

Don't be embarrassed to discuss your faith: You need not have attended seminary to have worthwhile opinions about your faith.

SHARING THE GOOD NEWS

Go, therefore, and make disciples of all nations, baptizing them in the name of the Father and of the Son and of the Holy Spirit, teaching them to observe everything I have commanded you. And remember, I am with you always, to the end of the age.

Matthew 28:19-20 Holman CSB

After His resurrection, Jesus addressed His disciples. As recorded in the 28th chapter of Matthew, Christ instructed His followers to share His message with the world. This "Great Commission" applies to Christians of every generation, including our own.

As believers, we are called to share the Good News of Jesus with our families, with our neighbors, and with the world. Christ commanded His disciples to become fishers of men. We must do likewise, and we must do so today. Tomorrow may indeed be too late.

Angels cannot preach the gospel; only beings such as Paul and you and I can preach the gospel.

Oswald Chambers

You can go to the mission field in person, by prayer, by provision, or by proxy. But remember, there is a mission field across the street as well as across the sea.

Vance Havner

A TIMELY TIP

God's Word clearly instructs you to share His Good News with the world. If you're willing, God will empower you to share your faith.

THE PATH

But grow in the special favor and knowledge of our Lord and Savior Jesus Christ. To him be all glory and honor, both now and forevermore. Amen.

2 Peter 3:18 NLT

When will you be a "fully-grown" Christian? Hopefully never—or at least not until you arrive in heaven! As a believer living here on planet earth, you're never "fully grown"; you always have the potential to keep growing.

In those quiet moments when you open your heart to God, the One who made you keeps remaking you. He gives you direction, perspective, wisdom, and courage.

Would you like a time-tested formula for spiritual growth? Here it is: keep studying God's Word, keep obeying His commandments, keep praying (and listening for answers), and keep trying to live in the center of God's will. When you do, you'll never stay stuck for long. You will, instead, be a growing Christian . . . and that's precisely the kind of Christian God wants you to be.

When it comes to walking with God, there is no such thing as instant maturity. God doesn't mass produce His saints. He hand tools each one, and it always takes longer than we expected.

Charles Swindoll

We set our eyes on the finish line, forgetting the past, and straining toward the mark of spiritual maturity and fruitfulness.

Vonette Bright

A TIMELY TIP

When it comes to your faith, God doesn't intend for you to stand still. He wants you to keep moving and growing.

THE WAY WE TREAT OUR NEIGHBORS

The whole law is made complete in this one command: "Love your neighbor as you love yourself."

Galatians 5:14 NCV

How should we treat other people? God's Word is clear: we should treat others in the same way that we wish to be treated. This Golden Rule is easy to understand, but sometimes it can be difficult to live by.

Because we are imperfect human beings, we are, on occasion, selfish, thoughtless, or cruel. But God commands us to behave otherwise. He teaches us to rise above our own imperfections and to treat others with unselfishness and love. When we observe God's Golden Rule, we help build His kingdom here on earth. And, when we share the love of Christ, we share a priceless gift; may we share it today and every day that we live.

If my heart is right with God, every human being is my neighbor.

Oswald Chambers

Wise Christians will be generous with their neighbors and live peaceably with them.

Warren Wiersbe

A TIMELY TIP

To be a good neighbor, follow the Golden Rule. So treat your neighbors like you want to be treated. No exceptions.

HAPPINESS IS . . .

Happy are the people who live at your Temple . . . . Happy are those whose strength comes from you.

Psalm 84:4-5 NCV

Do you seek happiness, abundance, and contentment? If so, here are some things you should do: Love God and His Son; depend upon God for strength; try, to the best of your abilities, to follow God's will; and strive to obey His Holy Word. When you do these things, you'll discover that happiness goes hand-in-hand with righteousness. The happiest people are not those who rebel against God; the happiest people are those who love God and obey His commandments.

What does life have in store for you? A world full of possibilities (of course it's up to you to seize them) and God's promise of abundance (of course it's up to you to accept it). So, as you embark upon the next phase of your journey, remember to celebrate the life that God has given you. Your Creator has blessed you beyond measure. Honor Him with your prayers, your words, your deeds, and your joy.

God cannot give us happiness and peace apart from Himself, because it is not there. There is no such thing.

C. S. Lewis

If you want to be truly happy, you won't find it on an endless quest for more stuff. You'll find it in receiving God's generosity and in passing that generosity along.

Bill Hybels

A TIMELY TIP

If you want to find lasting happiness, don't chase it. Instead, do your duty, obey your God, and wait for happiness to find you.

CHOICES PLEASING TO GOD

I am offering you life or death, blessings or curses. Now, choose life! Then you and your children may live. To choose life is to love the Lord your God, obey him, and stay close to him.

Deuteronomy 30:19-20 NCV

Because we are creatures of free will, we make choices—lots of them. When we make choices that are pleasing to our Heavenly Father, we are blessed. When we make choices that cause us to walk in the footsteps of God's Son, we enjoy the abundance that Christ has promised to those who follow Him. But when we make choices that are displeasing to God, we sow seeds that have the potential to bring forth a bitter harvest.

Today, as you encounter the challenges of everyday living, you will make hundreds of choices. Choose wisely. Make your thoughts and your actions pleasing to God. And remember: every choice that is displeasing to Him is the wrong choice—no exceptions.

Life is a series of choices between the bad, the good, and the best. Everything depends on how we choose.

Vance Havner

There is no one so far lost that Jesus cannot find him and cannot save him.

Andrew Murray

A TIMELY TIP

Sin is sin. There's no little sins, or big sins, or medium-sized sins. And lies don't come in colors.

MIRACLES GREAT AND SMALL

For nothing will be impossible with God.

Luke 1:37 Holman CSB

God is a miracle worker. Throughout history He has intervened in the course of human events in ways that cannot be explained by science or human rationale. And He's still doing so today.

God's miracles are not limited to special occasions, nor are they witnessed by a select few. God is crafting His wonders all around us: the miracle of the birth of a new baby; the miracle of a world renewing itself with every sunrise; the miracle of lives transformed by God's love and grace. Each day, God's handiwork is evident for all to see and experience.

Today, seize the opportunity to inspect God's hand at work. His miracles come in a variety of shapes and sizes, so keep your eyes and your heart open. Be watchful, and you'll soon be amazed.

Are you looking for a miracle? If you keep your eyes wide open and trust in God, you won't have to look very far.

Marie T. Freeman

Faith means believing in realities that go beyond sense and sight. It is the awareness of unseen divine realities all around you.

Joni Eareckson Tada

A TIMELY TIP

God has infinite power. If you're watchful, you'll observe many miracles. So keep your eyes, your heart, and your mind open.

A CHANGE OF HEART

The one who conceals his sins will not prosper, but whoever confesses and renounces them will find mercy.

Proverbs 28:13 Holman CSB

Who among us has sinned? All of us. But, God calls upon us to turn away from sin by following His commandments. And the good news is this: When we do ask God's forgiveness and turn our hearts to Him, He forgives us absolutely and completely.

Genuine repentance requires more than simply offering God apologies for our misdeeds. Real repentance may start with feelings of sorrow and remorse, but it ends only when we turn away from the sin that has heretofore distanced us from our Creator. In truth, we offer our most meaningful apologies to God, not with our words, but with our actions. As long as we are still engaged in sin, we may be "repenting," but we have not fully "repented."

Is there an aspect of your life that is distancing you from your God? If so, ask for His forgiveness, and—just as importantly—stop sinning. Then, wrap yourself in the protection of God's Word. When you do, you will be secure.

Repentance is among other things a sincere apology to God for distrusting Him so long, and faith is throwing oneself upon Christ in complete confidence.

A. W. Tozer

A TIMELY TIP

If you're engaged in behavior that is displeasing to God, repent today—tomorrow may be too late.

SMALL ACTS OF KINDNESS

Whatever you did for one of the least of these brothers of Mine, you did for Me

Matthew 25:40 Holman CSB

Kindness is a choice. Sometimes, when we feel happy or generous, we find it easy to be kind. Other times, when we are discouraged or tired, we can scarcely summon the energy to utter a single kind word. But, God's commandment is clear: He intends that we make the conscious choice to treat others with kindness and respect, no matter our circumstances, no matter our emotions.

In the busyness and confusion of daily life, it is easy to lose focus, and it is easy to become frustrated. We are imperfect human beings struggling to manage our lives as best we can, but we often fall short. When we are distracted or disappointed, we may neglect to share a kind word or a kind deed. This oversight hurts others, but it hurts us most of all.

Today, slow yourself down and be alert for people who need your smile, your kind words, or your helping hand. Make kindness a centerpiece of your dealings with others. They will be blessed, and you will be, too.

There are many timid souls whom we jostle morning and evening as we pass them by; but if only the kind word were spoken they might become fully persuaded.

Fanny Crosby

A TIMELY TIP

Kindness matters. When you make the decision to be a genuinely kind person, you'll make decisions that improve your own life and the lives of your family and friends.

MISTAKES:
THE PRICE OF BEING HUMAN

LORD, help! they cried in their trouble, and he saved them from their distress.

Psalm 107:13 NLT

Mistakes: nobody likes 'em but everybody makes 'em. Sometimes, even if you're a very good person, you're going to mess things up. And when you do, God is always ready to forgive you—He'll do His part, but you should be willing to do your part, too. Here's what you need to do:

1. If you've been engaging in behavior that is against the will of God, cease and desist (that means stop). 2. If you made a mistake, learn from it and don't repeat it (that's called getting smarter). 3. If you've hurt somebody, apologize and ask for forgiveness (that's called doing the right thing). 4. Ask for God's forgiveness, too (He'll give it whenever you ask, but you do need to ask!). Have you made a mistake? If so, today is the perfect day to make things right with everybody (and the word "everybody" includes yourself, your family, your friends, and your God).

Mistakes are the price you pay for being human; repeated mistakes are the price you pay for being stubborn. So don't be hardheaded: learn from your experiences—the first time!

I hope you don't mind me telling you all this? One can learn only by seeing one's mistakes.

C. S. Lewis

A TIMELY TIP

When you make a mistake, the time to make things better is now, not later. The sooner you address your problem, the better.

THE PLAN ACCORDING TO GOD

I will instruct you and teach you in the way you should go; I will guide you with My eye.

Psalm 32:8 NKJV

Maybe you've heard this old saying: "Look before you leap." Well, that saying may be old, but it still applies to you. Before you jump into something, you should look ahead and plan ahead. Otherwise, you might soon be sorry you jumped!

When you acquire the habit of planning ahead, you'll usually make better choices. So when it comes to the important things in life, make a plan and stick to it. When you do, you'll think about the consequences of your actions before you do something silly . . . or dangerous . . . or both.

It's incredible to realize that what we do each day has meaning in the big picture of God's plan.

Bill Hybels

The Father has a plan for you that no one else can fulfill. Although His ultimate goal of conforming you to Christ's image remains constant; He has custom-designed events, circumstances, and relationships that will lead you into His will.

Charles Swindoll

A TIMELY TIP

Think ahead—it's the best way of making sure you don't get left behind.

ETERNAL LIFE: GOD'S PRICELESS GIFT

I have written these things to you who believe in the name of the Son of God, so that you may know that you have eternal life.

1 John 5:13 Holman CSB

Christ sacrificed His life on the cross so that we might have eternal life. This gift, freely given from God's only begotten Son, is the priceless possession of everyone who accepts Him as Lord and Savior.

God is waiting patiently for each of us to accept the gift of eternal life. Let us claim Christ's gift today. Let us walk with the Savior, let us love Him, let us praise Him, and let us share His message of salvation with the world.

And because we know Christ is alive, we have hope for the present and hope for life beyond the grave.

Billy Graham

Let us see the victorious Jesus: the conqueror of the tomb, the one who defied death. And let us be reminded that we, too, will be granted the same victory!

Max Lucado

A TIMELY TIP

God has created heaven and given you a way to get there. The rest is up to you.

OUR FAMILIES ARE WATCHING

You must choose for yourselves today whom you will serve . . . as for me and my family, we will serve the Lord.

Joshua 24:15 NCV

How do people know that you're a Christian? Well, you can tell them, of course. And make no mistake about it: talking about your faith in God is a very good thing to do. But simply telling people about Jesus isn't enough. You must also be willing to show people how a radical Christian (like you) should behave.

Jesus never comes "next." He is always first. And, if you seek to follow Him, you must do so every day of the week, not just on Sundays. After all, you are indeed "the light that gives light to the world," and shouldn't your light all the time? Of course it should. God deserves no less, and neither, for that matter, do you.

Our walk counts far more than our talk, always!

George Mueller

In serving we uncover the greatest fulfillment within and become a stellar example of a woman who knows and loves Jesus.

Vonette Bright

A TIMELY TIP

Your life is a sermon. What kind of sermon will you preach? The words you choose to speak may have some impact on others, but not nearly as much impact as the life you choose to live. Today, pause to consider the tone, the theme, and the context of your particular sermon, and ask yourself if it's a message that you're proud to deliver.

POSSESSED BY FAITH

The Good News shows how God makes people right with himself—that it begins and ends with faith. As the Scripture says, "But those who are right with God will live by trusting in him."

Romans 1:17 NCV

Can you honestly say that you are an enthusiastic believer? Are you passionate about your faith and excited about your path? Hopefully so. But if your zest for life has waned, it is now time to redirect your efforts and recharge your spiritual batteries. And that means refocusing your priorities by putting God first.

Nothing is more important than your wholehearted commitment to your Creator and to His only begotten Son. Your faith must never be an afterthought; it must be your ultimate priority, your ultimate possession, and your ultimate passion.

Success or failure can be pretty well predicted by the degree to which the heart is fully in it.

John Eldredge

Am I ignitable? God deliver me from the dread asbestos of "other things." Saturate me with the oil of the Spirit that I may be aflame.

Jim Elliot

A TIMELY TIP

When you are passionate about your life and your faith . . . great things happen.

TIME: THE FABRIC OF LIFE

Lord, tell me when the end will come and how long I will live. Let me know how long I have. You have given me only a short life . . . . Everyone's life is only a breath.

Psalm 39:4–5 NCV

Every day, like every life, is composed of moments. Each moment of your life holds within it the potential to seek God's will and to serve His purposes. If you are wise, you will strive to do both.

An important part of wisdom is the wise use of time. How will you invest your time today? Will you savor the moments of your life, or will you squander them? Will you use your time as an instrument of God's will, or will you allow commonplace distractions to rule your day and your life?

The gift of time is a gift from God. Treat it as if it were a precious, fleeting, one-of-a-kind treasure. Because it is.

To choose time is to save time.

Francis Bacon

There were endless demands on Jesus' time. Still he was able to make that amazing claim of "completing the work you gave me to do." (John 17:4 NIV)

Elisabeth Elliot

A TIMELY TIP

Time management is a choice: Every day, you get to choose how you will spend your time. If you choose wisely, you'll improve yourself and your life.

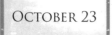

MAKING THE MOST OF OUR TALENTS

Do not neglect the gift that is in you.

1 Timothy 4:14 Holman CSB

Face it: you've got an array of talents that need to be refined. All people possess special gifts—bestowed from the Father above—and you are no exception. But, your gift is no guarantee of success; it must be cultivated—by you—or it will go unused . . . and God's gift to you will be squandered.

Today, make a promise to yourself that you will earnestly seek to discover the talents that God has given you. Then, nourish those talents and make them grow. Finally, vow to share your gifts with the world for as long as God gives you the power to do so. After all, the best way to say "Thank You" for God's gifts is to use them.

Employ whatever God has entrusted you with, in doing good, all possible good, in every possible kind and degree.

John Wesley

If you want to reach your potential, you need to add a strong work ethic to your talent.

John Maxwell

A TIMELY TIP

Each person possesses special abilities that can be nurtured carefully or ignored totally. The challenge, of course, is to do the former and to avoid the latter.

THE SOURCE OF STRENGTH

Happy are the people whose strength is in You, whose hearts are set on pilgrimage.

Psalm 84:5 Holman CSB

Have you "tapped in" to the power of God? Have you turned your life and your heart over to Him, or are you muddling along under your own power? The answer to this question will determine the quality of your life here on earth and the destiny of your life throughout all eternity.

The Bible tells us that we can do all things through the power of our risen Savior, Jesus Christ. But what does the Bible say about our powers outside the will of Christ? The Bible teaches us that "the wages of sin is death" (Romans 6:23). Our challenge, then, is clear: we must place Christ where He belongs: at the very center of our lives. When we do so, we will surely discover that He offers us the strength to live victoriously in this world and eternally in the next.

When God is our strength, it is strength indeed; when our strength is our own, it is only weakness.

St. Augustine

The same God who empowered Samson, Gideon, and Paul seeks to empower my life and your life, because God hasn't changed.

Bill Hybels

A TIMELY TIP

If you're energy is low or your nerves are frazzled, perhaps you need to slow down and have a heart-to-heart talk with God. And while you're at it, remember that God is bigger than your problems . . . much bigger.

THE SEARCH FOR TRUTH

You will know the truth, and the truth will set you free.

John 8:32 Holman CSB

The words of John 8:32 are both familiar and profound: the truth, indeed, will make you free. Truth is God's way: He commands His children to live in truth, and He rewards those who follow His commandment. Jesus is the personification of a perfect, liberating truth that offers salvation to mankind.

Do you seek to walk with God? Do you seek to feel God's peace? Then you must walk in truth, and you must walk with the Savior. There is simply no other way.

I would rather know the truth than be happy in ignorance. If I cannot have both truth and happiness, give me truth. We'll have a long time to be happy in heaven.

A. W. Tozer

Jesus differs from all other teachers; they reach the ear, but he instructs the heart; they deal with the outward letter, but he imparts an inward taste for the truth.

C. H. Spurgeon

A TIMELY TIP

Know the truth . . . and live it. Warren Wiersbe writes, "Learning God's truth and getting it into our heads is one thing, but living God's truth and getting it into our characters is quite something else." So don't be satisfied to sit on the sidelines and observe the truth at a distance—live it.

ENCOURAGING WORDS FOR FAMILY AND FRIENDS

Good people's words will help many others.

Proverbs 10:21 NCV

L ife is a team sport, and all of us need occasional pats on the back from our teammates. As Christians, we are called upon to spread the Good News of Christ, and we are also called to spread a message of encouragement and hope to the world.

Whether you realize it or not, many people with whom you come in contact every day are in desperate need of a smile or an encouraging word. The world can be a difficult place, and countless friends and family members may be troubled by the challenges of everyday life. Since you don't always know who needs our help, the best strategy is to try to encourage all the people who cross your path. So today, be a world-class source of encouragement to everyone you meet. Never has the need been greater.

When we bring sunshine into the lives of others, we're warmed by it ourselves. When we spill a little happiness, it splashes on us.

Barbara Johnson

He who becomes a brother to the bruised, a doctor to the despairing, and a comforter to the crushed may not actually say much. What he has to offer is often beyond the power of speech to convey. But, the weary sense it, and it is a balm of Gilead to their souls.

Vance Havner

A TIMELY TIP

Hang out with successful people. If you're constantly communicating with successful people, their good qualities will rub off on you, and vice versa.

KEEPING PROSPERITY IN PERSPECTIVE

If your wealth increases, don't make it the center of your life.

Psalm 62:10 NLT

In the demanding world in which we live, financial prosperity can be a good thing, but spiritual prosperity is profoundly more important. Yet our society leads us to believe otherwise. The world glorifies material possessions, personal fame, and physical beauty above all else; these things, of course, are totally unimportant to God. God sees the human heart, and that's what is important to Him.

As you establish your priorities for the coming day, remember this: The world will do everything it can to convince you that "things" are important. The world will tempt you to value fortune above faith and possessions above peace. God, on the other hand, will try to convince you that your relationship with Him is all-important. Trust God.

Have you prayed about your resources lately? Find out how God wants you to use your time and your money. No matter what it costs, forsake all that is not of God.

Kay Arthur

A TIMELY TIP

Material possessions may seem important at first, but they're nothing compared to the spiritual rewards that God gives to people (like you) who put Him first.

KEEPING UP APPEARANCES

Man does not see what the Lord sees, for man sees what is visible, but the Lord sees the heart.

1 Samuel 16:7 Holman CSB

The world sees you as you appear to be; God sees you as you really are. He sees your heart, and He understands your intentions. The opinions of others should be relatively unimportant to you; however, God's view of you—His understanding of your actions, your thoughts, and your motivations—should be vitally important.

Few things in life are more futile than "keeping up appearances" in order to impress your friends and your dates—yet the media would have you believe otherwise. The media would have you believe that everything depends on the color of your hair, the condition of your wardrobe, and the model of the car you drive. But nothing could be further from the truth. What is important, of course, is pleasing your Father in heaven. You please Him when your intentions are pure and your actions are just. When you do, you will be blessed today, tomorrow, and forever.

Fashion is an enduring testimony to the fact that we live quite consciously before the eyes of others.

John Eldredge

Outside appearances, things like the clothes you wear or the car you drive, are important to other people but totally unimportant to God. Trust God.

Marie T. Freeman

A TIMELY TIP

Don't be too worried about what you look like on the outside—be more concerned about the kind of person you are on the inside. And while you're at it, don't judge other people by their appearances, either.

THE WISDOM OF RIGHTEOUSNESS

As shameful conduct is pleasure for a fool, so wisdom is for a man of understanding.
Proverbs 10:23 Holman CSB

Are you a radically different person because of your decision to form a personal relationship with Jesus? Has Jesus made a BIG difference in your life, or are you basically the same person you were before you invited Him into your heart? The answer to these questions will determine the quality and the direction of your life.

If you're still doing all the same things you did before you became a Christian, it may be time to take an honest look at the current condition of your faith. Why? Because Jesus doesn't want you to be a run-of-the-mill, follow-the-crowd kind of guy. Jesus wants you to be a "new creation" through Him. And that's exactly what you should want for yourself, too.

Nobody is good by accident. No man ever became holy by chance.

C. H. Spurgeon

There may be no trumpet sound or loud applause when we make a right decision, just a calm sense of resolution and peace.

Gloria Gaither

A TIMELY TIP

Ask yourself if your behavior has been radically changed by your unfolding relationship with God. It the answer to this question is unclear to you—or if the honest answer is a resounding no—think of a single step you can take, a positive change in your life, that will bring you closer to your Creator.

FINDING YOUR WAY

In all your ways acknowledge him, and he will make your paths straight.

Proverbs 3:6 NIV

P roverbs 3:6 makes this promise: if you acknowledge God's sovereignty over every aspect of your life, He will guide your path. And, as prayerfully consider the path that God intends for you to take, here are things you should do: You should study His Word and be ever-watchful for His signs. You should associate with fellow believers who will encourage your spiritual growth. You should listen carefully to that inner voice that speaks to you in the quiet moments of your daily devotionals. And, as you continually seek God's unfolding purpose for your life, you should be patient. Your Heavenly Father may not always reveal Himself as quickly as you would like. But rest assured: God is here, and He intends to use you in wonderful, unexpected ways. He desires to lead you along a path of His choosing. Your challenge is to watch, to listen, to learn . . . and to follow.

You cannot be the person God meant you to be, and you cannot live the life he meant you to live, unless you live from the heart.

John Eldredge

My policy has always been to ask God to help me set goals because I believe God has a plan for every person.

Bill Bright

A TIMELY TIP

If your life has been turned upside down, you may find yourself searching for something new: a different direction, a new purpose, or a fresh start. As you make your plans, be sure to consult God because even now He is leading you toward a goal that only He can see. Your task is to pray, to listen, and to follow His lead.

WHEN WE STUMBLE

God is our refuge and strength, always ready to help in times of trouble. So we will not fear, even if earthquakes come and mountains crumble to the sea.

Psalm 46:1-2 NLT

From time to time, all of us face adversity, discouragement, or disappointment. And, throughout life, we must all endure life-changing personal losses that leave us breathless. When we do, God stands ready to protect us. Psalm 147 promises, "He heals the brokenhearted and bandages their wounds" (v. 3, NCV).

When we are troubled, we must call upon God, and, in His own time and according to His own plan, He will heal us.

Are you anxious? Take those anxieties to God. Are you troubled? Take your troubles to Him. Does your world seem to be trembling beneath your feet? Seek protection from the One who cannot be moved. The same God who created the universe will protect you if you ask Him . . . so ask Him.

God has never promised to keep us immune from trouble. He says, "I will be with you in trouble."

Oswald Chambers

Adversity is always unexpected and unwelcomed. It is an intruder and a thief, and yet in the hands of God, adversity becomes the means through which His supernatural power is demonstrated.

Charles Stanley

A TIMELY TIP

Remember that tough times are simply opportunities to trust God completely and to find strength in Him. And remember: Tough times can also be times of intense personal growth.

EARTHLY STRESS, HEAVENLY PEACE

And let the peace of the Messiah, to which you were also called in one body, control your hearts. Be thankful.

Colossians 3:15 Holman CSB

Stressful days are an inevitable fact of modern life. And how do we best cope with the challenges of our demanding, 21st-century world? By turning our days and our lives over to God. Elisabeth Elliot writes, "If my life is surrendered to God, all is well. Let me not grab it back, as though it were in peril in His hand but would be safer in mine!" Yet even the most devout Christian woman may, at times, seek to grab the reins of her life and proclaim, "I'm in charge!" To do so is foolish, prideful, and stressful.

When we seek to impose our own wills upon the world—or upon other people—we invite stress into our lives . . . needlessly. But, when we turn our lives and our hearts over to God—when we accept His will instead of seeking vainly to impose our own—we discover the inner peace that can be ours through Him.

Do you feel overwhelmed by the stresses of daily life? Turn your concerns and your prayers over to God. Trust Him. Trust Him completely. Trust Him today. Trust Him always. When it comes to the inevitable challenges of this day, hand them over to God completely and without reservation. He knows your needs and will meet those needs in His own way and in His own time if you let Him.

Satan does some of his worst work on exhausted Christians when nerves are frayed and the mind is faint.

Vance Havner

A TIMELY TIP

When in doubt, turn your worries over to God. He can handle them . . . and will.

PRAISE FOR THE FATHER; THANKS FOR HIS BLESSINGS

I will give You thanks with all my heart.

Psalm 138:1 Holman CSB

If you're like most folks on the planet, you're a very busy person. Your life is probably hectic, demanding, and complicated. And when the demands of life leave you rushing from place to place with scarcely a moment to spare, you may not take time to praise your Creator. Big mistake.

The Bible makes it clear: it pays to praise God. Worship and praise should be a part of everything you do. Otherwise, you quickly lose perspective as you fall prey to the demands of everyday life.

Do you sincerely desire to know God in a more meaningful way? Then praise Him for who He is and for what He has done for you. And please don't wait until Sunday morning—praise Him all day long, every day, for as long as you live . . . and then for all eternity.

The time for universal praise is sure to come some day. Let us begin to do our part now.

Hannah Whitall Smith

God is worthy of our praise and is pleased when we come before Him with thanksgiving.

Shirley Dobson

A TIMELY TIP

Remember that it always pays to praise your Creator. That's why thoughtful believers (like you) make it a habit to carve out quiet moments throughout the day to praise God.

PRAYING TO KNOW GOD

Teach me your ways, O Lord, that I may live according to your truth! Grant me purity of heart, that I may honor you.

Psalm 86:11 NLT

Andrew Murray observed, "Some people pray just to pray, and some people pray to know God." Your task, as maturing believer, is to pray, not out of habit or obligation, but out of a sincere desire to know your Heavenly Father. Through constant prayers, you should petition God, you should praise Him, and you should seek to discover His unfolding plans for your life.

Today, reach out to the Giver of all blessings. Turn to Him for guidance and for strength. Invite Him into every corner of your day. Ask Him to teach you and to lead you. And remember that no matter what your circumstances, God is never far away; He is here . . . always right here. So pray.

The purpose of all prayer is to find God's will and to make that will our prayer.

Catherine Marshall

Some people pray just to pray, and some people pray to know God.

Andrew Murray

A TIMELY TIP

God is everywhere you have ever been and everywhere you will ever be. If you seek Him sincerely and often, you will find Him.

THE COURAGE TO RISK FAILURE

The fear of human opinion disables; trusting in God protects you from that.

Proverbs 29:25 MSG

As we consider the uncertainties of the future, we are confronted with a powerful temptation: the temptation to "play it safe." Unwilling to move mountains, we fret over molehills. Unwilling to entertain great hopes for the tomorrow, we focus on the unfairness of the today. Unwilling to trust God completely, we take timid half-steps when God intends that we make giant leaps.

Today, ask God for the courage to step beyond the boundaries of your doubts. Ask Him to guide you to a place where you can realize your full potential—a place where you are freed from the fear of failure. Ask Him to do His part, and promise Him that you will do your part. Don't ask Him to lead you to a "safe" place; ask Him to lead you to the "right" place . . . and remember: those two places are seldom the same.

How beautiful it is to learn that grace isn't fragile, and that in the family of God we can fail and not be a failure.

Gloria Gaither

Our problem isn't that we've failed. Our problem is that we haven't failed enough. We haven't been brought low enough to learn what God wants us to learn.

Charles Swindoll

A TIMELY TIP

Setbacks are inevitable—your response to them is optional. You can turn your stumbling blocks into stepping stones . . . and you should.

WHEN HIS PEACE BECOMES OUR PEACE

But now in Christ Jesus, you who were far away have been brought near by the blood of the Messiah. For He is our peace, who made both groups one and tore down the dividing wall of hostility.

Ephesians 2:13-14 Holman CSB

Have you found the genuine peace that can be yours through Jesus Christ? Or are you still rushing after the illusion of "peace and happiness" that the world promises but cannot deliver?

The beautiful words of John 14:27 remind us that Jesus offers us peace, not as the world gives, but as He alone gives: "Peace I leave with you, My peace I give to you; not as the world gives do I give to you. Let not your heart be troubled, neither let it be afraid" (NKJV). Our challenge is to accept Christ's peace and then, as best we can, to share His blessings with our neighbors.

Today, as a gift to yourself, to your family, and to the world, let Christ's peace become your peace. Let Him rule your heart and your thoughts. When you do, you will partake in the peace that only He can give.

Peace with God is where all peace begins.

Jim Gallery

Jesus gives us the ultimate rest, the confidence we need, to escape the frustration and chaos of the world around us.

Billy Graham

A TIMELY TIP

Do you want to discover God's peace? Then do your best to live in the center of God's will.

SEARCHING FOR THE RIGHT KIND OF TREASURE

Wherever your treasure is, there your heart and thoughts will also be.

Luke 12:34 NLT

Is God a big priority for you . . . or is He an afterthought? Do you give God your best or what's left? Have you given Christ your heart, your soul, your talents, your time, and your testimony? Or are you giving Him little more than a few hours each Sunday morning?

In the book of Exodus, God warns that we should place no gods before Him (Exodus 20:3). Yet all too often, we place our Lord in second, third, or fourth place as we worship the gods of pride, money, or personal gratification. When we unwittingly place possessions or relationships above our love for the Creator, we must realign our priorities or suffer the consequences.

Does God rule your heart? Make certain that the honest answer to this question is a resounding yes. In the life of every radical believer, God comes first. And that's precisely the place that He deserves in your heart.

The work of God is appointed. There is always enough time to do the will of God.

Elisabeth Elliot

Action springs not from thought, but from a readiness for responsibility.

Dietrich Bonhoeffer

A TIMELY TIP

The priorities you choose will dictate the life you live. So choose carefully.

THE SIZE OF YOUR PROBLEMS

Ah Lord GOD! Behold, You have made the heavens and the earth by Your great power and by Your outstretched arm! Nothing is too difficult for You.

Jeremiah 32:17 NASB

If a temporary loss of perspective has left you worried, exhausted, or both, it's time to readjust your thought patterns. Negative thoughts are habit-forming; thankfully, so are positive ones. With practice, you can form the habit of focusing on God's priorities and your possibilities. When you do, you'll soon discover that you will spend less time fretting about your challenges and more time praising God for His gifts.

When you call upon the Lord and prayerfully seek His will, He will give you wisdom and perspective. When you make God's priorities your priorities, He will direct your steps and calm your fears. So today and every day hereafter, pray for a sense of balance and perspective. And remember: no problems are too big for God—and that includes yours.

God has plans—not problems—for our lives.

Corrie ten Boom

The Bible is a remarkable commentary on perspective. Through its divine message, we are brought face to face with issues and tests in daily living and how, by the power of the Holy Spirit, we are enabled to respond positively to them.

Luci Swindoll

A TIMELY TIP

Keep life in perspective: Your life is an integral part of God's grand plan. So don't become unduly upset over the minor inconveniences of life, and don't worry too much about today's setbacks—they're temporary.

NOVEMBER 8

STEERING CLEAR OF THE ROAD TO RUIN

Innocent people will be kept safe, but those who are dishonest will suddenly be ruined.

Proverbs 28:18 NCV

How hard is it to bump into temptation in this crazy world? Not very hard. The devil, it seems, is causing pain and heartache in more places and in more ways than ever before. We, as Christians, must remain vigilant. Not only must we resist Satan when he confronts us, but we must also avoid those places where Satan can most easily tempt us. And, if we are to avoid the unending temptations of this world, we must earnestly wrap ourselves in the protection of God's Holy Word.

The road to ruin is wide, long, and deadly. Avoid it, and help others do the same. When you do, God will smile—and the devil won't.

Good and evil both increase at compound interest. That is why the little decisions you and I make every day are of such infinite importance.

C. S. Lewis

Unconfessed sin in your life will cause you to doubt.

Anne Graham Lotz

A TIMELY TIP

Confess your sin as soon as you recognize it. God will forgive you, and then you can forgive yourself.

FROM THE INSIDE OUT

No one will say, "Look here!" or "There!" For you see, the kingdom of God is among you.

Luke 17:21 Holman CSB

I f we sincerely want to change ourselves for the better, we must start on the inside and work our way out from there. Lasting change doesn't occur "out there"; it occurs "in here." It occurs, not in the shifting sands of our own particular circumstances, but in quiet depths of our own hearts.

Do you desire to improve some aspect of your life? If so, don't expect changing circumstances to miraculously transform you into the person you want to become. Transformation starts with God, and it starts in the silent center of a humble human heart—like yours.

We're prone to want God to change our circumstances, but He wants to change our character. We think that peace comes from the outside in, but it comes from the inside out.

Warren Wiersbe

With God, it isn't who you were that matters; it's who you are becoming.

Liz Curtis Higgs

A TIMELY TIP

When it comes to making big changes or big purchases, proceed slowly. Otherwise, you may find yourself uncomfortably perched atop a merry-go-round that is much easier to start than it is to stop.

LEARNING FROM THE FAITHFUL

We have around us many people whose lives tell us what faith means. So let us run the race that is before us and never give up. We should remove from our lives anything that would get in the way and the sin that so easily holds us back.

Hebrews 12:1 NCV

It has been said on many occasions that life is a team sport. So, too, is learning how to live. If we are to become mature believers—and if we seek to discover God's purposes in our everyday lives—we need worthy examples and wise mentors.

Are you walking with the wise? Are you spending time with people you admire? Are you learning how to live from people who know how to live? If you genuinely seek to walk with God, then you will walk with those who walk with Him.

We urgently need people who encourage and inspire us to move toward God and away from the world's enticing pleasures.

Jim Cymbala

It's the things you learn after you know it all that really count.

Vance Havner

A TIMELY TIP

Today, spend a few minutes thinking about the lessons that God is trying to teach you. Focus on one area of your life that needs attention now. And remember, it's always the right time to learn something new.

IN SEARCH OF ANSWERS

You will seek Me and find Me when you search for Me with all your heart.
Jeremiah 29:13 Holman CSB

You've got questions? God's got answers. And if you'd like to hear from Him, here's precisely what you must do: petition Him with a sincere heart; be still; be patient; and listen. Then, in His own time and in His own fashion, God will answer your questions and give you guidance for the journey ahead.

Today, turn over everything to your Creator. Pray constantly about matters great and small. Seek God's instruction and His direction. And remember: God hears your prayers and answers them. But He won't answer the prayers that you don't get around to praying. So pray early and often. And then wait patiently for answers that are sure to come.

The story of every great Christian achievement is the history of answered prayer.

E. M. Bounds

Where there is much prayer, there will be much of the Spirit; where there is much of the Spirit, there will be ever-increasing power.

Andrew Murray

A TIMELY TIP

When God says "No," that's good! Why? Because God knows what's best; God wants what's best; and God is trying to lead you to a place that is best for you. So trust Him . . . especially when He says "No."

NOVEMBER 12

SERVING GOD . . . WITH HUMILITY

Jesus sat down and called the twelve apostles to him. He said, "Whoever wants to be the most important must be last of all and servant of all."

Mark 9:35 NCV

The teachings of Jesus are clear: We achieve greatness through service to others. But, as weak human beings, we sometimes fall short as we seek to puff ourselves up and glorify our own accomplishments. Jesus commands otherwise. He teaches us that the most esteemed men and women are not the self-congratulatory leaders of society but are instead the humblest of servants.

Today, you may feel the temptation to build yourself up in the eyes of your neighbors. Resist that temptation. Instead, serve your neighbors quietly and without fanfare. Find a need and fill it . . . humbly. Lend a helping hand and share a word of kindness . . . anonymously, for this is God's way.

As a humble servant, you will glorify yourself not before people, but before God, and that's what God intends. After all, earthly glory is fleeting: here today and all too soon gone. But, heavenly glory endures throughout eternity. So, the choice is yours: Either you can lift yourself up here on earth and be humbled in heaven, or vice versa. Choose vice versa.

In Jesus, the service of God and the service of the least of the brethren were one.

Dietrich Bonhoeffer

A TIMELY TIP

Wherever you happen to be—whatever your age, whatever your circumstances—you can find people to serve and ways to serve. So what are you waiting for?

FINDING PURPOSE THROUGH CHARITY

Happy is the person who thinks about the poor. When trouble comes, the Lord will save him.

Psalm 41:1 NCV

God's Words commands us to be generous, compassionate servants to those who need our support. As believers, we have been richly blessed by our Creator. We, in turn, are called to share our gifts, our possessions, our testimonies, and our talents.

Concentration camp survivor Corrie ten Boom correctly observed, "The measure of a life is not its duration but its donation." These words remind us that the quality of our lives is determined not by what are able to take from others, but instead by what we are able to share with others.

The thread of generosity is woven into the very fabric of Christ's teachings. If we are to be His disciples, then we, too, must be cheerful, generous, courageous givers. Our Savior expects no less from us. And He deserves no less.

Selfishness is as far from Christianity as darkness is from light.

C. H. Spurgeon

We can't do everything, but can we do anything more valuable than invest ourselves in another?

Elisabeth Elliot

A TIMELY TIP

Investing in God's work, including helping the poor, is always the right thing to do. Do something every day that helps another person have a better life.

WORDS WORTHY OF OUR SAVIOR

When you talk, do not say harmful things, but say what people need—words that will help others become stronger. Then what you say will do good to those who listen to you.

Ephesians 4:29 NCV

A re you a person who consistently strives to speak words that are pleasing to God? Hopefully so. If you genuinely desire to be godly, your words and your actions must demonstrate your faithfulness to the Creator.

Today, as you fulfill the responsibilities that God has placed before you, ask yourself this question: "Do my words and deeds bear witness to the ultimate truth that God has placed in my heart, or am I allowing the pressures of everyday life to overwhelm me?" It's a profound question that only you can answer.

Of course you must never take the Lord's name in vain, but it doesn't stop there. You must also strive to speak words of encouragement, words that lift others up, words that give honor to your Heavenly Father.

The Bible clearly warns that you will be judged by the words you speak, so choose those words carefully. And remember: God is always listening.

When you talk, choose the very same words that you would use if Jesus were looking over your shoulder. Because He is.

Marie T. Freeman

A TIMELY TIP

If you want to keep from hurting other people's feelings, don't open your mouth until you've turned on your brain.

A NEW DAY, A NEW PATH

Now that you are obedient children of God do not live as you did in the past. You did not understand, so you did the evil things you wanted. But be holy in all you do, just as God, the One who called you, is holy.

1 Peter 1:14–15 NCV

How will you respond to Christ's sacrifice? Will you take up His cross and follow Him (Luke 9:23), or will you choose another path? When you place your hopes squarely at the foot of the cross, when you place Jesus squarely at the center of your life, you will be blessed.

The 19th-century writer Hannah Whitall Smith observed, "The crucial question for each of us is this: What do you think of Jesus, and do you yet have a personal acquaintance with Him?" Indeed, the answer to that question determines the quality, the course, and the direction of our lives today and for all eternity.

Let us put down our old ways and pick up His cross. Let us walk the path that He walked.

No Christian can have a sacred ambition for holiness which the Lord is not prepared to fulfill.

C. H. Spurgeon

A TIMELY TIP

Following Christ is a daily journey. When you decide to walk in the footsteps of the Master, that means that you're agreeing to be a disciple seven days a week, not just on Sunday. Remember the words of Vance Havner: "We must live in all kinds of days, both high days and low days, in simple dependence upon Christ as the branch on the vine. This is the supreme experience."

SELECTING YOUR ROADMAP

Teach me, O Lord, the way of Your statutes, and I shall keep it to the end.

Psalm 119:33 NKJV

As you look to the future and decide upon the direction of your life, what will you use as your roadmap? Will you trust God's Holy Word and use it as an indispensable tool to guide your steps? Or will you choose a different map to guide your steps? The map you choose will determine the quality of your journey and its ultimate destination.

The Bible is the ultimate guide for life; make it your guidebook as well. When you do, you can be comforted in the knowledge that your steps are guided by a Source of wisdom and truth that never fails.

The Bible was not given to increase our knowledge but to change our lives.

D. L. Moody

Trust the past to God's mercy, the present to God's love, and the future to God's providence.

St. Augustine

A TIMELY TIP

If you have doubts, fears, or worries, talk things over with your most trustworthy friends and with your parents. And be sure to talk to God, too. It's better to talk about troubles than it is to worry about them.

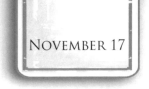
STEWARDSHIP OF YOUR TIME

Teach us to number our days carefully so that we may develop wisdom in our hearts.

Psalm 90:12 Holman CSB

Time is a nonrenewable gift from God. But sometimes, we treat our time here on earth as if it were not a gift at all: We may be tempted to invest our lives in trivial pursuits and petty diversions. But our Father beckons each of us to a higher calling.

An important element of our stewardship to God is the way that we choose to spend the time He has entrusted to us. Each waking moment holds the potential to do a good deed, to say a kind word, or to offer a heartfelt prayer. Our challenge, as believers, is to use our time wisely in the service of God's work and in accordance with His plan for our lives.

Each day is a special treasure to be savored and celebrated. May we—as Christians who have so much to celebrate—never fail to praise our Creator by rejoicing in this glorious day, and by using it wisely.

Our leisure, even our play, is a matter of serious concern. There is no neutral ground in the universe: every square inch, every split second, is claimed by God and counterclaimed by Satan.

C. S. Lewis

The work of God is appointed. There is always enough time to do the will of God.

Elisabeth Elliot

A TIMELY TIP

Feeling overwhelmed? Perhaps you're not doing a very good job of setting priorities—or perhaps you're allowing other people to set your priorities for you. In either case, perhaps it's time for a change.

TODAY'S BIBLE READING
Old Testament: Ezekiel 6-7
New Testament: James 1

A GOD OF POSSIBILITIES

But Jesus looked at them and said, "With men this is impossible, but with God all things are possible."

Matthew 19:26 Holman CSB

If you really want to know God, you must be willing to worship Him seven days a week, not just on Sunday.

God has a wonderful plan for your life, and an important part of that plan includes the time that you set aside for praise and worship. Every life, including yours, is based upon some form of worship. The question is not whether you will worship, but what you worship.

If you choose to worship God, you will receive a bountiful harvest of joy, peace, and abundance. But if you distance yourself from God by foolishly worshipping earthly possessions and personal gratification, you're making a huge mistake. So do this: Worship God today and every day. Worship Him with sincerity and thanksgiving. Write His name on your heart and rest assured that He, too, has written your name on His.

The fact that we were created to enjoy God and to worship him forever is etched upon our souls.

Jim Cymbala

Worship is wonder, love, and praise. Not only does it cause us to contemplate and appreciate our holy God, but it gives us vitality, vigor, and a desire to obey Him.

Franklin Graham

A TIMELY TIP

When you worship God with a sincere heart, He will guide your steps and bless your life.

THE REWARDS OF RIGHTEOUSNESS

Test all things; hold fast what is good. Abstain from every form of evil.

1 Thessalonians 5:21-22 NKJV

When we seek righteousness in our own lives—and when we seek the companionship of those who do likewise—we reap the spiritual rewards that God intends for us to enjoy. When we behave ourselves as godly young men and women, we honor God. When we live righteously and according to God's commandments, He blesses us in ways that we cannot fully understand.

Today, as you fulfill your responsibilities, hold fast that which is good, and associate yourself with believers who behave themselves in like fashion. When you do, your good works will serve as a powerful example for others and as a worthy offering to your Creator.

Our souls were made to live in an upper atmosphere, and we stifle and choke if we live on any lower level. Our eyes were made to look off from these heavenly heights, and our vision is distorted by any lower gazing.

Hannah Whitall Smith

Christianity says we were created by a righteous God to flourish and be exhilarated in a righteous environment. God has "wired" us in such a way that the more righteous we are, the more we'll actually enjoy life.

Bill Hybels

A TIMELY TIP

You shouldn't be overly fearful of displeasing your friends, but you should be very fearful of displeasing God.

PRAYERFUL HEARTS AND WILLING HANDS

So you may walk in the way of goodness, and keep to the paths of righteousness. For the upright will dwell in the land, And the blameless will remain in it.

Proverbs 2:20-21 NKJV

The old adage is both familiar and true: We must pray as if everything depended upon God, but work as if everything depended upon us. Yet sometimes, when we are weary and discouraged, we may allow our worries to sap our energy and our hope. God has other intentions. God intends that we pray for things, and He intends that we be willing to work for the things that we pray for. More importantly, God intends that our work should become His work.

Are you willing to work diligently for yourself and for your God? And are you willing to engage in work that is pleasing to your Creator? If so, you can expect your Heavenly Father to bring forth a rich harvest.

And if you have concerns about the inevitable challenges of everyday living, take those concerns to God in prayer. He will guide your steps, He will steady your hand, He will calm your fears, and He will reward your efforts.

Great relief and satisfaction can come from seeking God's priorities for us in each season, discerning what is "best" in the midst of many noble opportunities, and pouring our most excellent energies into those things.

Beth Moore

A TIMELY TIP

When your good works speak for themselves, don't interrupt.

QUIET CHARITY

Be careful not to practice your righteousness in front of people, to be seen by them. Otherwise, you will have no reward from your Father in heaven.

Matthew 6:1 Holman CSB

Hymn writer Fanny Crosby wrote, "To God be the glory; great thing He hath done!" But sometimes, because we are imperfect human beings, we seek the glory. Sometimes, when we do good deeds, we seek to glorify our achievements in a vain attempt to build ourselves up in the eyes of our neighbors. To do so is a profound mistake.

God's Word gives specific instructions about how we should approach our acts of charity: The glory must go to God, not to us. All praise belongs to the Giver of all good gifts: our Father in heaven. We are simply conduits for His generosity, and we must remain humble . . . extremely humble.

Abundant living means abundant giving.

E. Stanley Jones

No matter how heavy the burden, daily strength is given, so I expect we need not give ourselves any concern as to what the outcome will be. We must simply go forward.

Annie Armstrong

A TIMELY TIP

Today, challenge your faith by thinking of at least one small, practical step you can take to help someone in need.

CONCERNING THE LOVE OF MONEY

Keep your lives free from the love of money, and be satisfied with what you have.

Hebrews 13:5 NCV

In our modern society, we need money to live. But as Christians, we must never make the acquisition of money the central focus of our lives. Money is a tool, but it should never overwhelm our sensibilities. The focus of life must be squarely on things spiritual, not things material.

Whenever we place our love for material possessions above our love for God—or when we yield to the countless other temptations of everyday living—we find ourselves engaged in a struggle between good and evil, a clash between God and Satan. Our responses to these struggles have implications that echo throughout our families and throughout our communities. Let us choose wisely by freeing ourselves from that subtle yet powerful temptation: the temptation to love the world more than we love God.

Servants of God are always more concerned about ministry than money.

Rick Warren

When we put people before possessions in our hearts, we are sowing seeds of enduring satisfaction.

Beverly LaHaye

A TIMELY TIP

Everything we have is on loan from God. Holocaust survivor Corrie ten Boom writes, "I have held many things in my hands, and I have lost them all; but whatever I have placed in God's hands, that I still possess." Remember: your real riches are in heaven, so conduct yourself accordingly.

THE SEARCH FOR WISDOM

If you don't know what you're doing, pray to the Father. He loves to help. You'll get his help, and won't be condescended to when you ask for it. Ask boldly, believingly, without a second thought. People who "worry their prayers" are like wind-whipped waves. Don't think you're going to get anything from the Master that way, adrift at sea, keeping all your options open.

James 1:5-8 MSG

Do you seek the wisdom that only God can give? If so, ask Him for it! If you ask God for guidance, He will not withhold it. If you petition Him sincerely, and if you genuinely seek to form a relationship with Him, your Heavenly Father will guide your steps and enlighten your heart. But be forewarned: You will not acquire God's wisdom without obeying His commandments. Why? Because God's wisdom is more than just a collection of thoughts; it is, first and foremost, a way of life.

Wisdom is as wisdom does. So if you sincerely seek God's wisdom, don't be satisfied to learn something; make up your mind to become something. And then, as you allow God to remake you in the image of His Son, you will most surely become wise.

Wise people listen to wise instruction, especially instruction from the Word of God.

Warren Wiersbe

A TIMELY TIP

If you'd like to become a little wiser, the place to start is with God. And His wisdom isn't very hard to find; it's right there on the pages of the Book He wrote.

GIVING AN ACCOUNT
OF OURSELVES

Yes, each of us will have to give a personal account to God.

Romans 14:12 NLT

For most of us, it is a daunting thought: one day, perhaps soon, we'll come face-to-face with our Heavenly Father, and we'll be called to account for our actions here on earth. Our personal histories will certainly not be surprising to God; He already knows everything about us. But the full scope of our activities may be surprising to us: some of us will be pleasantly surprised; others will not be.

Today, do whatever you can to ensure that your thoughts and your deeds are pleasing to your Creator. Because you will, at some point in the future, be called to account for your actions. And the future may be sooner than you think.

Don't worry about what you do not understand. Worry about what you do understand in the Bible but do not live by.

Corrie ten Boom

God provides the ingredients for our daily bread but expects us to do the baking. With our own hands!

Barbara Johnson

A TIMELY TIP

Success according to God requires perseverance, prayer, and patience—if you want to be successful, you'll need all three.

THE TIME TO PLANT SEEDS

Those who wait for perfect weather will never plant seeds; those who look at every cloud will never harvest crops. Plant early in the morning, and work until evening, because you don't know if this or that will succeed. They might both do well.

Ecclesiastes 11:4,6 NCV

Once the season for planting is upon us, the time to plant seeds is when we make time to plant seeds. And when it comes to planting God's seeds in the soil of eternity, the only certain time that we have is now. Yet because we are fallible human beings with limited vision and misplaced priorities, we may be tempted to delay.

If we hope to reap a bountiful harvest for God, for our families, and for ourselves, we must plant now by defeating a dreaded human frailty: the habit of procrastination. Procrastination often results from our shortsighted attempts to postpone temporary discomfort.

A far better strategy is this: Whatever "it" is, do it now. When you do, you won't have to worry about "it" later.

Do noble things, do not dream them all day long.

Charles Kingsley

We spend our lives dreaming of the future, not realizing that a little of it slips away every day.

Barbara Johnson

A TIMELY TIP

Pick out one important obligation that you've been putting off. Then, take at least one specific step toward the completion of the task you've been avoiding. Even if you don't finish the job, you'll discover that it's easier to finish a job that you've already begun than to finish a job that you've never started.

TODAY'S BIBLE READING
Old Testament: Ezekiel 25-27
New Testament: 1 Peter 4

WHAT WE BELIEVE
AND HOW WE BEHAVE

Not everyone who says to me, "Lord, Lord," will enter the kingdom of heaven, but only he who does the will of my Father who is in heaven.

Matthew 7:21 NIV

Face facts: this world is inhabited by quite a few people who are very determined to do bad things. The devil and his human helpers are working 24/7 to cause pain and heartbreak in every corner of the globe . . . including your corner. So you'd better beware.

Your job, if you choose to accept it, is to recognize bad behavior and fight it. How? By standing up for your beliefs, that's how!

The moment that you decide to fight mischief whenever you see it, you can no longer be a lukewarm, halfhearted Christian. And, when you are no longer a lukewarm Christian, God rejoices (and the devil doesn't).

So stand up for your beliefs. And remember this: in the battle of good versus evil, the devil never takes a day off . . . and neither should you.

To believe God is to worship God.

Martin Luther

Believe and do what God says. The life-changing consequences will be limitless, and the results will be confidence and peace of mind.

Franklin Graham

A TIMELY TIP

When you live in accordance with your beliefs, God will guide your steps and protect your heart.

SPIRITUAL MATURITY, DAY BY DAY

When I was a child, I spoke and thought and reasoned as a child does. But when I grew up, I put away childish things.

1 Corinthians 13:11 NLT

The path to spiritual maturity unfolds day by day. Each day offers the opportunity to worship God, to ignore God, or to rebel against God. When we worship Him with our prayers, our words, our thoughts, and our actions, we are blessed by the richness of our relationship with the Father. But if we ignore God altogether or intentionally rebel against His commandments, we rob ourselves of His blessings.

Today offers yet another opportunity for spiritual growth. If you choose, you can seize that opportunity by obeying God's Word, by seeking His will, and by walking with His Son.

God's goal is that we move toward maturity—all our past failures and faults notwithstanding.

Charles Swindoll

One of the marks of Spiritual maturity is a consistent, Spirit-controlled life.

Vonette Bright

A TIMELY TIP

Spiritual maturity is a journey, not a destination. A growing relationship with God should be your highest priority.

BEYOND STUBBORNNESS

Pride comes before destruction, and an arrogant spirit before a fall.

Proverbs 16:18 Holman CSB

Since the days of Adam and Eve, human beings have been strong-willed and rebellious. Our rebellion stems, in large part, from an intense desire to do things "our way" instead of "God's way." But when we pridefully choose to forsake God's path for our lives, we do ourselves a sincere injustice . . . and we are penalized because of our stubbornness.

God's Word warns us to be humble, not prideful. God instructs us to be obedient, not rebellious. God wants us to do things His way. When we do, we reap a bountiful harvest of blessings—more blessings than we can count. But when we pridefully rebel against our Creator, we sow the seeds of our own destruction, and we reap a sad, sparse, bitter harvest. May we sow—and reap—accordingly.

God uses broken things: broken soil and broken clouds to produce grain; broken grain to produce bread; broken bread to feed our bodies. He wants our stubbornness broken into humble obedience.

Vance Havner

Much bending breaks the bough; much unbending the mind.

Francis Bacon

A TIMELY TIP

If you're stubbornly rebelling against God, you're heading for trouble, and fast.

THE ART OF GODLY ACCEPTANCE

People may make plans in their minds, but the Lord decides what they will do.

Proverbs 16:9 NCV

Sometimes, we must accept life on its terms, not our own. Life has a way of unfolding, not as we will, but as it will. And sometimes, there is precious little we can do to change things.

When events transpire that are beyond our control, we have a choice: we can either learn the art of acceptance, or we can make ourselves miserable as we struggle to change the unchangeable.

We must entrust the things we cannot change to God. Once we have done so, we can prayerfully and faithfully tackle the important work that He has placed before us: the things we can change.

Our Lord never asks us to decide for Him; He asks us to yield to Him—a very different matter.

Oswald Chambers

We honor God by asking for great things when they are a part of His promise. We dishonor Him and cheat ourselves when we ask for molehills where He has promised mountains.

Vance Havner

A TIMELY TIP

Acceptance means learning to trust God more. Today, think of at least one aspect of your life that you've been reluctant to accept, and then prayerfully ask God to help you trust Him more by accepting the past.

WHEN WE DO OUR PART, GOD DOES HIS

And we know that in all things God works for the good of those who love him, who have been called according to his purpose.

Romans 8:28 NIV

L ife can be challenging, but fear not. God loves you, and He will protect you. In times of trouble, He will comfort you; in times of sorrow, He will dry your tears. When you are troubled, or weak, or sorrowful, God is as near as your next breath. Build your life on the rock that cannot be shaken . . . trust in God.

We have ample evidence that the Lord is able to guide. The promises cover every imaginable situation. All we need to do is to take the hand he stretches out.

Elisabeth Elliot

No matter what we are going through, no matter how long the waiting for answers, of one thing we may be sure. God is faithful. He keeps His promises. What He starts, He finishes . . . including His perfect work in us.

Gloria Gaither

A TIMELY TIP

God can handle it. Corrie ten Boom advised, "God's all-sufficiency is a major. Your inability is a minor. Major in majors, not in minors." Enough said.

LIFETIME LEARNING

Above all and before all, do this: Get Wisdom! Write this at the top of your list: Get Understanding!

Proverbs 4:7 MSG

Whether you're fifteen or a hundred and fifteen, you've still got lots to learn. Even if you're a very wise person, God isn't finished with you yet. Why? Because lifetime learning is part of God's plan—and He certainly hasn't finished teaching you some very important lessons.

Do you seek to live a life of righteousness and wisdom? If so, you must continue to study the ultimate source of wisdom: the Word of God. You must associate, day in and day out, with godly men and women. And, you must act in accordance with your beliefs. When you study God's Word and live according to His commandments, you will become wise . . . and you will be a blessing to your friends, to your family, and to the world.

While chastening is always difficult, if we look to God for the lesson we should learn, we will see spiritual fruit.

Vonette Bright

Wisdom is the God-given ability to see life with rare objectivity and to handle life with rare stability.

Charles Swindoll

A TIMELY TIP

Never stop learning. Think of it like this: when you're through learning, you're through.

HABITS THAT ARE PLEASING TO GOD

I the Lord search the heart and examine the mind, to reward a man according to his conduct, according to what his deeds deserve.

Jeremiah 17:10 NIV

It's an old saying and a true one: First, you make your habits, and then your habits make you. Some habits will inevitably bring you closer to God; other habits will lead you away from the path He has chosen for you. If you sincerely desire to improve your spiritual health, you must honestly examine the habits that make up the fabric of your day. And you must abandon those habits that are displeasing to God.

If you trust God, and if you keep asking for His help, He can transform your life. If you sincerely ask Him to help you, the same God who created the universe will help you defeat the harmful habits that have heretofore defeated you. So, if at first you don't succeed, keep praying. God is listening, and He's ready to help you become a better person if you ask Him . . . so ask today.

You will never change your life until you change something you do daily.

John Maxwell

Since behaviors become habits, make them work with you and not against you.

E. Stanley Jones

A TIMELY TIP

Choose your habits carefully. Habits are easier to make than they are to break, so be careful!

FOLLOWING HIS FOOTSTEPS

But whoever keeps His word, truly in him the love of God is perfected. This is how we know we are in Him: the one who says he remains in Him should walk just as He walked.

1 John 2:5-6 Holman CSB

Life is a series of decisions and choices. Each day, we make countless decisions that can bring us closer to God . . . or not. When we live according to God's commandments, we reap bountiful rewards: abundance, hope, and peace, for starters. But, when we turn our backs upon God by disobeying Him, we bring needless suffering upon ourselves and our families.

Do you seek to walk in the footsteps of the One from Galilee, or will you choose another path? If you sincerely seek God's peace and His blessings, then you must strive to imitate God's Son.

Thomas Brooks spoke for believers of every generation when he observed, "Christ is the sun, and all the watches of our lives should be set by the dial of his motion." Christ, indeed, is the ultimate Savior of mankind and the personal Savior of those who believe in Him. As His servants, we should walk in His footsteps as we share His love and His message with a world that needs both.

It is the highest duty of religion to imitate Him whom you adore.

St. Augustine

A person who gazes and keeps on gazing at Jesus becomes like him in appearance.

E. Stanley Jones

A TIMELY TIP

If you are a Christian, the One you should seek to imitate is Christ.

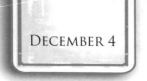

AIMING HIGH

I am able to do all things through Him who strengthens me.

Philippians 4:13 Holman CSB

Are you willing to dream big dreams? Hopefully so; after all, God promises that we can do "all things" through Him. Yet most of us, even the most devout among us, live far below our potential. We take half measures; we dream small dreams; we waste precious time and energy on the distractions of the world. But God has other plans for us. Our Creator intends that we live faithfully, hopefully, courageously, and abundantly. He knows that we are capable of so much more; and He wants us to do the things we're capable of doing; and He wants us to start doing those things now.

You cannot out-dream God.

John Eldredge

It would be a dreadful thing to hand one's confidence in such a fragile thing as a dream.

C. H. Spurgeon

A TIMELY TIP

You can dream big dreams, but you can never out-dream God. His plans for you are even bigger than you can imagine.

ACCORDING TO GOD

The counsel of the LORD stands forever, the plans of His heart from generation to generation.

Psalm 33:11 NASB

When you have a question that you simply can't answer, whom do you ask? When you face a difficult decision, to whom do you turn for counsel? To friends? To mentors? To family members? Or do you turn first to the Ultimate source of wisdom? The answers to life's Big Questions start with God and with the teachings of His Holy Word.

God's wisdom stands forever. God's Word is a light for every generation. Make it your light as well. Use the Bible as a compass for the next stage of your life's journey. Use it as the yardstick by which your behavior is measured. And as you carefully consult the pages of God's Word, prayerfully ask Him to reveal the wisdom that you need. When you take your concerns to God, He will not turn you away; He will, instead, offer answers that are tested and true. Your job is to ask, to listen, and to trust.

God Himself is what enlightens understanding about everything else in life. Knowledge about any subject is fragmentary without the enlightenment that comes from His relationship to it.

Beth Moore

Let him who wants a true church cling to the Word by which everything is upheld.

Martin Luther

A TIMELY TIP

God's wisdom is perfect, and it's available to you. So if you want to become wise, become a student of God's Word and a follower of His Son.

PRAISE AND CRITICISM

Our only goal is to please God whether we live here or there, because we must all stand before Christ to be judged.

2 Corinthians 5:9-10 NCV

Rick Warren observed, "Those who follow the crowd usually get lost in it." We know those words to be true, but oftentimes we fail to live by them. Instead of trusting God for guidance, we imitate our friends and suffer the consequences. Instead of seeking to please our Father in heaven, we strive to please our peers, with decidedly mixed results. Instead of doing the right thing, we do the "easy" thing or the "popular" thing. And when we do, we pay a high price for our shortsightedness.

Would you like a time-tested formula for successful living? Here is a simple formula that is proven and true: don't give in to peer pressure. Period.

Instead of getting lost in the crowd, you should find guidance from God. Does this sound too simple? Perhaps it is simple, but it is also the only way to reap all the marvelous riches that God has in store for you.

When we are set free from the bondage of pleasing others, when we are free from currying others' favor and others' approval—then no one will be able to make us miserable or dissatisfied. And then, if we know we have pleased God, contentment will be our consolation.

Kay Arthur

It is impossible to please everybody. It's not impossible to please God. So try pleasing God.

Criswell Freeman

A TIMELY TIP

If you're more concerned with pleasing people than pleasing God, it's time for a change—a BIG change.

THE ULTIMATE PARTNER

For we are God's co-workers. You are God's field, God's building.

1 Corinthians 3:9 Holman CSB

I f you want to be successful—genuinely successful in the things that really matter—you need a partner. That Partner is God. And the good news is this: When you humbly and sincerely ask God to become your partner, He will grant your request and transform your life.

Is your life a testimony to the personal relationship that you enjoy with your Heavenly Father? Or have you compartmentalized your faith to a few hours on Sunday morning? If you genuinely wish to make God your fulltime partner, you must allow Him to reign over every aspect of your life and every day of your week. When you do, you'll be amazed at the things that the two of you, working together, can accomplish.

God does not want us to work for Him, nor does He want to be our helper. Rather, He wants to do His work in and through us.

Vonette Bright

You get the most out of your work when you view yourself as a servant.

Charles Stanley

A TIMELY TIP

Goofing off is contagious. That's why it's important for you to hang out with people who are interested in getting the job done right—and getting it done right now!

GOD IS PERFECT; WE ARE NOT

Since we've compiled this long and sorry record as sinners (both us and them) and proved that we are utterly incapable of living the glorious lives God wills for us, God did it for us. Out of sheer generosity he put us in right standing with himself. A pure gift. He got us out of the mess we're in and restored us to where he always wanted us to be. And he did it by means of Jesus Christ.

Romans 3:23 MSG

When God made you, He equipped you with an array of talents and abilities that are uniquely yours. It's up to you to discover those talents and to use them, but sometimes your own perfectionism may get in the way.

If you're your own worst critic, give it up. After all, God doesn't expect you to be perfect, and if that's okay with Him, then it should be okay with you, too.

When you accepted Christ as your Savior, God accepted you for all eternity. Now, it's your turn to accept yourself. When you do, you'll feel a tremendous weight being lifted from your shoulders. And that's as it should be. After all, only one earthly being ever lived life to perfection, and He was the Son of God. The rest of us have fallen short of God's standard and need to be accepting of our own limitations as well as the limitations of others.

The greatest destroyer of good works is the desire to do great works.

C. H. Spurgeon

A TIMELY TIP

One of the wisest choices you can make is the choice to take care of your body. That means saying "Yes" to a healthy lifestyle and "No" to any substance that has the potential to harm you.

APART FROM THE WORLD

Don't love the world's ways. Don't love the world's goods. Love of the world squeezes out love for the Father. Practically everything that goes on in the world— wanting your own way, wanting everything for yourself, wanting to appear important—has nothing to do with the Father. It just isolates you from him. The world and all its wanting, wanting, wanting is on the way out—but whoever does what God wants is set for eternity.

1 John 2:15-17 MSG

We live in the world, but we must not worship it. Our duty is to place God first and everything else second. But because we are fallible beings with imperfect faith, placing God in His rightful place is often difficult. In fact, at every turn, or so it seems, we are tempted to do otherwise.

The 21st-century world is a noisy, distracting place filled with countless opportunities to stray from God's will. The world seems to cry, "Worship me with your time, your money, your energy, and your thoughts!" But God commands otherwise: He commands us to worship Him and Him alone; everything else must be secondary.

Our joy ends where love of the world begins.

C. H. Spurgeon

As we have by faith said no to sin, so we should by faith say yes to God and set our minds on things above, where Christ is seated in the heavenlies.

Vonette Bright

A TIMELY TIP

The world's power to distract, detour, and destroy is formidable. Thankfully, God's power is even greater.

A PERFECT TIMETABLE

He has made everything beautiful in its time.

Ecclesiastes 3:11 NIV

Upon this we can trust: God's sense of timing is without error. God's timing may not coincide with our timing—which, by the way, is perfectly fine with God because He knows precisely what He's doing, even if we do not.

Perhaps you are impatient for God to reveal His plans for your life. If so, it is time to reread the third chapter of Ecclesiastes. Solomon's words will remind you that there is a time for every purpose under God's heaven—and that includes your purpose.

Will not the Lord's time be better than your time?

C. H. Spurgeon

God has a designated time when his promise will be fulfilled and the prayer will be answered.

Jim Cymbala

A TIMELY TIP

You should always trust God, and you should wait patiently for His plans to unfold. God's timing is best.

GOD'S PERSPECTIVE

He will teach us His ways, and we shall walk in His paths.

Isaiah 2:3 NKJV

For most of us, life is busy and complicated. Amid the rush and crush of the daily grind, it is easy to lose perspective . . . easy, but wrong. When our world seems to be spinning out of control, we must simply seek to regain perspective by slowing ourselves down and then turning our thoughts and prayers toward God.

The familiar words of Psalm 46:10 remind us to "Be still, and know that I am God" (NKJV). When we do so, we encounter the awesome presence of our loving Heavenly Father, and we are blessed beyond words. But, when we ignore the presence of our Creator, we rob ourselves of His perspective, His peace, and His joy.

Today and every day, set aside a time to be still before God. When you do, you can face the day's complications with the wisdom and power that only He can provide.

When considering the size of your problems, there are two categories that you should never worry about: the problems that are small enough for you to handle, and the ones that aren't too big for God to handle.

Marie T. Freeman

Earthly fears are no fears at all. Answer the big question of eternity, and the little questions of life fall into perspective.

Max Lucado

A TIMELY TIP

When you focus on the world, you lose perspective. When you focus on God's promises, you gain clearer perspective.

HELPING TO BEAR THE BURDENS

Carry each other's burdens, and in this way you will fulfill the law of Christ.

Galatians 6:2 NIV

Neighbors. We know that we are instructed to love them, and yet there's so little time . . . and we're so busy. No matter. As Christians, we are commanded by our Lord and Savior Jesus Christ to love our neighbors just as we love ourselves. We are not asked to love our neighbors, nor are we encouraged to do so. We are commanded to love them. Period.

This very day, you will encounter someone who needs a word of encouragement, or a pat on the back, or a helping hand, or a heartfelt prayer. And, if you don't reach out to that person, who will? If you don't take the time to understand the needs of your neighbors, who will? If you don't love your brothers and sisters, who will? So, today, look for a neighbor in need . . . and then do something to help. Father's orders.

He climbs highest who helps another up.

Zig Ziglar

In spite of our high-tech world and efficient procedures, people remain the essential ingredient of life. When we forget that, a strange thing happens: we start treating people like inconveniences instead of assets.

Charles Swindoll

A TIMELY TIP

Once you realize that Christianity is about serving other people, you focus less on yourself and more on other people.

GOD'S STRENGTH FOR THE DAY AHEAD

The Lord is my rock, my fortress, and my deliverer, my God, my mountain where I seek refuge. My shield, the horn of my salvation, my stronghold, my refuge, and my Savior.

2 Samuel 22:2-3 Holman CSB

God is a never-ending source of support and courage for those of us who call upon Him. When we are weary, He gives us strength. When we see no hope, God reminds us of His promises. When we grieve, God wipes away our tears.

Do the demands of this day threaten to overwhelm you? If so, you must rely not only upon your own resources, but also upon the promises of your Father in heaven. God will hold your hand and walk with you every day of your life if you let Him. So even if your circumstances are difficult, trust the Father. His love is eternal and His goodness endures forever.

If we take God's program, we can have God's power—not otherwise.

E. Stanley Jones

By ourselves we are not capable of suffering bravely, but the Lord possesses all the strength we lack and will demonstrate His power when we undergo persecution.

Corrie ten Boom

A TIMELY TIP

Because God is faithful, you can—and should—live courageously. When in doubt, do the courageous thing.

WALKING THE CHRISTIAN PATH

And don't be wishing you were someplace else or with someone else. Where you are right now is God's place for you. Live and obey and love and believe right there.

1 Corinthians 7:17 MSG

Each day, as we awaken from sleep, we are confronted with countless opportunities to serve God and to follow in the footsteps of His Son. When we do, our Heavenly Father guides our steps and blesses our endeavors.

As citizens of a fast-changing world, we face challenges that sometimes leave us feeling overworked, overcommitted, and overwhelmed. But God has different plans for us. He intends that we slow down long enough to praise Him and to glorify His Son. When we do, He lifts our spirits and enriches our lives.

Today provides a glorious opportunity to place yourself in the service of the One who is the Giver of all blessings. May you seek His will, may you trust His word, and may you walk in the footsteps of His Son.

The Bible says that being a Christian is not only a great way to die, but it's also the best way to live.

Bill Hybels

Life is a glorious opportunity.

Billy Graham

A TIMELY TIP

Life is a priceless gift from God. Spend time each day thanking God for His gift.

HAPPY TOMORROW

Whereas you do not know what will happen tomorrow. For what is your life? It is even a vapor that appears for a little time and then vanishes away.

James 4:14 NJKV

When will you rejoice at God's marvelous creation? Today or tomorrow? When will you accept His abundance: now or later? When will you accept the peace that can and should be yours? In the present moment or in the distant future? The answer, of course, is straightforward: the best moment to accept God's gifts is the present one.

Will you accept God's blessings now or later? Are you willing to give Him your full attention today? Hopefully so. He deserves it. And so, for that matter, do you.

Submit each day to God, knowing that He is God over all your tomorrows.

Kay Arthur

Our time is short! The time we can invest for God, in creative things, in receiving our fellowmen for Christ, is short!

Billy Graham

A TIMELY TIP

Take time to celebrate another day of life. And while you're at it, encourage your family and friends to join in the celebration.

BUSY WITH OUR THOUGHTS

So prepare your minds for service and have self-control.

1 Peter 1:13 NCV

Because we are human, we are always busy with our thoughts. We simply can't help ourselves. Our brains never shut off, and even while we're sleeping, we mull things over in our minds. The question is not if we will think; the question is how will we think and what will we think about.

Today, focus your thoughts on God and His will. And if you've been plagued by pessimism and doubt, stop thinking like that! Place your faith in God and give thanks for His blessings. Think optimistically about your world and your life. It's the wise way to use your mind. And besides, since you will always be busy with your thoughts, you might as well make those thoughts pleasing (to God) and helpful (to you and yours).

Do you feel the world is treating you well? If your attitude toward the world is excellent, you will receive excellent results. If you feel so-so about the world, your response from that world will be average. If you feel badly about your world, you will seem to have only negative feedback from life.

John Maxwell

Developing a positive attitude means working continually to find what is uplifting and encouraging.

Barbara Johnson

A TIMELY TIP

If you want to improve the quality of your thoughts, ask God to help you.

COMPASSION AND COURTESY IN A DISCOURTEOUS WORLD

Finally, all of you should be of one mind, full of sympathy toward each other, loving one another with tender hearts and humble minds.

1 Peter 3:8 NLT

As Christians, we are instructed to be courteous and compassionate. As believers, we are called to be gracious, humble, gentle, and kind. But sometimes, we fall short. Sometimes, amid the busyness and confusion of everyday life, we may neglect to share a kind word or a kind deed. This oversight hurts others, and it hurts us as well.

Today, slow yourself down and be alert for those who need your smile, your kind words, or your helping hand. Make kindness a centerpiece of your dealings with others. They will be blessed, and you will be, too. So make this promise to yourself and keep it: honor Christ by obeying His Golden Rule. He deserves no less. And neither, for that matter, do they.

If we have the true love of God in our hearts, we will show it in our lives. We will not have to go up and down the earth proclaiming it. We will show it in everything we say or do.

D. L. Moody

When you extend hospitality to others, you're not trying to impress people, you're trying to reflect God to them.

Max Lucado

A TIMELY TIP

The Golden Rule starts with you, so when in doubt, be a little kinder than necessary.

WHOM WE SHOULD JUDGE

Stop judging others, and you will not be judged. Stop criticizing others, or it will all come back on you. If you forgive others, you will be forgiven.

Luke 6:37 NLT

Even the most devoted Christians may fall prey to a powerful yet subtle temptation: the temptation to judge others. But as faithful believers, we are commanded to refrain from such behavior. The warning of Luke 6:37 is clear: "Judge not."

We are warned that to judge others is to invite fearful consequences: to the extent we judge them, so, too, will we be judged by God. Let us refrain, then, from judging our neighbors. Instead, let us forgive them and love them in the same way that God has forgiven us.

Christians think they are prosecuting attorneys or judges, when, in reality, God has called all of us to be witnesses.

Warren Wiersbe

Don't judge other people more harshly than you want God to judge you.

Marie T. Freeman

A TIMELY TIP

When you catch yourself being overly judgmental, try to stop yourself and interrupt your critical thoughts before you become angry.

WISDOM FROM THE HEART

But what happens when we live God's way? He brings gifts into our lives, much the same way that fruit appears in an orchard—things like affection for others, exuberance about life, serenity. We develop a willingness to stick with things, a sense of compassion in the heart, and a conviction that a basic holiness permeates things and people. We find ourselves involved in loyal commitments, not needing to force our way in life, able to marshal and direct our energies wisely. Legalism is helpless in bringing this about; it only gets in the way.

Galatians 5:22-23 MSG

When we genuinely open our hearts to God, He speaks to us through a small, still voice within. When He does, we can listen, or not. When we pay careful attention to the Father, He leads us along a path of His choosing, a path that leads to abundance, peace, joy, and eternal life. But when we choose to ignore God, we select a path that is not His, and we must endure the consequences of our shortsightedness.

Today, focus your thoughts and your prayers on the path that God intends for you to take. When you do, your loving Heavenly Father will speak to your heart. When He does, listen carefully . . . and trust Him.

Wisdom is knowledge applied. Head knowledge is useless on the battlefield. Knowledge stamped on the heart makes one wise.

Beth Moore

A TIMELY TIP

The more important the decision . . . the more carefully you should listen to your conscience.

THINK NOW, ACT LATER

Enthusiasm without knowledge is not good. If you act too quickly, you might make a mistake.

Proverbs 19:2 NCV

Are you, at times, just a little bit impulsive? Do you sometimes fail to look before you leap? If so, God wants to have a little chat with you.

God's Word is clear: as believers, we are called to lead lives of discipline, diligence, moderation, and maturity. But the world often tempts us to behave otherwise. Everywhere we turn, or so it seems, we are faced with powerful temptations to behave in undisciplined, ungodly ways.

God's Word instructs us to be disciplined in our thoughts and our actions; God's Word warns us against the dangers of impulsive behavior. As believers in a just God, we should act and react accordingly.

The man who prays ceases to be a fool.

Oswald Chambers

The first thing we have to do to receive God's guidance is to reevaluate our current guidance systems.

Bill Hybels

A TIMELY TIP

If you can't seem to put the brakes on impulsive behavior . . . you're not praying hard enough.

THE GIFT OF GRACE

For by grace you are saved through faith, and this is not from yourselves; it is God's gift—not from works, so that no one can boast.

Ephesians 2:8-9 Holman CSB

God has given us so many gifts, but none can compare with the gift of salvation. We have not earned our salvation; it is a gift from God. When we accept Christ into our hearts, we are saved by His grace.

The familiar words of Ephesians 2:8 make God's promise perfectly clear: It is by grace we have been saved, through faith. We are saved not because of our good deeds but because of our faith in Christ.

God's grace is the ultimate gift, and we owe to Him the ultimate in thanksgiving. Let us praise the Creator for His priceless gift, and let us share the Good News with all who cross our paths. We return our Father's love by accepting His grace and by sharing His message and His love. When we do, we are eternally blessed . . . and the Father smiles.

The life of faith is a daily exploration of the constant and countless ways in which God's grace and love are experienced.

Eugene Peterson

Grace is an outrageous blessing bestowed freely on a totally undeserving recipient.

Bill Hybels

A TIMELY TIP

Developing an attitude of gratitude is key to a joyful and satisfying life. So ask yourself this question: "Am I grateful enough?"

PROBLEM-SOLVING 101

People who do what is right may have many problems, but the Lord will solve them all.

Psalm 34:19 NCV

Life is an exercise in problem-solving. The question is not whether we will encounter problems; the real question is how we will choose to address them. When it comes to solving the problems of everyday living, we often know precisely what needs to be done, but we may be slow in doing it—especially if what needs to be done is difficult or uncomfortable for us. So we put off till tomorrow what should be done today.

The words of Psalm 34 remind us that the Lord solves problems for "people who do what is right." And usually, doing "what is right" means doing the uncomfortable work of confronting our problems sooner rather than later. So with no further ado, let the problem-solving begin . . . now.

Faith does not eliminate problems. Faith keeps you in a trusting relationship with God in the midst of your problems.

C. H. Spurgeon

The closer we are to God, the more confidence we place in him when we are under fire.

C. H. Spurgeon

A TIMELY TIP

When tough times arrive, you should work as if everything depended on you and pray as if everything depended on God.

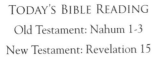

YOUR SHINING LIGHT

You are the light of the world. A city situated on a hill cannot be hidden. No one lights a lamp and puts it under a basket, but rather on a lampstand, and it gives light for all who are in the house. In the same way, let your light shine before men, so that they may see your good works and give glory to your Father in heaven.

Matthew 5:14-16 Holman CSB

Whether we like it or not, we are role models. Hopefully, the lives we lead and the choices we make will serve as enduring examples of the spiritual abundance that is available to all who worship God and obey His commandments.

Ask yourself this question: Are you the kind of role model that you would want to emulate? If so, congratulations. But if certain aspects of your behavior could stand improvement, the best day to begin your self-improvement regimen is this one. Because whether you realize it or not, people you love are watching your behavior, and they're learning how to live. You owe it to them—and to yourself—to live righteously and well.

It is a great deal better to live a holy life than to talk about it. Lighthouses do not ring bells and fire cannons to call attention to their shining—they just shine.

D. L. Moody

We must mirror God's love in the midst of a world full of hatred. We are the mirrors of God's love, so we may show Jesus by our lives.

Corrie ten Boom

A TIMELY TIP

Your friends are watching: so be the kind of example that God wants you to be—be a good example.

GOD'S PERFECT LOVE

This is what real love is: It is not our love for God; it is God's love for us in sending his Son to be the way to take away our sins.

1 John 4:10 NCV

If God had a refrigerator in heaven, your picture would be on it. And that fact should make you feel very good about the person you are and the person you can become.

God's love for you is bigger and more wonderful than you can imagine, So do this, and do it right now: accept God's love with open arms and welcome His Son Jesus into your heart. When you do, you'll feel better about yourself . . . and your life will be changed forever.

God proved his love on the cross. When Christ hung, and bled, and died it was God saying to the world—I love you.

Billy Graham

God wants to emancipate his people; he wants to set them free. He wants his people to be not slaves but sons. He wants them governed not by law but by love.

Max Lucado

A TIMELY TIP

When you invite the love of God into your heart, everything changes . . . including you.

SUCCESS ACCORDING TO GOD

Live the way the Lord your God has commanded you so that you may live and have what is good.

Deuteronomy 5:33 NCV

How do you define success? Do you define it as the accumulation of material possessions or the adulation of your neighbors? If so, you need to reorder your priorities. Genuine success has little to do with fame or fortune; it has everything to do with God's gift of love and with His promise of salvation.

If you have allowed Christ to reign over your life, you are already a towering success in the eyes of God, but there is still more that you can do. You task—as a believer who has been touched by the Creator's grace—is to accept the spiritual abundance and peace that He offers through the person of His Son. Then, you can share the healing message of God's love and His abundance with a world that desperately needs both. When you do, you have reached the pinnacle of success.

The battles of life are not easy, but God has given us the equipment we need to succeed.

Warren Wiersbe

In essence, my testimony is that there is life after failure: abundant, effective, spirit-filled life for those who are willing to repent hard and work hard.

Beth Moore

A TIMELY TIP

How do you define success? If you're wise, you define it in accordance with God's Word.

NEW AND IMPROVED

Your old life is dead. Your new life, which is your real life—even though invisible to spectators—is with Christ in God. He is your life.

Colossians 3:3 MSG

Has your relationship with Jesus transformed you into an extremely different person? Hopefully so! Otherwise, you're missing out on the joy and abundance that can be yours through Christ.

Think, for a moment, about the "old" you, the person you were before you invited Christ to reign over your heart. Now, think about the "new" you, the person you've become since then. Is there a difference between the "old" version of you and the "new-and-improved" version? There should be! And that difference should be evident to you, to your family, and to your friends.

When you invited Christ to reign over your heart, you became a radically new creation. This day offers yet another opportunity to behave yourself like that new person. When you do, God will guide your steps and bless your endeavors . . . forever.

Are you willing to make radical changes for Jesus? If so, you may be certain of this fact: He's standing at the door of your heart, patiently waiting to form an extreme, life-altering relationship with you.

Believe and do what God says. The life-changing consequences will be limitless, and the results will be confidence and peace of mind.

Franklin Graham

A TIMELY TIP

Jesus made radical sacrifices for you, and now He's asking you to make radical changes for Him. Are you willing to be a radical Christian? If so, you will be blessed for your willingness to serve God and to walk faithfully and closely in the footsteps of His only begotten Son.

HUMILITY IN THE PRESENCE OF THE SAVIOR

We love because He first loved us.

1 John 4:19 Holman CSB

As we consider Christ's sacrifice on the cross, we should be profoundly humbled. And today, as we come to Christ in prayer, we should do so in a spirit of humble devotion.

Christ humbled Himself on a cross—for you. He shed His blood—for you. He has offered to walk with you through this life and throughout all eternity. As you approach Him today in prayer, think about His sacrifice and His grace. And be humble.

Do you wish to be great? Then begin by being humble. Do you desire to construct a vast and lofty fabric? Think first about the foundations of humility. The higher your structure is to be, the deeper must be its foundation.

St. Augustine

Nothing sets a person so much out of the devil's reach as humility.

Jonathan Edwards

A TIMELY TIP

You must remain humble or face the consequences. Pride does go before the fall, but humility often prevents the fall.

TRUSTING GOD'S PROVIDENCE

*Naked I came from my mother's womb, naked I'll return to the womb of the earth.
God gives, God takes. God's name be ever blessed.*

Job 1:21 MSG

When Jesus confronted the reality of His impending death on the cross, He asked God that this terrible burden might be lifted. But as He faced the possibility of a suffering that was beyond description, Jesus prayed, "Nevertheless not my will, but Yours, be done" (Luke 22:42 NKJV). As Christians, we too must be willing to accept God's will, even when we do not fully understand the reasons for the hardships that we must endure.

Grief and suffering visit all of us who live long and love deeply. When we lose a loved one, or when we experience any other profound loss, darkness overwhelms us for a while, and it seems as if we cannot summon the strength to face another day—but, with God's help, we can. When we confront circumstances that trouble us to the very core of our souls, we must trust God. When we are worried, we must turn our concerns over to Him. When we are anxious, we must be still and listen for the quiet assurance of God's promises. And then, by placing our lives in His hands, we learn that He is our shepherd today and throughout eternity. Let us trust the Shepherd.

Trust the past to God's mercy, the present to God's love, and the future to God's providence.

St. Augustine

A TIMELY TIP

God is in control of our world . . . and your world.

PERSISTENT PRAYER

Watch therefore, and pray always. . . .

Luke 21:36 NKJV

When we weave the habit of prayer into the very fabric of our days, we invite God to become a partner in every aspect of our lives. When we consult God on an hourly basis, we avail ourselves of His wisdom, His strength, and His love. Today, instead of turning things over in your mind, turn them over to God in prayer. Instead of worrying about your next decision, decide to let God lead the way. Don't limit your prayers to meals or to bedtime. Pray constantly about things great and small. God is listening, and He wants to hear from you. Now.

I learned as never before that persistent calling upon the Lord breaks through every stronghold of the devil, for nothing is impossible with God. For Christians in these troubled times, there is simply no other way.

Jim Cymbala

Nothing is clearer than that prayer has its only worth and significance in the great fact that God hears and answers prayer.

E. M. Bounds

A TIMELY TIP

When you are praying, the position of your eyelids makes little or no difference. Of course it's good to close your eyes and bow your head whenever you can, but it's also good to offer quick prayers to God with your eyes—and your heart—wide open.

PART OF GOD'S FAMILY

How good and pleasant it is when brothers live together in unity!

Psalm 133:1 NIV

As human beings with limited understanding, we can never fully understand the will of God. But as believers in a benevolent God, we must always trust the will of our Heavenly Father.

As this day unfolds, seek God's will for your own life and obey His Word. When you entrust your life to Him completely and without reservation, He will give you the strength to meet any challenge, the courage to face any trial, and the wisdom to live in His righteousness and in His peace.

The center of power is not to be found in summit meetings or in peace conferences. It is not in Peking or Washington or the United Nations, but rather where a child of God prays in the power of the Spirit for God's will to be done in her life, in her home, and in the world around her.

Ruth Bell Graham

To walk out of His will is to walk into nowhere.

C. S. Lewis

A TIMELY TIP

When God's will becomes your will, good things happen.

GOD IS LOVE

We know how much God loves us, and we have put our trust in him. God is love, and all who live in love live in God, and God lives in them.

1 John 4:16 NLT

St. Augustine observed, "God loves each of us as if there were only one of us." Do you believe those words? Do you seek to have an intimate, one-on-one relationship with your Heavenly Father, or are you satisfied to keep Him at a "safe" distance?

Sometimes, in the crush of our daily duties, God may seem far away, but He is not. God is everywhere we have ever been and everywhere we will ever go. He is with us night and day; He knows our thoughts and our prayers. And, when we earnestly seek Him, we will find Him because He is here, waiting patiently for us to reach out to Him.

Let us reach out to Him today and always. And let us praise Him for the glorious gifts that have transformed us today and forever. Amen.

The essence of God's being is love—He never separates Himself from that.

Kay Arthur

The life of faith is a daily exploration of the constant and countless ways in which God's grace and love are experienced.

Eugene Peterson

A TIMELY TIP

Remember: God's love for you is too big to understand with your brain . . . but it's not too big to feel with your heart.

NOTES AND FAVORITE SCRIPTURE

NOTES AND FAVORITE SCRIPTURE

NOTES AND FAVORITE SCRIPTURE

NOTES AND FAVORITE SCRIPTURE

NOTES AND FAVORITE SCRIPTURE

NOTES AND FAVORITE SCRIPTURE